HOME before DAYLIGHT

STEVE PARISH

WITH JOE LAYDEN

HOME before DAYLIGHT

My Life on the Road with
THE GRATEFUL DEAD

St. Martin's Press ≈ New York

HOME BEFORE DAYLIGHT. Copyright © 2003 by Steve Parish. Foreword copyright © 2003 by Bob Weir. All rights reserved. Printed in the United States of America. No part of this book may be used or reproduced in any manner whatsoever without written permission except in the case of brief quotations embodied in critical articles or reviews. For information, address St. Martin's Press, 175 Fifth Avenue, New York, N.Y. 10010.

The names of some of the people described in this book have been changed.

www.stmartins.com

Design by Kathryn Parise

LIBRARY OF CONGRESS CATALOGING-IN-PUBLICATION DATA

Parish, Steve.
    Home before daylight : my life on the road with the Grateful Dead / Steve Parish with Joe Layden ; foreword by Bob Weir.
        p.   cm.
    ISBN 0-312-30353-X
        1. Grateful Dead (Musical group)   2. Rock musicians—United States—Biography.   I. Layden, Joseph, 1959–   II. Title.

ML421.G72P37 2003
782.421266'092'2—dc21
[B]
                                                                    2003053855

First Edition: September 2003

10   9   8   7   6   5   4   3   2   1

Foreword

Let's be clear about this: Steve Parish is definitively a mixed blessing. After twenty-some years and a million or so miles working with him as our roadie, our old pal Jerry Garcia took him on as manager for his solo band expressly as his "revenge on the music industry." It was an excellent choice and description. This arrangement went on for a number of years to the infernal chagrin of music industry "suits" who had to deal with him until ol' Jer checked out. To better understand the kind of bollix Steve would do to a normal businessman, you're going to need to read this book.

Steve as a roadie, well, so-so. I recall a time in Texas, I think it was, as I was walking on stage, and he handed me my guitar with the B and G strings strung inverted in a big, lazy X. Incidents like this were not altogether uncommon, but he made up for them with his ability to enliven a conversation and dispel the drudgery of travel. A *Rolling Stone* writer once described him as "the official loudmouth for the [Grateful Dead] crew." He then went on to quote him at some length. Steve is at the very least quotable, though it's probably a good thing that not much of what was said in the guitar tent on the back of the stage—"The Hacienda"—ever found its way to gentle public ears. We'd have been hanged.

The Grateful Dead was all about improvisation, and Steve spoke that language with flourish. One night we were traveling by charter jet to the next gig. I was seated with my girlfriend across the table from Jerry and his lady. It was my girlfriend's birthday. As Steve walked by our seats to the back of the airplane, the lights went down and he began conducting everyone in a late-night rendition of "Happy Birthday." He looked festive but a little tense. Down the aisle came the stewardesses with the cake, looking more than a little tense. They placed the cake on the table in front of us, then disappeared quickly back into the galley.

He then told us that when he saw the cake up in the galley, he told the stewies that the rhythm guitar player's girlfriend was "a little unstable, if you know what I mean. I think tonight her name's gonna be Natascha, and she likes to have a birthday every night; otherwise, big trouble. So, let's get these candles lit, girls."

Another time, I walked into the Hacienda to see Steve holding an ugly little wiggly plastic demon doll, the kind one finds in toy stores. He was holding it gently, looking at it in a deep and pensive manner. Sitting next to him was Jerry, who informed me that Steve had just coughed up his higher self.

These kinds of incidents might be the "You had to have been there" sort of deal, but these are the kinds of things that kept us going, as much as the music. It was the same kind of interaction as the music, only we had no instruments in our hands or microphones in front of us. One of us, often as not Steve, would offer a theme, and off we'd go.

And so it was that we yukked our way back and forth across the country and 'round and about the world, and Steve was a central figure, often in the lead of what was going on backstage, in the hotels, on the airplanes, busses, boats, or whatever. If ever I get around to writing a book, you'll be reading plenty more about Steve.

OK. I've gotta get some rest; I have a show tomorrow.

R. Weir
05-07-03
Tulsa, OK

Acknowledgments

The process of writing a book is a long one and is something that I had thought about a lot over the years. I never thought I would be one to write a book, but my life was drastically changed by being subpoenaed into court and forced to talk about Jerry, which was shown nationwide on Court TV.

No book like this could ever have been writtten without the encouragement of friends and family. It was powerful at times to remember certain things, but the support I received helped me get through the difficult memories. For me, friendship is everything, and I have been blessed with the best. As with most things in my life, the path of this book revealed itself daily to me. My friend, Phil DeGuerre, got the process started by working with me on another project. He then introduced me to the literary agent Mickey Freiberg, who introduced me to my gifted cowriter, Joe Layden.

I must acknowledge my deep feelings for the band, the crew, and our families. We have had so many experiences together over my thirty-plus years with the Grateful Dead that it was difficult to choose which stories to include in this book. In 1969, when I was nineteen and basically raw material, I was ready to be shaped by my experiences with this amazing new family. These experiences included learning to drive and load trucks, learning to fix amps, learing to make cables, learning to build the "Wall of Sound" PA system, and, of course, learning the ins and outs of traveling the world with the greatest party ever. When the Grateful Dead bought the Alembic PA, along with it came Bob Matthews, Kidd Candelario, Joe Winslow, Sparky Raizene, and myself. We joined with veterans Ramrod, Jackson, and Heard to form the crew.

I would especially like to thank the following people: Jerry Garcia, Bob and Natascha Weir, Mickey Hart, Bill Kreutzman, Phil Lesh, Robert Hunter, Alan Trist, Joe and Sandi Winslow, Ramrod Shurtliff, Kid Candelario, Billy Grillo, George Vaara, Alan Caplan, Al Abono, Angelo Barbaria, Danny Schow, Dennis McNally, Jan Simmons, Eileen Law, David Lemieux, Jeff Norman, Cameron, Cassidy, and Harrison Sears, Sue Stallkup, Jackie LaBranch, Gloria Jones, Melvin Sears, Dave Kemper, Freddie and Sandie Herrera, Danny Rifkin, Oley Hendriksen, Denise Hanson, Herbie Herbert, Louis Rosenbaum, Arthur and Lauren Moshlak, Phil and Allison DeGuerre, Mickey Freiberg, Linda Sue Smith, Norma Parish, Ellen Mines, Ruth Fahrman, Marc Resnick and everyone at St. Martin's Press, and my family: Lauren, Tony, and Marilyn. There are so many more (you know who you are)—I thank you all.

HOME before DAYLIGHT

Prologue

AUGUST 8, 1995-

The call comes late in the morning. I'm surprised by the buoyancy in his voice—the excitement, the way he seems to have recaptured some of that zeal for life, even now, after all the pain and abuse, all the aborted attempts to get clean and healthy, the junkie kicks that failed and chipped away at his genius—and for a moment it seems like the magic has returned, that perhaps this isn't the end . . . that maybe the long, strange trip ain't over just yet.

"Meet me at the studio," he says. "Let's talk."

The highs and lows run through my mind during the drive-in, a quarter of a century with the greatest band in the world, the irony of my life having been saved, quite literally, by a band known as the Grateful Dead. I think of the fun we've all had (those of us who are left, anyway), the friends I've made . . . and the ones I've lost, the casualties of the rock 'n' roll life: keyboardist Ron "Pigpen" McKernan, whose liver gave out back in '73; his successors, Keith Godchaux (auto accident, 1980) and Brent Mydland (drug overdose, 1990); my buddies on the road crew, Jackson and Heard; my first wife, Lorraine, and my two children.

All gone.

But I'm still here, and so is the band. So is Jerry, and now he wants to meet me, to talk about the future, perhaps, and what we'll do next. I find myself smiling as the breeze blows through the open windows, the clean, crisp air of another beautiful day in Northern California. A day of hope.

For nearly three decades the unofficial home of the Dead has been a Front Street studio in San Rafael, but that's not where I'm going. My destination is a new building the band has just purchased, a cavernous place on five acres of land in Novato, empty and waiting. The plan is to transform this warehouse into our new studio, as well as the ultimate boys' club, a place where we'll all hang out, conduct business, and make music. Great music. Just like in the old days.

He's waiting when I arrive, and although he looks pale and weak, there is an enthusiasm, an energy, that I haven't seen in some time. I manage his band now, and in many ways I'm his closest confidante and friend—the best man at his wedding, the guy who had flown to the Betty Ford Clinic with him just a few weeks earlier, and who had picked him up when he bolted halfway through his allotted twenty-eight days. But he's still the boss, a man I admire and respect and love, and for whom I would do almost anything, so I let him take the lead. We walk through the building, and he keeps talking and pointing, designing the floor plan in his head.

Right here . . . see it? A big guitar room . . . where we can lay everything out, the whole collection, every instrument I own . . . a place where I can just sit and play . . . anytime I want.

His eyes are wide, slightly yellow at the edges. He's heavy, heavier than he should be, and his gait and breathing are labored. But he's animated, gesturing with his hands, trying to keep busy, busy, busy, as if he knows that he needs something, that without the heroin and the morphine his armor is gone and he's just a sick man trying to get well, and what better prescription than art? Music had made him, and maybe it could save him.

He'll need help, though, he explains. Help from the rest of the band, help from his legion of fans, help from everyone in our extended family, including me, if he is to make this clean, bright future a reality. I nod in agreement, for he's right. We've all gotten a little sloppy, lazy.

He glances again at the empty room that will become his sanctuary, a home for all those once-glorious guitars that have been locked away in closets, silently, sadly, gathering dust.

Can I count on you?

I tell him he can.

With a smile parting his thick, gray beard, he thanks me. His eyes reflect a mix of apprehension and anticipation, maybe even desperation. I want to believe it's possible, that he can pull himself out of that dark place once and for all, but he seems so fragile, so weak. We shake hands and agree to meet again the next day, to put the plan into action. As the door closes behind me, I have no way of knowing that I will never see him again. By morning, Jerry Garcia, my friend and mentor, the heart and soul of the Grateful Dead, will be gone.

Chapter 1

I grew up in Flushing Meadow, Queens, not far from where the World's Fair was held in 1939/1940 and 1964/1965. The fairgrounds, overgrown and abandoned in the years in between, provided an oasis for me and my prepubescent buddies, a place where we could hang out and engage in mischievous behavior of one type or another. Safely out of range of our parents and the authorities, we'd paddle boats out onto a little pond and shoot off firecrackers, shatter bottles with our BB guns, maybe smoke a few cigarettes. As we grew older and the sixties became "THE SIXTIES," with all that the term and the decade implies, cigarettes gave way to marijuana, and marijuana to LSD. It was a time and a place of wild experimentation, and we were about as open-minded and empty-headed as a bunch of kids could possibly be.

Let me give you an example. My Uncle Fred was a dermatologist and allergy specialist who practiced medicine in Boston, and periodically he'd send samples to my parents. There was nothing illicit about these transactions—I'm sure Uncle Fred looked at it as an innocent way to help some relatives through the cold and flu season. Over the years my parents accumulated quite a stash of medication, and for the longest time I never considered touching it. But I was fascinated by the human body (Uncle Fred had given me a copy of *Gray's Anatomy,* and I'd devoured the whole thing by the age of ten), which I saw not so much as a temple, but as a playground.

One day after school, when I was about sixteen years old, I came home with a couple friends of mine, Arthur and Mike, and after hanging out and listening to music for a while, we decided to rummage around in Uncle Fred's pharmacy. We found some little blue-and-white capsules, filled with Carbitol, and began drinking them. Carbitol, I later learned, was a powerful barbiturate, as strong as Seconal, and it hit us like a ton of bricks, largely, of course, because we ingested so much. I remember leaving the house that day, my legs getting rubbery, and staggering down the street in what felt like slow motion. I remember carrying Arthur and Mike (who were smaller than me) after they passed out, and leaving them at a bus stop and then hiding out for a while at Willie Blye's Luncheonette, afraid I was going to get into trouble, but not really sure exactly what I'd done wrong.

Later, I woke up in my own bed, in my own house, with a New York City cop kneeling on my chest.

"You stupid fool!" he yelled. "If you want to kill yourself, do it like a man. Like this!"

The cop pulled out a .38 service revolver and pressed it hard against my temple. I could smell the gun, feel the cold steel against my skin, and suddenly I realized I wasn't dreaming.

"Heeeeyyyy," I slurred. "What's goin' on?"

The cop looked at his watch. "Your two friends are in the hospital right now. Within a half hour they should both be dead, and we're going to arrest you for murder."

I was too stoned to know whether he was serious or just trying to scare me. I knew only that I wanted to see my friends. Later that night, after I'd passed out again, our family doctor came to examine me. When his stethoscope touched my flesh, I bolted upright, imagined the cop with his gun, and smacked the doctor right in the jaw. Realizing what I'd done—seeing this dear old man who had cared for me since I was a baby crumbling to the floor—I panicked and ran shirtless out of the house. I remember bits and pieces of the next hour, snapshots of a crazy kid careening half-naked through the streets, crying, screaming, looking for his friends. I remember bursting through the doors of the hospital like a madman and being chased from floor to floor by orderlies and nurses and security men, and avoiding them by diving under beds and over tables, like something out of a Marx Brothers movie. I remember throwing up in a telephone booth on the third floor of Queens General Hospital (I think it was the third floor, anyway), which greatly pissed off one of the orderlies, and I remember stumbling out of a basement door, just in time to see another of my relatives, my Uncle Joe, driving up in his '58 Pontiac, and screaming "Get in!"

Arthur and Mike both lived (in fact, Arthur has been coming to Grateful Dead shows for years, and remains a good friend of mine to this day), and we received only a slap on the wrists from the authorities, but my parents were pretty pissed. My father, you see, knew something about the consequences of breaking the law, and he was determined that his son would follow the path of the righteous. Dad was a union guy, vice-president of Teamsters Local 757. It was the kind of work that brought out his best qualities. He was great with people, capable of being smooth and charming, but tough enough to stand up to bosses and hoodlums. Dad was mechanically inclined, too—he could fix anything. And he passed these skills on to me. I learned how to use my hands, and by accompanying my father to union meetings (where I met all kinds of interesting characters, including Jimmy Hoffa), I gained insight into the process of negotiation and the power of the spoken word. I also inherited from my father a deep stubborn streak, and while I had great love and respect for him, it was inevitable that we'd eventually butt heads.

What I didn't know for the longest time was that my father was a self-made man who had overcome some severe setbacks earlier in his life—that he'd spent the better part of seven years battling a life-threatening bout of ileitis, and that he'd later run a tavern in Bayonne, New Jersey. This was just after Prohibition ended, when the bar business was not for the faint of heart. My dad got pretty good with his fists, although he would later claim that he never went looking for a fight, but merely did what he had to do in order to protect the honor of his business. Regardless, he collected some thirteen counts of disorderly conduct over the years and eventually wound up in prison. When he got out, he moved to New York, met my mother, and started a new life. A life that he swore would never involve prison or crime— for himself or anyone in his family.

Like a lot of people, Dad was caught off guard by the counter-culture revolution of the 1960s, with its emphasis on free love and altered states of consciousness. My friends and I embraced the new world with reckless abandon. We smoked pot, experimented with LSD and various other types of drugs, and embraced the work of free-thinking artists of all types—from the writings of Ken Kesey and William Burroughs to the music of the Jefferson Airplane and the Grateful Dead, two bands that hailed from the San Francisco area, which seemed to be ground zero in this whole psychedelic movement. I knew by the time I was seventeen that I wanted to live in California, and that one day I would.

My father hated what he saw happening to the country he knew and loved, and especially hated what it all seemed to be doing to his son. Filled with wanderlust and stoked by massive amounts of chemicals and a healthy disrespect for authority, I began getting into trouble. My alleged involvement in a case involving a stolen car cost me my driver's license. Although I was a fairly intelligent and well-read kid, my grades began to slip, primarily because I stopped going to school. All I could think about was moving out West. But how to do it? The answer came in a series of conversations with a friend of mine named Curtis who had already moved to San Francisco, and who talked endlessly about the weather, the girls, and the drugs (which were far easier to obtain than they were in New York). So a few of us came up with this brilliant idea: I'd fly out to San Francisco, hang out with Curtis, score some illicit material, and bring it back East. We'd cut it up, sell it, and use whatever profit we made to help fund an eventual relocation to the West Coast. There was just one problem: we weren't criminals. In fact, we were pathetically naive and ignorant.

To fund this doomed adventure I waited until my parents went away on vacation, and then I stole four hundred dollars from a peanut butter jar that my father kept hidden on a closet shelf, beneath his winter underwear. They'd be gone for ten days, which I figured was plenty of time for the scheme to be played out. I stayed at Curtis's apartment on Brady Alley in San Francisco, and quickly came to the realization that he wasn't exactly a big-time dealer, either. But he had contacts, and it wasn't long before I scored an ounce of what I thought was LSD (but which later turned out to be mostly speed). I flew back to New York, strolled right through the airport (this being long before the advent of drug-sniffing dogs and tight security), and proceeded to set up shop in my house. We expected to triple our money—and still have a little left over for personal use, of course. But as the clock began to tick and the phone failed to ring, my goal quickly changed. Moving an ounce of acid was not as easy as we had been led to believe, and pretty soon I was concerned only with breaking even, so that I could put the four hundred dollars back in that peanut butter jar before my father came home.

With time running out, and me getting desperate, I got a call from an acquaintance in the neighborhood who said he had found a couple buyers.

"Come on over," I said. They arrived within just a few minutes and quickly offered me four times what I had expected. Being too stupid and panicked to give this much thought, I closed the deal. The money was immediately returned to the peanut butter jar—I'd written down the exact denominations of the bills, and the order in which they were stacked, so that my father would never discover my theft. As luck would have it, though, my fumbling adolescent hands fucked up the perfect crime: the jar slipped out of my grasp just as I was replacing the lid and fell to the floor of the closet, hitting a shelf on the way down. I scooped the jar up and examined it for damage.

Please . . . please . . . please . . .

At first I saw nothing, but then . . . there it was . . . the thinnest of cracks—a long, jagged line stretching from the rim to the base.

Shit!

Stupidly and futilely, I wiped the jar with my shirtsleeve, as if that would erase the evidence. Then I tightened the lid and placed the jar back on the shelf, turning the crack toward the wall before I left. Maybe, if I was lucky, Dad wouldn't notice. Then again, maybe he would.

Pretty soon I was on my way to San Francisco—this time, I thought, for good. I went out with my friend Louis and the two of us moved in with Curtis on Brady Alley. It was during this time, in the summer of 1968, that fate stepped in and introduced me to the life I would lead. Curtis's apartment was just around the corner from a club known as the Carousel Ballroom, which the legendary promoter Bill Graham would one day transform into the equally legendary Fillmore West. Across the street from the Carousel was a recording studio, where the Grateful Dead were working on a new album, and sometimes I'd just hang around outside and listen, maybe talk to some of the guys on the crew. They seemed to be having a good time living the rock 'n' roll life: working odd hours, listening to music, smoking weed, charming the hordes of groupies that were an integral part of the scene. Best of all, I noticed, these guys, most of whom were only a few years older than me, seemed to be more than just employees. They seemed to be family, brothers-in-arms with the boys in the band. They were united in some great cause. Whether their mission was to make great music, to change the world, or to simply have a hell of a good time, I didn't know. And I didn't really care. I just wanted to be a part of it.

Chapter 2

Within a few short months, unfortunately, I had returned to New York, not because I had grown tired of San Francisco or the laid-back hippie lifestyle, but simply because I had run out of money and lacked the ambition to seek any type of employment. I was into hanging out, getting high, listening to music, and generally absorbing as much of Northern California's counterculture atmosphere as I possibly could. But even that meager goal required funding, and I had none available. So, in November of 1968, I reluctantly headed back home.

My father didn't exactly welcome me with open arms—he was pretty sure I was on the verge of screwing up my life for good—but my mom was relieved to have me in the house, safe and sound. At the very least, she thought, I'd go back to school and complete the requirements for a degree. But that never happened. I had friends who were pretty bright and had graduated early, but I'd fallen too far behind to catch up at this point—not that I wanted to anyway. Although I enjoyed literature and reading about places I wanted to visit and great characters who had carved out their places in history, I wasn't much of a student. My last couple years in school I'd gotten into a bit of trouble, mostly silly shit involving vandalism and other typically stupid adolescent behavior. There was the time, for example, during my high school junior year, when I jumped up and slapped the ceiling—I don't even remember why—and wound up putting my fist through a tile. I stood there, dumbfounded, as the other kids laughed and white powder rained down on my head. Within a few seconds I'd been dragged off to the principal's office, and the next thing I knew they were talking about having me arrested. My mother didn't put up much of a fight. Mom was the sweetest, dearest person you could imagine; unfortunately, she was totally submissive to any type of authority, so, when it came to my wild behavior, she would just wring her hands and say, "I can't do a thing with him!" (In fairness, I should point out that my parents had no real experience in these matters. My older sister, Ellen, had been a perfect child, the kind who always did her homework, never talked back, and was admired and respected by just about everyone. She, too, was naturally exasperated by my behavior.) In the end, my mother and the principal agreed that it wouldn't be a terrible idea for me to visit the school psychologist. So I endured a few annoyingly reflective sessions, during which I was asked to describe my feelings while looking at a variety of pictures: a boy sitting next to a tree, a man sitting all alone on a bed. I drew pictures of my own, completed dexterity tests, and chatted with the psychologist about my attitude and outlook on life. In the end, the school psychologist came to the predictable conclusion that I was a young man with some serious . . . *issues.*

"Steve could be a nuclear physicist," the psychologist told my mother. "Or he could be a truck driver. But there's no question that there's a fire burning inside him."

A fire burning inside him . . .

He made it sound like a bad thing, like the flames had to be doused to prevent me from burning myself. But I kind of liked that idea—that I was a furnace, with tremendous energy and potential.

The psychologist convinced my parents that I'd probably benefit from at least a brief round of psychiatric care, so I spent a few hours with a shrink and to my surprise found it enlightening. I came away from those sessions with the understanding that I was my own person, that I was in control of my destiny. Sure, I was just an aimless, fucked-up sixteen-year-old kid, but I didn't have to remain that way. I was my own person, and it was up to me to decide how I wanted to live my life. I liked living on the edge, which most people—my parents included—viewed as a liability, a character flaw. The doctor told me this wasn't necessarily true. The trick, he said, was to find a way to take all that excess energy and turn it into something positive. I liked the sound of that, and I've used it as a guiding principle ever since. Admittedly, along the way there have been side trips down some seriously dark alleys. I've made mistakes, some big, some small. Trying to move an ounce of acid, I discovered, was a very big mistake. I wanted to make some quick money by selling drugs, and I was not someone who ever should have tried something like that. I was a sorry excuse for a criminal, destined to get caught. And that's precisely what happened.

Within a few days of returning to New York, I came home one afternoon to discover a gray Volkswagen parked in front of our house. Sitting in the car were two men. I'd never seen the car before and immediately suspected trouble. The hair on the back of my neck bristled as I walked into the house and saw my parents talking quietly. My mother paused, then said, nervously, "Steve, someone named Bill called for you earlier."

"Thanks, Mom," I responded as I walked up the stairs, trying not to betray the nervousness I felt. I had no friends named Bill, and I mulled that over as I walked upstairs to use the bathroom. Suddenly there was heavy knock at the door.

"Open up!" someone yelled.

I hadn't even responded when the door flew open and in rushed the two men I'd seen sitting outside in the Volkswagen. One of them threw me against the bathroom wall while the other fell to his knees, rolled up his sleeve, and prepared to go fishing in the toilet. At that moment I realized what was happening. These guys were cops—narcotics officers, probably—and they thought I had just flushed evidence down the toilet.

"Easy, man," I said. "I was just taking a piss."

"Shut up!"

He curled my arm up behind my back and pressed my face into the wall. Then he dragged me out of the bathroom, steered me down the stairs, and told me to take a seat on the couch. With my mother screaming hysterically and my father doing his best to get in their faces and stand up for me (even though I'm sure he felt I'd done *something* to deserve this), the cops turned the house upside down in a futile search for drugs. That, of course, only made them angrier.

"Where is it?" one of the men asked, his face turning red.

"Where's what?"

He smacked the sofa with his fist. "Don't bullshit me! If you've got speed in this house, we're going to find it, so you might as well just make it easy on yourself."

Speed?

Now I was really confused. When the assault had begun, I was reasonably certain it had something to do with the acid we'd sold months earlier. But I wasn't positive. After all, so much time had passed, and I was stupid enough to think that what we'd done really wasn't that big a deal. I mean, it wasn't like I was a *dealer*. Not in my mind anyway. And now here they were screaming about speed. I didn't sell any speed. Hell, I didn't even *own* any speed.

"I don't know what you're talking about, man. You must have me confused with someone else."

The cop leaned into me, put his mouth against my ear. "Listen, you mother-fucker," he said softly, but with malicious intent. "We're going downtown to talk about this. Now, I don't want to handcuff you in front of your mother, because I don't want to see you break her heart, so I'm going to let you walk outside to the car on your own. But if you try to run . . . if you even take a step in the wrong direction . . . I will shoot you." He paused, looked at my mother. "Is that clear?"

I nodded.

"Good. Let's go."

Thus began my descent into "the system." They cuffed me in the back seat of the car and drove me to the precinct house. They questioned me for hours on end without offering me a chance to make a phone call or asking if I wanted legal representation. They threatened and harassed me in all kinds of ways. I didn't know they were doing anything wrong. They were cops—I figured they could do whatever they wanted. And, after they'd told me that the LSD I'd sold was laced with speed, I came to the conclusion that they had me nailed. Not that I admitted anything. I just sat there and kept my mouth shut, tried to act like a tough guy. A stoic.

Finally, the interrogation ceased. They led me out of the room and down a flight of stairs, to the basement of the Queens House of Detention. We walked down a long, dark hallway, illuminated only by a single bare lightbulb, and then down another short flight of stairs, at the bottom of which was a single row of cells. There was water on the floor, nearly ankle deep, and the place reeked of urine and puke. The guard unlocked my cuffs, pushed me into a cell, and slammed the door behind me.

"Enjoy yourself," he said, and then he was gone.

The cell was nearly pitch black, and the darkness had precisely the desired effect: it scared the shit out of me. I leaned into the bars, like a caged animal, and looked up the stairs toward a sliver of light, praying that it wouldn't go away, and that my stay here would be brief. Suddenly, there was a noise from the back of the cell, a snort, like the sound of someone clearing his throat. With my heart racing, I whirled around and saw something in the far corner of the cell, a shadow moving slowly, deliberately.

"Who's there?"

No response. Then the shadow moved again, and now I could see its head, big and black and toothless, and its eyes, glowing red. He was a huge, wild-looking man, at least as tall as me (I was six-foot-four), and probably fifty pounds heavier, with thick round shoulders and . . . and . . .

Holy shit! He's buck naked!

"Get me outta here!" I yelled, just as the man charged at me, laughing and snorting and pawing like an animal. I could smell his breath, feel the hot stink of his body as he chased me around the cell. Bouncing off the walls, climbing the bars, kicking and punching and doing everything I could to keep him off me, I screamed until my voice went raw.

"*Somebody help me! Please!*"

With the beast on my back, about to have his way with me, two cops came strolling casually down the stairs and up to the door of the cell. One of them reached into his back pocket and withdrew a hip flask.

"Here you go, Curly," he said, tossing the flask into the cell. Curly, who was, of course, nothing more than a big drunk, stumbled after it. By now the cops were laughing uncontrollably. I guess they were just playing with me, having some fun, trying to make me a bit more pliable. And it worked.

The next stop was another cell on a cleaner, drier floor. Right away the guy in the next cell struck up a conversation with me. I couldn't see him, but I could tell by his voice and the way he acted that he was older and more experienced in these matters than I was. Unlike me, he seemed not to be the least bit frightened or intimidated. Not only that, but he seemed like a genuinely nice guy.

"Don't worry, kid," he said. "You'll be fine. They're just trying to scare you."

He asked my name, where I was from, what I had done. He asked if I was cold or hungry, and when I said that I was, he said he'd talk to one of the guards and see if they could get me a blanket, maybe some hot soup. Before long I was talking to him like he was my best buddy, sharing lifelong secrets with a man I couldn't even see. Some convict, huh? After hours of playing hard-ass, acting like Jimmy Cagney with the cops upstairs, I was spilling my guts to a complete stranger. Well, guess what? He wasn't a prisoner. He was an undercover cop, and by the time he was through with me, they had nearly enough information to close their case. I told him everything: where we got the acid, how much we sold, how much money we'd made. It wasn't exactly a confession, given the circumstances under which the information had been obtained, but it was enough to get a conviction.

The next morning I was arraigned. The judge, a hard-looking man with a square jaw and a perpetual scowl, scolded me as a teacher would a disruptive child. "What's wrong with you, son?" he asked, his voice rising. "Selling LSD? You want to spend the rest of your life in prison?"

The fact that I had pleaded not guilty seemed utterly irrelevant to this man. In his eyes, I was guilty. (Yeah, I know—I *was* guilty, but I didn't feel like a criminal, and the fact that I'd been so quickly labeled as one was startling.)

"Get out of my courtroom," the judge spat, and with that they whisked me away to a holding cell with more than a dozen other inmates, where I would wait for bail to be posted. Then I could go home and forget all about this humiliating nightmare. Imagine my shock when one of the officers walked in and told us all to stand up. He began reading names, ordering us around, putting us in handcuffs. As we marched outside, I could see a bus waiting in the street, spewing exhaust into the air.

"Whoa," I said to the prisoner next to me, a kid maybe a year or two older than I was. "What's going on? I'm supposed to be going home."

The kid laughed. "Mother-fucker, you ain't going home. You're going to the Rock!"

The Rock, as everyone in New York knew, was Rikers Island, an absolute shithole of a jail, worse in many ways than a maximum security penitentiary.

"Wait a minute," I stammered. "There must be some mistake."

The kid laughed again. "Ain't no mistake," he said as we climbed the stairs of the bus.

"You're fucked."

And so it seemed.

Chapter 3

As the gates parted and the bus pulled into Rikers, I felt like my heart was going to leap out of my chest. I kept fidgeting, squirming, mumbling under my breath.

This can't be happening . . .

The chain of events that had led me to this moment seemed inconsistent with the surroundings. Had I done anything so terrible as to deserve a ticket to Rikers? Was I really no different than the rest of the convicts on this bus? My head swiveled from side to side as I tried to get a glimpse of the prison.

"Hey, man," said the kid next to me. "Sit the fuck still!"

I did as I was told. He seemed like someone who had a bit of experience in this area, so maybe it was best to just follow his lead. I closed my eyes, tried to think of all the prison movies I'd seen. I was a fish out of water, no question about it, but maybe I could at least play the part well enough to survive a day or two. By then, I figured, someone would have bailed me out and the whole nightmare would be over.

Like every other facility in the New York County jail system, Rikers Island was a horrible place, big and nasty and brutal. In fact, it was occupied primarily by hardened criminals, repeat offenders mostly, who were on their way to Attica, Dannemora, Great Meadow, or some other forsaken upstate fortress. Rikers was a giant, bestial holding tank where the petty thief and the hapless, inexperienced drug dealer (yours truly) rubbed elbows with some of the biggest, meanest convicts on the planet.

Let's put it this way: it's not the kind of place where you'd want to send your adolescent son for a night of a sensitivity training.

But there I was, eighteen years old and scared shitless, standing at the sally port, listening to the sound of thousands of doors slamming and locking, separating me from the outside world. I knew I wasn't long for this place, that somehow I'd get out in fairly short order; nevertheless, at that moment, as we were ordered to strip naked and stand at attention while a crew of corrections officers inspected us from head to toe, I felt like I was going away forever.

Back then the guards carried canes. They were longer and more impressive than the batons favored in today's prisons, and I sensed right away that the guards wouldn't hesitate to use them as weapons. You could see it in their eyes, in the way they walked and talked, constantly berating the inmates, practically daring them to get out of line. To the guards every day was a battle, and they weren't about to lose. Just in case there was any confusion about the matter, they presented to us—the new arrivals—a young Hispanic inmate who had been badly beaten. His jumpsuit was torn, his eyes practically swollen shut. His nose had been whacked out of line and blood trickled from his mouth. He appeared to be nearly unconscious and would no doubt have slumped to the floor if not for the firm grip of the mountainous CO who held him by the collar.

"You want to try to escape?" one of the guards said. "Go ahead. But you'd better succeed. Because this is what happens if we catch you."

Practically speaking, there was no escaping from the Rock. Armed guards patrolled the walls that rose above the jail and the polluted waterways beyond. That anyone thought it possible to break out of Rikers only served as a reminder of what a hellhole the place really was. Drowning, getting shot or beaten—after a few days at Rikers, these became risks worth taking.

To some people, anyway. Not to me. I just wanted to mind my own business and do my time—whatever that might mean—as quietly as possible. That proved to be more difficult than I'd anticipated. I was tall and weighed more than two hundred pounds, so I wasn't the immediate target that some kids become when they enter a jail or prison. Yes, I was scared, anxious, and I'm sure the older cons noticed that. But they also knew, just by looking at me, that I wouldn't be punked out without a fight. There was easier prey, skinny little kids who whimpered and cried from the moment they got on the bus. I was more concerned with doing something wrong, with violating some unwritten code of conduct that would lead to a confrontation with other inmates and maybe punishment at the hands of the guards and, inevitably, a longer stay at Rikers. That was the last thing I wanted. My only goal was to blend into the background, to be as inconspicuous as possible. And to make sure that I was ready to go the minute my father came to his senses and bailed me out.

Life in jail is more complicated than that, though. A few hours after I arrived I went to the chow hall, and for some reason the first thing I noticed was the coffee, how it poured from the pot in a thick, caramel-colored stream because it had already been laced with cream and sugar. Just to keep things simple. Then I noticed there were no knives, only spoons. As I slid my tray along the serving track, another inmate approached me and began to strike up a conversation. He was a black guy, several years older than me, and he seemed friendly enough. We talked for only a minute or two and then I retreated to a table to eat in private. No sooner had I sat down when I was surrounded by a group of five white men—some with glistening, anvil-shaped heads, some with long greasy hair swept back over reptilian brows, all tattooed, and all built like NFL linemen.

"What are you doing?" one of them said.

"Eating."

"Don't be a wiseass. You know what I mean."

"No, I don't."

He shook his head in disgust and put his nose inches from mine. "Stay away from the niggers . . . or you're gonna have a big problem."

This was baffling to me. I'd grown up in New York. I'd been around black people my whole life. This was the sixties, obviously, so I'm not going to lie and say I was blind to the problem of race relations in the United States, but I sure didn't think of myself as a bigot. I got along with almost everyone. I had friends who were black, white, Hispanic, Jewish, Catholic. It never seemed like much of a big deal to me.

At Rikers, however, the rules were different. "If you know what's good for you," one of the white guys told me, "you'll stick with your own."

I'd like to say that I bravely and righteously told them to go fuck themselves, that I proudly and defiantly identified them as the assholes they were. But I was eighteen and scared and more than willing to do what I was told. I understood immediately that these guys meant business, and that I'd be wise to take their advice. Rikers was populated not only by kids like me, but also by men who had been incarcerated for much of their adult lives, and they ran the place in conjunction with the guards. There were two sets of rules, and neither was to be violated without serious consideration of the consequences.

As they got up to leave, the obvious leader, the one who had done all the talking, or threatening, locked eyes with me. He didn't say anything. He just stood there for a moment, waiting for some sort of acknowledgment. Slowly, subtly, I nodded. And then they went away.

The first night was the worst. They threw me in a cell on the third tier with some poor junkie who was clearly not enjoying the experience of kicking heroin cold turkey. Like me, this guy had just been processed and so was new to the ways of Rikers Island. Unlike me, he didn't really give a rat's ass about who he offended or what anyone thought of him. Heroin, as I later discovered, will do that to a man: rob him of everything he owns—his money, his family, his livelihood, his dignity.

Darkness somehow illuminates the sadness of jail. When the lights go out and the inmates are instructed to "shut the fuck up and go to sleep!" that's when the craziness begins in earnest. Grown men weeping out loud, screaming for their mothers. Psychopaths carrying on bizarre conversations with themselves. You get used to it after a while, I guess, and you're able to sleep through most of the distractions. On this night, however, the loudest noise emanated from my cell. The periodic retching and incessant wailing of my cellmate drowned out everything else, and did nothing to endear me to my neighbors on the third tier. At first I felt bad for him—he was so sick and pathetic and obviously in terrible pain. After a while, though, he started to get on my nerves, not only because I couldn't sleep, but because of the threats cascading down on us. The whole cell block, it seemed, was united in its anger.

"Stop crying or I'll kick your sorry ass, you mother-fucker!"

"Quiet down, bitch!"

It went on like that all night, him curled up on the floor, whimpering and convulsing and begging for help . . . and me sitting crosslegged on my bunk, making promises to myself, swearing that if I got out of this place alive I'd never do anything so stupid that it would warrant a return trip. (In many ways I've made good on that promise. I never again accepted money for drugs, and I never spent more than

a few hours in jail. I've done stupid things now and then, but hell . . .
no one's perfect.)

The next morning, as soon as the cells were opened, there was a
mad rush in my direction. Guys were pushing me, cursing at me,
threatening me.

"You fuckin' junkie . . . you kept us up all night!"

A few of them began slapping me, then punching me. I covered up
and tried to defend myself, while at the same time trying to make
them aware of their mistake.

"It wasn't me!" I shouted. "It wasn't me!"

Finally, as they backed me into my cell, one of the inmates noticed
my cellmate on the floor, practically comatose, and immediately the
assault ebbed. He was such a mess that the others didn't even bother
with him. They just cursed at him and walked away. A few minutes
later the guards showed up. They laughed at the junkie and they
laughed at me. As I nursed the bruises on my arms and ribs, one of the
guards offered me a bit of advice: "Keep it quiet tonight." Then he
smiled and walked out.

My father had his own take on the theory of relativity: "If a pretty girl is
sitting on your lap, an hour feels like a minute," he used to say. "If
you're sitting on a hot stove, a minute feels like an hour." I spent less
than a week at Rikers, but it felt like a year. Time dripped that slowly. I
was surrounded by convicts, men who had become completely institu-
tionalized and jail-minded. Just as I couldn't imagine a life behind these
bars that was worth living, they couldn't imagine life on the outside.

Did I say the first night was the worst? Actually, that's not true. In
some ways the second night was worst, for it was on the second night,
just after lights out, that the guards came rumbling down the tier,
canes at the ready, and yanked every man out of his cell.

"You fucking thieves!" shouted the captain as he sauntered up and
down the rows of men, all standing at attention, trying not to make

25

any movement that might result in a beating. "You think it's acceptable to steal blankets in my jail? You think we won't notice?"

Rikers was a cold and drafty old place, uncomfortable even in the most temperate of times. In late November it was miserable. Each inmate was issued one crummy blanket with which to cover himself while trying to sleep on a musty cot that unfolded from the wall. I hadn't taken any extra blankets, and I didn't know who had. But I applauded their decision.

"You guys got your own system in here, huh?" the captain said. "Think you run the place." He continued walking, staring at each inmate as he passed. Finally he got to me. I tried not to make eye contact. "I want that blanket back!" he said. *"Now!"* The last word echoed in my head, delivered as it was only inches from my right ear. And then I panicked. In an act of sublime stupidity, I decided to speak.

"Please, sir," I stammered. "I'm just a victim of circumstances."

The guard stared at me for a moment, as if shocked that I'd had the audacity to say anything. Then, almost without moving, he drove his stick into my stomach, a short, sharp jab that left me gasping and doubled over in pain. As I tried to catch my breath, I watched him walk away, still barking at the other inmates, promising to bring the fugitive blanket thief to justice. To drive home his point, he ordered a sweep of all cells, and the confiscation of all blankets.

That night I felt like a character in some 1930s prison movie: shivering in a dark and dank jail, sharing a fetid cell with a sick junkie. To shut him the hell up, and to prevent a replay of the previous night, I resorted to threatening him with bodily harm, which worked only so well since the guy was hurting so bad that he really didn't care whether he lived or died. Throughout the tier men screamed and wailed and demanded to be treated like human beings, which, of course, they weren't. Not as long as they were within these walls. The whole thing was like some awful Heronymous Bosch depiction of hell. I kept my sanity, believe it or not, by talking to myself, by repeating the sort of flaccid daily affirmations that make millionaires out of self-help gurus: *I do not belong here. I made a stupid mistake, but I'm a good person.*

Three or four days went by, and like most anyone who winds up in a correctional facility I started to get the rhythm down. To be honest, that might have been the scariest part of all: the ease with which you could sink into the brain-dead routine of prison life. Basically, this is what you did at Rikers: you'd get out of bed, go to the chow hall, eat some tepid shit, then sit around and play cards and smoke cigarettes until it was time to eat more tepid shit. There were no jobs, no weights, no exercise of any kind. You just hung out and counted the minutes. Day after fucking day. I saw some people playing checkers, chess, things like that, but I didn't dare seek entry into their games or their world. Games, like everything else at Rikers, were dominated by various cliques, and I wanted no part of that. I didn't want to be affiliated with anyone; I just wanted to mind my own business. Soon, I figured, the call would come and I'd be on my way home.

It happened on the fifth day. I was leaning against a wall, all by myself, silently reciting poetry to calm my nerves, when one of the officers shouted my name.

"Let's go, Parish!"

I didn't know what he wanted at first, but everyone else seemed to have a pretty good idea of what was happening. As I walked along the tier several of the inmates gathered around me. A few tried to press notes into my hands and pockets. One threw an arm around my neck and said, with desperation in his voice, "Nobody knows I'm in here, man. Can you call my sister?"

Then it hit me: *Holy shit! I'm being released!* I began to walk more swiftly, pushing the men away from me as I drew closer to the gate. And then I was on the other side, retrieving my meager belongings and signing release forms, and getting a tearful kiss from my mother and a hug from a man named Pete Clark, a union buddy of my father who had driven Mom to Rikers to bail me out. Behind me I could still hear the inmates shouting, pleading for help. I felt for them, wondered what would become of them, but more than anything else I just wanted to leave them behind, to put as much distance as I possibly could between me and this place.

Walking across the parking lot I was amazed by the way my senses came to life. Not only did the air smell clean, it tasted clean.

"Never again," I whispered to no one in particular. "Never again."

Chapter 4

On the drive home I discovered that the reason I hadn't been bailed out right away was that mine had been one of only two crises facing the Parish family that week. Shortly after the cops had hauled me away, my father had fallen ill with a recurrence of ileitis. He'd been rushed by ambulance to the hospital, where doctors told my mother that without immediate surgical intervention he would probably die. In fact, the intestinal blockage was so bad that he nearly died anyway, right there on the operating table.

Hearing this news from my mother, who had just come from the hospital, where my father was still in the intensive care unit, brought a flood of conflicting emotions. I felt guilty for putting my mother through so much pain and hardship when she obviously already had enough on her plate. Nevertheless, I was intensely pissed at having been left in that cesspool for nearly a week. Surely someone could have taken a few hours to bail me out. I mean, once Dad was off the operating table and out of danger. Or was I merely being selfish and self-centered?

The answer came roughly a week later, when my father came home from the hospital. He was still very sick. Despite our disagreements (and there had been many in recent years), I'd always known him as a strong man, a leader, and it was hard to see him this way, so weak and frail, his body ravaged by age and illness. I'd been moping around the house for days, angry over having been left at Rikers and probably suffering from what would now be referred to as post-traumatic stress syndrome. I wanted answers from my father, some explanation as to what had happened, but I really didn't want to ask, because it didn't seem right to badger him when he could barely stand up. Fortunately, my father took control of the situation. He sat me down in the living room and proceeded to tell me all about his past. I'd never heard any of this before—the stories about his younger, wilder days in Bayonne, and the time he spent in prison—and I was shocked to hear it now. I'd always thought of my father as a real straight-arrow, the kind of man who knew right from wrong and never crossed the line. He could be a hard-ass, of course—you don't reach that level of union leadership without having the courage to stand up to some pretty tough people—but it had never occurred to me that my dad had once lived a very different kind of life . . . a life that involved boozing and brawling; the idea that he'd ever been incarcerated was almost beyond my comprehension. And not just for a few days or weeks, either: two years, he'd been locked up.

Two years!

I'd been at Rikers for five days and had found it to be by far the worst experience of my life, so horrible and depressing and frightening that I was certain I'd lead a crime-free life from that day forward.

Which was precisely what my father had hoped to accomplish when he stopped my mother from bailing me out.

"I'm sorry," he said, his voice breaking. "I know it was hard in there, but I thought if you got a taste of it, maybe you'd learn something."

"Learn something? Like what?"

My father shook his head, and then he did something I'd never see him do: he started to cry.

"I look at you and I see myself twenty-five years ago," he said. "I just don't want you making the same mistakes I made."

As an adult—as a father and a husband—I can look back on that incident now and say without question that my father's instincts were right, that by letting me rot behind bars for a few days and by revealing to me his own dark past, he taught me an invaluable lesson. It's no stretch to say that he saved my life. If I'd gotten off easy—if I'd been bailed out that first day and never served any time at Rikers—I might well have failed to grasp the seriousness of the situation. Dad allowed life to give me a cold slap to the face, and it did indeed wake me up.

Not that I became a model citizen right away. You don't spend thirty years in the world of rock 'n' roll without sacrificing a brain cell here and there, but I certainly lost any inclination to become a garden-variety criminal. I liked having a good time and occasionally I used my fists to get a point across. And God knows I've ingested just about every chemical substance known to man at one time or another. But I never sold the stuff again. In that sense I experienced what can only be called an epiphany. And for that I have Rikers Island and my father to thank.

The gratitude was far from instantaneous, however. My father may have been right, but that didn't mean I was happy about it, or that I respected or admired him for it. Not then, anyway. I wanted more than ever to get away from home and away from New York, to return to Northern California, to the beautiful Bay Area, and to once again become entrenched in that scene. I didn't know what I would do when

I got there, or how I would make a life for myself, but somehow I knew I belonged there.

Unfortunately, I wasn't allowed to leave the state until my case came to trial, which took nearly a year. I was under a dark cloud that whole time, for not only was I restless and bored, but I was scared to death about what might happen when I stood before the judge. Mine was not a petty crime; it was a major felony, with the potential to put me in prison for twenty years. I preferred not to think about that, and I didn't really believe it would happen, but it was a possibility.

To help distract me from the anxiety surrounding my case, and because I knew it would look good when it came time to be sentenced, I began looking for work. Arthur called one day and said he had seen an advertisement in which "tall people" were being recruited to help out with some sort of project at the New York State Pavilion at Flushing Meadows. Apparently, the Pavilion was going to be hosting rock shows, plays, that sort of thing, and they needed a crew. At six-foot-four I figured I'd have a pretty good shot at landing a position, and I was right. I started out at the very bottom—cleaning toilets, hauling equipment—and then graduated to helping out with security and setup. If that sounds mundane enough, it proved to be a life-saving opportunity for me. I learned the theater arts, which includes much more than standing on stage and performing. The average show, be it a symphony, a rock concert, or a play, lasts a couple hours. Setup and teardown can take the better part of a day. The artists, the musicians—they're the stars, but they can't put on a show by themselves. They need help, lots of it, and I was proud to be a part of the support system.

I was a sponge, really, eager to soak up as much knowledge as I possibly could. My first day on the job I met a guy named Keith Kevin, a veteran stage hand who immediately began teaching me about electronics and sound and public address systems, the lifeblood of a rock 'n' roll show, of any show, for that matter. I started hanging out with Kevin at the legendary Fillmore East, and I got to see what was involved in preparing a bare theater for a live performance. It was, to say the least, enlightening. I couldn't believe how hard these guys worked, and how much they seemed to enjoy their work. I'd always sort of thought of roadies, when I thought of them at all, as being little more than hired muscle, but that was so far off the mark. Sure, it took a strong back and boundless energy to load in and load out, but the intricacy of it all was mind-boggling: the wiring of a sound system, the setting up of instruments, the raising of scaffolding. It was like building a small city each and every night. Strength and technical expertise were required on the part of the stage crew; blind faith was required of the band. What surprised me most was how rarely mistakes were made, and how simple it all must have seemed to the people in the audience.

In an interesting twist of fate, the very first show I worked at the Pavilion, in July of 1969, featured the Grateful Dead. I spent a lot of time that day talking with Larry "Ramrod" Shurtliff, Johnny Hagen, and William "Kid" Candelario, three wild and crazy guys who formed the nucleus of what would become the greatest road crew in rock 'n' roll history. We shared a few tokes off a nitrous tank, and I liked all of these guys from the get-go. I was having a ball setting up for the show. But I was nervous, too, for I was scheduled to appear in court the very next day, and I thought there was a reasonable chance I might end up going back to jail, at least for a little while. To be honest, one day might have been more than I could handle. Some of this anxiety I shared with Keith Kevin as the day and night wore on. Finally, he looked at me, laughed, and said, "What are you talking about, man? Just relax. It'll all work out."

"You think so?"

"Sure . . . just look at these guys."

He gestured toward the stage, where the band was in the middle of a typically generous set. Jerry Garcia stood in the center of the action, playing his guitar, a look of pure joy on his face, radiating energy that I'd never felt before from any music or any person. Their music was subdued, but incredibly powerful, and I fell in love with it instantly. At that moment, I became a Deadhead.

The next day, in court, the judge emerged from his chambers with a big smile on his face, which completely confused me. My limited experience with judges led me to believe that they were completely incapable of seeing the humor in anything, and that you were wise never to even try to make them laugh. Compounding my anxiety was the fact that my attorney, who had been hired by my father, had convinced me to enter a plea of guilty. I'd been reluctant to follow his advice, not because I wanted to proclaim my innocence, which would have been laughable, but because I didn't want to admit guilt and accept a prison sentence. The attorney had simply nodded, smiled, and said, "Relax. It'll be all right."

And now here was the judge, preparing to pass sentence. And he, too, was smiling. I tried not to read too much into it. Instead, I just stood quietly and waited for him to address me.

The judge sat down, rifled through some papers, looked around the courtroom, and finally spoke.

"You look like a nice kid to me," he said.

I didn't respond. After all, it wasn't a question.

"You going to college, son?" he asked.

"Yes, sir," I lied.

"You gonna stay out of trouble?"

"Absolutely."

"Good."

Next thing I knew he was saying something about my being a juvenile offender and sealing the records and releasing me on my own recognizance. Then he slammed the gavel, and that was that. Stunned, I walked out of the courtroom a free man. Better than that even. By granting me youthful offender status, the judge was essentially saying the crime had never occurred. I was too numb to speak, and too naive to understand what had really just transpired.

As we got into the car to go home, my father shook his head.

"College, huh?" he said.

I shrugged. "Sure."

"Well, I hope you're paying for it, because I just spent your whole college account to get you out of trouble."

I looked at Dad with amazement. Had he really greased the judge? What other explanation could there have been for his leniency? I guess I'll never know for sure.

I nodded. "That's okay, Dad."

And it really was. I had other plans.

Chapter 5

It didn't take long for me to become immersed in the East Coast music scene. When I wasn't working shows at the Pavilion or the Capital Theater in Port Chester, New York, I was hanging out around the stage at the Fillmore East, soaking up as much of the culture and atmosphere as I possibly could. (I was there many times to hear Bill Graham give his nightly speech. Little did I realize, as I listened to him, that this man, who was so full of creative energy and enthusiasm, would have such a tremendous impact on my life and career; that I would be invited to his house for a multitude of Christmas dinners; that he would one day try to coax me into dancing on stage while the Grateful Dead performed at the U.S. Festival; that together we would take the

Garcia Band to Broadway; and that in 1971, at Winterland, he would exuberantly promote a sandlot football game known as the Toilet Bowl between his crew and the crew of the Grateful Dead, and that he'd present us with an oak toilet seat in honor of our illustrious victory.)

There were so many brilliant and unusual artists who seemed to call the Fillmore their second home. I got to know Alan Arkush, an aspiring film director who went on to make such cult hits as *Rock 'n' Roll High School,* starring the Ramones; John Noonan, a really colorful playwright who favored tattered overalls and scatological jokes, but who was clearly a man of significant talent—this, after all, was a guy who wrote the Broadway hit *A Coupla White Chicks Sitting Around Talking*; and, perhaps most important of all, Candace Brightman, a gifted lighting technician who taught me so much about life and love and the craft of putting on a rock 'n' roll show. Candace was a few years older than me, but we clicked right away and I wound up falling in love with her. Our relationship ended when I went out west and she stayed at behind to work the East Coast theater scene, but our friendship endured. Candace later joined the Dead as a lighting tech and we spent what seemed like a lifetime on the road together.

I couldn't get enough of this world, a world of music and literature and, yes, drugs. These were people who worked hard and played hard, and I was totally captivated by them. This was especially true of the Grateful Dead, a band that hailed from the Bay Area of California, but spent an enormous amount of time in the Northeast. The Dead had a huge following in New York, so their touring schedule frequently brought them to my backyard. I loved working alongside these guys, being a part of their ensemble. They were a team in every sense of the word. The crew would swagger into town, acting like they owned the place, and then they'd just move in and take over the venue. They worked furiously, but almost poetically. There was magic in the way they could transform an empty space into a perfectly wired stage in a matter of hours, and they would do it while harassing each other mercilessly, the way brothers and teammates do. These guys loved each other and supported each other and got on each other's nerves. This wasn't a job to them—it was a calling, a way of life.

It was while watching the Dead crew, and helping them, that I first got the idea that I'd like to work for a single band, rather than a theater. And what better band than the Grateful Dead? So when I had an opportunity to make a little trip upstate that summer, to help a fellow stagehand named Ray bring a truckload of super-trooper spotlights to a big outdoor festival, I was only too happy to oblige. I felt guilty about leaving my bosses at the Pavilion hanging for a few days, but I viewed the invitation from Ray to be too good an opportunity to pass up. The fact that I wasn't going to be paid a dime didn't matter in the least. It was a chance to learn more about the craft, and to be part of something that had the potential for greatness: Woodstock.

Well, enough has been written about Woodstock that I won't belabor the point here. It was, of course, less about music than about cultural and spiritual bonding. The guys in the Dead weren't happy with their set, and they've never considered Woodstock to be one of the more memorable performances in their long and storied careers. For me, though, a wide-eyed teenager whose experience had been limited to small theaters in New York, it was incredible to help erect scaffolding and lights on a stage that would be surrounded by hundreds of thousands of mud-soaked flower children. I was little more than a hired hand at Woodstock, someone who did whatever was asked of him, which mainly meant hauling heavy equipment. It was a seminal moment in American pop culture history, and to be a small part of it was kind of cool.

By the time I returned to New York from Woodstock I was tired of the theatre scene and was itching for something bigger. What I wanted, specifically, was to work for the Grateful Dead. It's hard to explain exactly why I felt this way: maybe it was the music, maybe it was the romantic way I viewed the lives of the guys on the crew. In some ways I was just like a kid who wants to run away and join the circus. The Grateful Dead was a vehicle for me to see the world outside, to be part of something bigger, something that seemed important. Sure they were just a band, but in 1969 there was something mystical about making music, and no one had a purer, more noble attitude toward the art of performing than the Grateful Dead. This was a fiercely independent band, one that refused to bend to the whims of record company executives and promoters, and one that viewed its mission as something other than just selling records and making money. I didn't know shit about the business of rock 'n' roll, but I could tell by watching the Dead, and Jerry Garcia in particular, that this was a band with a higher purpose. For them it was all about playing and performing and connecting with the audience. It wasn't an act, and it wasn't just a show. These guys genuinely loved to play.

The enthusiasm extended to the crew, which was unlike any other in rock 'n' roll. Even then, in the embryonic days, the crew was a special part of the Dead. The band enjoyed being around them and treated them with respect and dignity. In return, the guys on the crew seemed to work harder and more passionately than the roadies who passed through the Capital Theater and the Pavilion. These guys, particularly Ramrod, Clifford Dale "Sonny Boy" Heard, and Donald "Rex" Jackson (the three members of the crew with whom I spent most of my time in the early years), were different. And they knew it.

Sonny Heard, whose nickname stemmed from the fact that he loved a good time, was the first to befriend me. Heard introduced me to the greatest marijuana I'd ever smoked. It was mind-boggling in its intensity and purity. We smoked together during shows, after shows, whenever we had some down time, and it wasn't long before Heard extended an invitation to join him in California.

"You can work for the band and stay with me," he said. "It'll be great."

Heard was quick to add, however, that there would be no salary. Not right away, anyway. He was talking less about a career than a philosophy of life, an attitude reflected in the writing of such Beat Generation artists as William Burroughs and Jack Kerouac, and, more recent, in the work of Ken Kesey, who would of course become a prominent Deadhead himself. It was about blending life and work and friendship and art and music on a daily basis. It was about freedom of expression, rejection of traditional material values; it was about sex and drugs and rock 'n' roll.

It was about the sixties.

I woke one morning after the Dead left town and felt a clarity I'd never known. It was time to leave, to embark on a new adventure. I told my parents of my plan and they were predictably nonplused.

"You're going to do *what?*" my mother asked. Then she began to cry.

My father's response was less emotional. He threw his head back and laughed. "You'll be back."

Their skepticism was understandable, considering what a flop my previous attempt at self-sufficient California living had been. But this was different. This was my break. I had my own way of thinking about things, my own strange little way of looking at the world, and nothing was going to change my mind. When I was a small child I used to have these vivid dreams, almost like nightmares, in which my bed would drift away on an ice floe. I never knew where I was going, only that I was leaving everything far behind—my home and family and friends—and that I had but two choices: fall into the frigid water or hang on for the ride. After a while the fear would dissipate and I'd be filled with excitement, like a kid on a magic carpet, with a vison of a new and expanding universe. I was maybe six or seven years old at the time, but I sensed even then that my destiny was out there on the open road, somewhere far away. You may think that sounds crazy, but it's the way I felt.

I'm proud to say that I took not a single penny from anyone. Along with a friend named Stu, I boarded a plane in New York with a beat-up duffel bag and a single hundred dollar bill in my back pocket, representative of my entire life savings. I don't remember the farewell being a particularly tearful one—I think my parents looked at me as a fool dancing on the precipice; they just hoped I wouldn't get hurt too badly before coming back home and settling into some shitty job. In retrospect, I can sympathize with them. I had limited skills, practically no money, and only a handful of contacts. I'd been a borderline fuck-up most of my life. At that moment, though, as the plane roared down the runway and lifted off the ground, I wasn't the least bit apprehensive. New York was behind me, below me. A new adventure awaited. I was drunk with freedom.

Chapter 6

Stu and I took a bus from the San Francisco airport to the Grateful Dead's office in San Rafael. When we arrived, the only person in the building was John McIntire, the band's manager. I later discovered that this was a particularly weird and uncomfortable period in the business life of the Dead (which was always somewhat turbulent). The previous manager, who was the father of Grateful Dead drummer Mickey Hart, had recently departed, allegedly taking with him a sizable chunk of the band's money. McIntire, though, was a good-hearted and level-headed man, intellectual and eclectic in his tastes, open to new ideas and experiences. He seemed unfazed by my arrival and said I could find the band and the crew at a club called the Family Dog, located on the Great Highway in San Francisco.

Stu and I went straight to the Family Dog to watch the Dead play. After the show, exhausted from a long day of travel, I went home with Ramrod and his girlfriend Frances, and they were quick to open their lives and hearts to me, which I found rather extraordinary. Ramrod was no more than five-foot-seven but with strong, calloused hands, the hands of a working man. He had blond, bushy hair and often wore cowboy boots and a poncho, remnants of his days growing up in the high desert of Eastern Oregon. Like a lot of the guys who worked on the Dead crew over the years, he had a crusty exterior, but he was capable of immense compassion. Ramrod, for whatever reason, took me under his wing. Maybe it was because I was five years younger than him, and he saw me as some sort of younger brother. I don't really know. I know only that I owe just about everything to him.

Ramrod was living at the time with a man named Augustus Owsley Stanley, a brilliant sound technician who had worked for the band but whose primary focus now was avoiding jail time. "Bear," as he was known to just about everyone, was one of the great acid kings of the 1960s, a genius who had become adept at manufacturing LSD at a time when it was not only legal, but downright fashionable. Times were changing, though, and the attitude toward LSD, at least among law enforcement officials, was evolving rapidly, which was bad news for Bear. As a result, he was a bit paranoid; understandably, he wasn't thrilled with the idea of strangers hanging out at his home. Bear trusted Ramrod completely, but when he got up the next morning and found me sleeping on his floor, he was more than a little agitated.

Bear had a beautiful, rambling home in the Oakland hills, with lots of land and a neighbor whose pet cougar wailed incessantly. To me, a kid from New York, it seemed like a fairly weird setup, but then, Bear was an unusual man. In the coming months we became very good friends, but at that moment he wasn't happy to have me in his house.

I can still see him looking up at me, this big rangy kid from the East, and shaking his head.

"This ain't good, man," he said to Ramrod. "Not good at all."

Despite his trepidation Bear let me hang out at his place for another day. Then Ramrod took me to where Sonny Heard was staying, Rucka Rucka Ranch, a communal compound in Marin County where Dead guitarist Bob Weir lived. Rucka Rucka wasn't really a ranch, although there were horses and some other animals there. It took its silly, sophomoric name (I believe Ramrod was responsible) from something you'd say when you walked up to a girl and gave her breast a little tweak, imaginary or otherwise: *"Rucka Rucka!"* It was a real hippie place, and it represented my introduction to the Grateful Dead scene and the Grateful Dead family, where roadies and children and wives and girlfriends and groupies all lived together with the band. Life there was remarkably open and free, like the Summer of Love in full bloom. We had a lot of fun, to say the least, and I realized quickly that I had somehow found a life that millions of young people dreamed about; I had stumbled upon the World of the Lost Boys, and I never wanted to leave.

The guys from Pendleton, Oregon, all a little older than me, but still young enough to have a real taste for the wild life, were the primary source of my education. They'd come a few years earlier, through Kesey and the Merry Pranksters, and their cowboy attitude and image had a real influence on the band. Jackson would call me a "New Yawker," in kind of a sarcastic way, and occasionally he'd give me shit about my "New York attitude." Really, though, he was very curious about New York, which must have seemed as strange and distant to him as Pendleton did to me. Pendleton was a Western town, as opposed to a Pacific town. It had a great cowboy heritage and its citizens rightly considered themselves to be strong, hard-working people. Interestingly, Jackson, Heard, and Ramrod didn't even live in Pendleton; they lived in a little town called Hermiston, which was sort of across the tracks from Pendleton and was known to be even smaller and harder. So these guys had grown up tough together. They'd been high school buddies. Jackson and Ramrod had even spent time in reform school together—six months for stealing a bottle of liquor from a farmhand's truck. Not much of an offense, really, but they'd run into a hard-ass judge who wanted to make an example out of them. The same thing had nearly happened to me, but my father had gotten me off the hook. Jackson and Ramrod weren't so lucky.

Anyway, the agenda at Rucka Rucka was mainly this: have fun—from the time we woke up in the morning until the sun set . . . and afterward. Not that we didn't work. On a typical day Heard, Jackson, and I would get up around 9 A.M., and we'd begin loading this old silver Metro with gear. Ramrod would show up about ten o'clock, and we'd jump in the truck, all four of us, and drive to the studio, where we'd help the band set up. When we were at Rucka Rucka, though, we'd mainly do country boy things, which was all new to me. These guys fashioned themselves as real cowboys, and they loved teaching me about life in the wide open spaces, a side of life I barely knew existed. If not for my love of books and movies, through which I'd at least gotten a glimpse of Western life, I'd have been totally out of it.

Sometimes we'd go into town and buy a bunch of ammo and get all these guns and start shooting at cans. Some of the band guys would join in this, too, most notably Jerry Garcia and Pigpen McKernan. They'd bring their little handguns and we'd have a shootout. We considered safety to be a primary factor, but the truth was, target practice was rarely conducted without copious amounts of pot, so I suppose there was some risk involved. But it sure did make for an interesting time. One day, for example, we were hanging around, having a big Western-style shootout, and one of the guns we were using was a huge Blackhawk .44 magnum, a double-action six-shooter owned by Jackson that was very much like the kind of gun used in the old West. Bob Weir was sitting on a step, holding the gun, waiting for his turn to shoot, talking with Heard and Jackson, when all of a sudden—like something out of a Saturday morning cartoon—the ground beneath the muzzle of the gun began to rumble. Then a gopher poked his head out of the earth, just inches from the barrel, and looked right up at Weir. It was the strangest and funniest thing, but it also said a lot about the kind of guy Weir is. The gun was loaded and ready to go—all he had to do was cock and pull the trigger. But Bobby is a very gentle soul, incapable of hurting anyone or anything, so he just sat there and smiled at the gopher.

They watched each other for more than a minute, until finally Heard couldn't stand it any longer.

"What the fuck is this?!" he yelled. Then he reached over, took the gun from Bobby, and stuck it down the hole, just as the gopher disappeared.

BAM! BAM! BAM!

The ground blew apart, sending chunks of dirt and stone in all direction—but no gopher guts. The little guy apparently got away, much to Weir's delight and Heard's dismay.

Bobby loved animals. He owned a horse named Apache Chipper, a big Appaloosa that lived in a stall right behind the bunk I shared with Heard. Every morning this horse would wake us up in violent fashion, kicking the walls of the barn and farting as loudly as he could. Outside, in the corral, he'd run around in tight circles, snorting and bucking and spitting at anyone who dared to get near him. This was an uncut stallion, a true wild horse. I'd never seen anything like it. The only horses I'd seen were the chunky, bow-legged kind that hauled carriages filled with tourists around Central Park and dumped steaming piles of crap on the New York streets. Bobby would occasionally get up on Apache Chipper, but you could see right away it was not man riding horse, but rather, horse taking man for a ride. This was a powerful, nasty animal, with strong, muscular legs and a thick, straight back. I rarely had the nerve to go near him. He'd kick down walls, fences, anything that got in his way. I'd try to mend them and Apache Chipper would look at me as I hammered and it was like he was laughing at me: *I'm gonna knock that shit down as soon as you're through, man. So don't even bother.*

I swear, sometimes he'd walk over and just lean on the fence with his body, right after I'd finished repairing it. I was in awe of that damn horse, and I was afraid of him. In fact, about the only person at Rucka Rucka who didn't fear Apache Chipper was Jackson. He was an honest-to-God cowboy whose father had been a horse trader. I'd watch with wonder as Jackson would grab this powerful horse by the reins and take complete command of it. It was fascinating. With his boots, his buckskin shirt and Stetson hat, his steel blue eyes, his strength, his confidence, his ability to communicate with that horse . . . Jackson looked like Wild Bill Hickok.

Hanging out with Jackson and the other Pendleton boys at Rucka Rucka was like being transported to another era. We all had long hair, we smoked a ton of dope, we did what we wanted. It was a world in which the norm included Heard sucking down a six-pack of Olympia beer every day at four, like clockwork, just shotgunning the whole thing in a matter of seconds; and Jackson leading tours of the best burger joints in town, wolfing his down in a single bite, then, just for fun, grabbing yours and squeezing all the juice out before handing back to you a mangled patty in the shape of his fist. Around these boys you constantly had to be on your toes, for they'd always be pranking you, hot-footing you, literally ripping the shirt off your back.

There were few rules or regulations at Rucka Rucka. It was the kind of place where you'd wake up in the morning to find a billy goat standing on the hood of your car, pissing all over your windshield. There was a peacock at Rucka Rucka that attacked Heard every morning, for no particular reason that I could ascertain, although Heard's response, which usually involved a baseball bat and a storm of feathers, probably didn't help matters any. For a guy who grew up in the country and lived on a ranch, Heard wasn't great with animals He had a dog named Irene, but the dog hated him, because Heard had a nasty habit of kicking the mutt whenever it got in his way.

"Sonny Boy," I'd say. "Why are you kicking that poor dog?"

"Because I named him after my mother and it just makes me feel good," Heard would respond. True or not, it was a great answer.

There were strong women in our circle, too, women like Bob Weir's girlfriend, Frankie, who kept order on the ranch and who made sure we all stayed in line. And a lifelong friend and employee of the band Eileen Law, who was pregnant the summer I arrived. I held Eileen's hand while she was in labor, as Frankie helped the doctor deliver a little girl named Cassidy while Bobby played guitar. My mind was blown by the sight of this little child, so frail and helpless and beautiful, and by the courage of Eileen and the support of her friends. It was such a magical moment, such a burst of life and energy. I'd never seen anything like it. Cassidy became part of the family, too, and has been such her entire life. She's married to Cameron Sears, who became a Grateful Dead manager, and they have a child of their own.

Even though the other band members all had their own homes, Rucka Rucka was for a time the social center of the Grateful Dead. If nothing was happening as far as work or rehearsals, people would just stop by and hang out. They stayed for a few hours or a few days. Whatever. It was at the ranch that I first got to know Jerry a little bit. Jerry liked to joke about my East Coast heritage. "Look at you," he'd say. "Hanging out with the crew. You're our New York karma, man." The fact that Jerry would talk me up once in a while helped break down the barriers that naturally arose between me and the predominantly West Coast crew and band. He took a liking to me right away, maybe because I had a good and sometimes dark sense of humor, and I shared his fascination with the strange and the bizarre. And, of course, we both had a fondness for marijuana. I remember sitting around with Jerry and a few of the guys one day shortly after I arrived from New York, talking about pot smoking, sharing our various views and expertise, when Jerry pulled out a little machine and showed me how to make a perfect cigarette, one that bore a striking resemblance to an unfiltered Camel, which was the brand favored by just about all of us. I was amazed. Here was a joint that could pass for a cigarette, and thus could be taken and toked almost anywhere, which was precisely the point.

I don't want to give the impression that we did nothing but sit around and get high all day. The truth is, although we were high a lot of the time—drugs were a communal experience and an integral part of the Grateful Dead family—we also managed to get quite a lot of work done. In hindsight, I realize that my first year or two with the Grateful Dead was a time of transition for the band, as well for me. They'd been around for five years already, and they were finally becoming more than just a group of guys who loved to hang out together and play music, although they still were that, to be sure. By 1970, the Grateful Dead had become something more, something they had never really explicitly aspired to be: a hard-working, professional, career-oriented band, a band that had a chance to do what only the greatest bands do—make money and sell records without losing its identity and its integrity along the way.

Chapter 7

My apprenticeship was perhaps longer than it might have been because, as a New Yorker, I was viewed with a degree of skepticism. In time, though, my sense of humor and my willingness to embrace whatever work came my way—without worrying about compensation—helped win them over. I watched, I listened, I learned.

In time I got over being starstruck, because the guys in the band were so laid back and down to earth. They treated us not as employees, but as friends and comrades, as if we were all united in some great cause. I spent most of my time in those first few months hanging out with Ramrod and Heard. The three of us would go down to Jerry's house in Larkspur most mornings and loosely plan the day's events. At night we'd either have a show or go to a party. We hung out at Alembic, a small warehouse on Judah and Ninth, in which we built a massive public address system and recording studio. Bear had been the brains and driving force behind Alembic, but his escalating legal problems had driven him out of the picture, and his place was now taken by a man named Bob Matthews. In this world I met people like Janis Joplin, who lived down the street from Jerry in Larkspur, where he was living with Robert Hunter. Visitors to our studio included Ken Kesey and the Merry Pranksters. (The first time we met, Kesey slapped me on the back, laughed, and said, "Good! I like new blood!" He was, to say the least, a character.)

Every day was an amusement park ride, with tons of great drugs and an assortment of easy, guilt-free sexual encounters, all accompanied by a soundtrack supplied by the Grateful Dead and the many artists who became their friends. In many ways, it was like living in a movie: you know, life . . . with the boring parts taken out.

When I called home, which wasn't very often, I was careful to present a more mature, responsible picture of life in the Bay Area. I told my parents I was learning a set of skills that would last a lifetime: how to drive a truck, set up equipment, handle and even tune expensive musical instruments. I was learning how to work at a pace that most people would find unmanageable. Most of the hedonistic details I left out, the stories of debauchery that made life with the Dead so amazing. I just wanted them not to worry, to think that I was making it on my own in a strange and distant land. Which was true. Although I had yet to begin collecting a salary, I was able to survive off the kindness of the band and crew. I had a place to stay, food to eat, work that I enjoyed, and friends whose company I cherished. Occasionally, someone would throw me a few bucks for working so hard and asking so little in return. I knew if I hung in there long enough and kept paying attention, there would be a place for me on the payroll. For the time being, though, I was content to be merely an intern. After all, even if the pay sucked, the benefits were hard to beat. In terms of compensation, you had to look at the whole package.

How many nineteen-year-old kids were doing the kinds of things I was doing? In so many ways it was a fantasy that I was living. Picture this: me and Ramrod driving from Rucka Rucka to Pacific High Recording, across from Brady Alley, where I'd lived when I first came to the Bay Area a few years earlier, with a five-foot tank of nitrous oxide in the back of our truck. Nitrous tends to get short shrift when cultural historians discuss the great hallucinogenic fervor of the 1960s and early 1970s. It was actually a very popular and commonly used drug, especially in and around the world of the Grateful Dead. Nitrous had an interesting background. It had been invented by a doctor in the deep South and was one of the first commonly used anesthetics. Like a lot of painkillers, though, nitrous developed an avid following among people who neither needed surgery nor had any identifiable ache that needed numbing. In other words, it became a recreational drug, carted from town to town in the Old West, and hawked by the equivalent of frontier medicine men and carnival barkers. A stage would be erected in the center of town, and several of the community's more influential and highfalutin citizens—the mayor, the sheriff, president of the local bank—would be invited to the stage and offered an opportunity to take a toke, which they usually accepted. The results were immediate and wondrous, and before long the entire town would on the equivalent of a frontier acid trip.

To understand the remarkable hallucinogenic properties of nitrous oxide, it helps to understand a little about the body's chemistry, and the effect that an inflated level of nitrogen can have on the brain. Deep-sea divers, for example, sometimes experience a physiological phenomenon known as nitrogen narcosis, which is also known as "rapture of the deep." When your brain receives a sudden and dramatic influx of nitrogen, a strange and beautiful feeling of euphoria comes over you, and the sheath that envelopes your mind, separating reality from fantasy, is peeled away. Admittedly, this sort of trip can have its consequences when you're deep beneath the surface of the ocean, floating around in blackness; it is not, generally speaking, something the average diver seeks to experience.

But for landlocked, music-loving Deadheads, nitrogen narcosis was an altered state of mind that was pursued with almost religious fervor. It was a cheap, easy high, one that could be indulged several times a day, usually without consequences. I'm not saying it wasn't danger-ous—obviously, when you're depriving your body of oxygen, bad shit can happen, but we tried to exercise caution. We always kept a supply of pure oxygen nearby, and we vehemently discouraged the practice of going solo on nitrous. See, the gas makes you pass out a little bit, and if you imbibe too heavily and lose consciousness for too long, you can do some serious harm to your brain and body. I know of a few instances in which people came very close to permanently damaging themselves. But it only happened when you did it alone. That's why we had nitrous "parties," because the buddy system worked. One time in the early 1980s Jerry and I decided to do some nitrous together at our studio on Front Street; we sat there on little boxes, just him and me, passing the hose back and forth, toking together, and we both passed out at the exact same time. We each fell forward and banged our heads together—*Wham!*—and that woke us up. We sat there for a moment or two, rubbing our bruised foreheads, waiting for the fog to lift, and then suddenly we looked at each other and got really spooked. Without saying a word we jumped up and ran out the front door and locked the place up and got into our cars and drove away. It was just too weird.

On a nitrous high you go into these deep, mind-bending dreams, and if you come out of it cleanly—without cracking your skull, for instance—there is a sudden rush of confidence and knowledge, a heightened sense of awareness, and you instantly say, "Yes! I've got it!" as if you suddenly understand the meaning of life . . . as if the uni-verse is no longer infinite and incomprehensible, but small enough to fit in the palm of your hand. In reality, of course, you've just gone to a place where your brain is starved for oxygen. It's a pretty simple thing, really.

Another great thing about nitrous oxide was that in the 1970s it was viewed as a rather benign substance by law enforcement officials, especially when compared to LSD, speed, and even pot (cocaine and heroin were in a league of their own). Although it was a controlled substance, with restrictions on how easily it could be obtained, we rarely had a problem getting all we needed. We'd just go to any one of several dozen gas companies in the Bay Area, tell the salesperson we needed a few tanks of nitrous oxide for testing our equipment (which was, in fact, one of the many legitimate functions of nitrous), and he'd give it to us. After a while word got out that nitrous was gaining favor among the party set, and it did become slightly more difficult to acquire. As with anything, though, where there's a will, there's a way. One time after a recording session I was riding home with Heard and Ramrod, when all of a sudden we spotted a truck parked in front of a building. Strapped onto the bed of the truck, standing erect and proud and just waiting to be released, were more than a dozen six-foot tanks of nitrous oxide! We'd happened upon a deliveryman making his legal and appointed rounds. Well, since no one was guarding the truck, we pulled over to the side of the road and Heard quickly jumped out, freed one of the tanks, and, despite the fact that a full tank of nitrous weighed close to two hundred pounds, handed it off to me. Then we pulled away.

"Shit!"

I glanced back. Heard was fiddling with the tank's valve.

"What's the problem?" I asked.

"It's empty!"

"You're kidding?"

"Nope. This fucker's kicked."

Well, that explained why Heard tossed that baby so easily, anyway. Ramrod turned right at the next light, then right again . . . and again, until we'd completed a square and we were parked right next to the delivery truck all over again. Heard jumped out, placed the empty tank back on the bed of the truck, and exchanged it for one that had a few good trips left in it. Then we drove away.

Later Ramrod and I wound up at Pacific High Recording, a studio where Jerry was helping David Crosby with a solo album called *If I Could Only Remember My Name.* An appropriate title considering that one of the first times I saw David he was in the process of snorting up a long line of cocaine that he had used to spell out Jerry's name on a coffee table. Jokes aside, though, that was a pivotal day for me, because I learned how to set up some of Jerry's equipment and was treated like a member of the Grateful Dead entourage, not only by Jerry, but by Crosby, who was one of the most gifted and well-known performers of his time—hell, of any time. He was brilliant. The well-documented drug addiction that would later nearly cost him his life hadn't yet exacted much of a toll, Crosby seemed no more seduced by chemicals than anyone else in our vast circle. And he seemed to be a genuinely warm and friendly human being.

If there was anything unusual about Crosby, it was his choice of drugs. In the late sixties and early seventies, cocaine had yet to gain much of a foothold in American culture. Certainly it wasn't very popular among the Grateful Dead (although that would change). I had no interest in joining the party that day, not because I was prudish or concerned about the potential danger of cocaine, but simply because Ramrod and I had a full tank of nitrous oxide to keep us happy. So we toked and worked and listened, and generally had a great day.

As was often the case with nitrous, however, the delivery system was problematic. There were basically two ways to inhale nitrous: directly through a hose attached to the tank, or through some type of receptacle into which nitrous had been pumped. We were using the latter method on this day. We started out with balloons, but they were cheap and they kept popping, and we ended up running to the nearby Hub

Pharmacy in the Haight every fifteen minutes to buy more. Eventually we switched to condoms, but they didn't work either. Finally we bought some large latex gloves, which did the trick, although it made for an outrageous scene. Picture the two of us, sitting there in the studio, blowing up these giant gloves, tying off the ends, and sitting there sucking nitrous through a tiny hole in the thumb. Jerry was the first to come out. He practically fell over laughing. Then he went back inside and retrieved Crosby. They both stood there for a few moments, shaking their heads, convulsing with laughter. Finally, though, they stopped, looked at each other, and then looked at us.

"Hey, man," Jerry said with a smile. "Give me a tug on that."

Ramrod handed him the glove. Jerry took a toke, then passed it to Crosby. And then they went back to work.

It may not be fashionable to say this, but the truth is when you do drugs with people, you form a bond with them, and my generally adventurous and open nature when it came to chemicals, particularly hallucinogenics, made it easier for me to fit in. Not just with the guys on the crew, but with the band as well. The more you were willing to expose yourself, to share in the culture of the Dead, the more likely you were to gain acceptance. Nitrous was part of that culture. So was LSD.

Acid was everywhere at this time, and while my brief, terrifying trip to Rikers Island had done a great job of convincing me that I neither wanted nor was qualified for a career in LSD trafficking, I had no compunction about being a recreational user. To my delight it seemed that everyone in my new world shared that attitude. So common was acid among the Dead and its followers that you had to exercise a bit of caution and have a heightened sense of awareness just to keep from getting more than you'd bargained for. Everyone was dosing you all the time in those days, so if you didn't pay attention you'd find yourself wandering around backstage, moving in slow motion, suddenly and inexplicably in the middle of an unscheduled acid trip. It was, as Kesey noted, the Electric Kool-Aid Acid Test. Only sometimes it was Pepsi . . . or ginger ale . . . or coffee. Didn't matter. One minute you'd be feeling fine, sober, and the next you'd be flying high, and you'd realize later, *Oh, yeah, man . . . they got me again.*

There wasn't anyone on the crew who didn't go through it—I was dosed several times in the early days. It was a rite of passage, not so much a hazing (like sadistic frat boys making pledges drink till they puke) as a polygraph of the soul: *Okay, you want to hang with us? Let's see what you're really like. Let's see who you really are.* See, LSD has a phenomenal ability to break down the barriers that your mind places between you and the world. It strips away ego and inhibition, leaving you emotionally naked (sometimes physically, too, which is why you'd so often see kids removing their clothes and running on stage at concerts in the sixties and early seventies). You are who you are on LSD. There is no hiding.

That was the thinking, anyway.

All of us involved with the Grateful Dead became afficionados of LSD. Sometimes before a show we'd just take a giant garbage can and use a garden hose to mix up Kool-Aid and LSD, and it would sit there throughout the night, a vat of acid available to anyone and everyone. At virtually every performance several members of the band played while high on acid; those of us on the crew routinely worked while we were high. It was just part of what we did, as normal as having a hot dog during intermission. I never experienced any horrific trips, anything that made me want to fly off a building. But the trip—the high—was only part of the rationale for taking acid; it also served as a stimulant, and as such allowed those of us on the crew to stay awake and work long hours, tearing down sets and packing away equipment and driving to the next town for the next show. Day blended into night, night into day. It was a remarkable life, being tested all the time on physical, emotional, and spiritual levels. We melded together and learned everything about each other.

And I loved it.

Chapter 8

Sometimes only distance can make you realize how much something means to you. Or, as Dorothy said in *The Wizard of Oz,* "There's no place like home."

Home, in my case, was a variety of places: Rucka Rucka, a friend's apartment, a hotel room, even the backseat of my car, where I spent many nights during my first couple years in the Bay Area. Mainly, though, it was wherever the Grateful Dead happened to be hanging out. As much as I enjoyed that life, however, there were times when I grew frustrated at having no money, no tangible career path, no bed to call my own.

Once, when Heard went back up to Oregon for a while, he gave me permission to borrow his clothes, and I gladly took him up on the offer. Before going out one evening I put on what I thought was Heard's leather coat, and when I stuffed my hands in the pocket I was shocked to discover a huge wad of bills. I had no idea how Heard had managed to get his hands on so much cash, and quite frankly I didn't want to know. I knew only that I was dead broke and hungry, and I figured Heard wouldn't mind if I took out a small loan. So I peeled off a single fifty-dollar bill, which I replaced a few days later. I later discovered that neither the money nor the coat belonged to Heard—in fact the coat was the property of John McIntire, and the money belonged to the Dead. John had seen me in that coat, and he knew I could have walked off with a big chunk of cash. But I hadn't, and he later told me he was impressed by my honesty.

More important to me, for a while anyway, was the generosity extended by Dan Healy, a brilliant technician and electronics wizard who was something of a guru to all of us on the Dead crew. Some of the other guys, Bob Matthews in particular, had sort of a snotty attitude about the technical aspects of the business, as if they were engineers and we were merely hired hands—they were the brains, we were the brawn. (Although I should point out that Bob was a true brother who once bailed me out of jail when I got arrested for having some outstanding traffic tickets.) Healy wasn't like that. He took pleasure not only in doing his work, but in sharing his knowledge with others who seemed genuinely interested in learning. He was a teacher, in the truest sense of the word. Dan was the first person who showed me how to work a Fender amp. He taught me about electricity and building and buying speaker cabinets. I admired and liked Healy, so when he went off for a while too work with a band called Quicksilver Messenger Service, I was only too happy to join him (it happened when one of their roadies took off his clothes at a show at Winterland, lay down naked on the stage, and then walked off, never to be seen again). The pay was minimal and sporadic, but the compensation included free room and board, which sounded pretty good to me at the time.

Quicksilver was a Bay Area band that had been formed in 1965 by a folk singer and songwriter named Dino Valenti, but did not release its first album until 1968. By that time Valenti had left the band and been imprisoned on a drug charge. By 1970, when Healy and I went to work for Quicksilver, Valenti had returned and taken over the reins of the band that was rightfully his. I'd gotten to know some of the guys in Quicksilver, because our paths often crossed in the studio (just as they crossed with other San Francisco artists, such as Janis Joplin and the Jefferson Airplane), and so I thought I knew what I was getting into. But I really didn't. My frame of reference was the Grateful Dead, and I quickly discovered that no other band operated in such a democratic fashion. Certainly not Quicksilver, which at the time I arrived was Dino Valenti's personal fiefdom.

Dino had been a carny, and it showed in just about everything he did. A nice way of putting it would be to say that he had a dynamic personality; another way of putting it would be to say that he was something of an asshole. Regardless, I wasn't accustomed to working for someone who treated people the way Dino did. Let me give you an example. I lived at the rehearsal hall where the band practiced and stored its gear. My primary job was to drive a truck for the band, to shepherd equipment and instruments wherever they were needed. I'd been there only a few days when I got a strange call from Dino.

"Come over right now," he said, "and bring me some wood."

"Wood?"

"Yeah, I want to make a fire in my house."

He hung up, leaving me standing there, dumbfounded, with the receiver dangling from my hand. Suddenly I had no idea what my job was. I had hoped to be a stagehand, to learn more about music and equipment—about the *business* of rock 'n' roll—by working alongside Dan Healy. Instead, apparently, I was some sort of servant.

Bring me some wood?

Not wanting to get fired in the first week on the job, I went out and picked up some firewood and drove to Dino's house in the middle of the night. I rang the doorbell and waited nearly ten minutes for someone to answer. When the door opened I was treated to the sight of Dino, stark naked except for the gold chain around his neck, holding a glass of wine in his hand.

"Come in, Steve," he said, gesturing with his free hand.

As I crossed the threshold I could see that Dino wasn't alone. Far from it. Behind him were two stunningly curvaceous and beautiful blonde women who looked to be in their early twenties. They, too, had shed their clothes, and now they were leaning on each other, smiling, stroking each other's hair. I'd been around musicians long enough by now to know that attractive women were one of the perks—maybe the best perk—but I was still taken aback. For one thing, these were not your garden-variety, run-of-the-mill groupies. These were the type of women you'd see in *Playboy*—flawless, airbrushed women. A fantasy come to life. Not only that, but it was abundantly clear to me from the looks on their faces, and the look on Dino's face, that this display of flesh was primarily for my amusement. I'll be honest—for the first thirty seconds or so I harbored some small hope that I was about to be invited into an orgy. But as Dino began ordering me around—"Set the wood down over there. The matches are on the mantel. Come on, man, it's cold in here, get the fire going!"—it became abundantly clear that their exhibitionism was designed primarily to cause me discomfort. They wanted to watch me squirm. They wanted to tease and to taunt me, and send me home blue-balled and baffled.

When the door closed behind me and I heard the girls laughing, I knew all I needed to know about Dino Valenti, and I found myself wondering, *What have I gotten myself into?*

My initial assessment of Dino was confirmed on a daily basis. He was a talented but extremely unusual man who craved nothing so much as power. A true megalomaniac, he made a practice of berating the people in his circle: bandmates, crew, management, girlfriends, *everyone.* He seemed to enjoy torturing people, making their lives miserable. I couldn't believe what a bad decision I'd made, and I wondered what I would do when the inevitable happened and Quicksilver fell apart; actually, I wondered if I'd even last long enough to see the band unravel.

By the fall of 1970, Quicksilver Messenger Service was in turmoil. John Cipollina, the band's guitar player, declared his dissatisfaction with Dino and announced that he was going to quit. Then Healy began getting into arguments with Dino, and finally he quit. Well, once Dan left there was no way in hell I was going to stay. By December I was preparing to move back into my car. Things were so bad with Dino that even being homeless and jobless was preferable to working for Quicksilver.

Fortunately, the Grateful Dead came to my rescue again. On what turned out to be my last day of work for Quicksilver, I took a ride with Rex Jackson down to El Monte, where the Dead were playing a show. The band and crew were staying together at the Tropicana, one of the all-time great rock 'n' roll hotels, a legendary place that catered to virtually every big band that passed through Los Angeles. There seemed to be almost no rules at the Tropicana: bad behavior, the hallmark of the working band, was not only tolerated, but encouraged. Jackson and I got to our room and did what we always did: we made it ours. This was something that Bear had started, back in the days when he traveled with the band. Bear believed that one way you kept your sanity on the road was to transform your surroundings, to rid the hotel room of its sterile atmosphere and make it feel like home, whatever that meant to you. In Bear's case—and Jackson followed his example—that meant removing most of the lightbulbs from lamps and lighting a bunch of scented candles, hanging pictures and paintings, laying embroidered cloths and rugs and quilts all over the room. Like Bear, Jackson had this down to a science. He could break a hotel room down and turn it into his own private pad in about ten minutes.

Anyway, we went to the venue and I helped set up for the show (Jackson showed me how to do Billy Kreutzmann's drums that night). While watching the band I realized how much I missed being around these guys. True, it wasn't like I never saw them anymore. Quicksilver and the Dead shared some of the same studio space and occasionally, as on this night, I pitched in and helped the crew. But I didn't really belong there anymore. I had left. And now I wanted nothing more than to come back.

Jackson and I returned to the Tropicana to discover that his room had been gutted. Apparently one of the candles had tipped over and set fire to a quilt, which then ignited the mattress, which then . . . well, you get the picture. Remarkably enough, the fire department had arrived almost instantly and prevented the fire from spreading beyond our room. Even more remarkable was the fact that I don't even remember anyone getting all that worked up about the whole incident. We had destroyed a room and nearly burned down the hotel, and yet they didn't even throw us out. It was just another day in the life of the Tropicana Hotel.

We ended up staying with Phil Lesh, the Dead's bass player. See, that's the way it was with this band, especially in the early days. These guys opened their hearts and minds and homes to so many people. I'd seen that at Rucka Rucka Ranch, where Bob Weir provided a warm bed and food for just about everyone on the crew at one time or another. Even now Bill Kreutzmann, the band's drummer, was sharing a place with William "Kid" Candelario, another member of the crew. When I'd been working at the theaters back East I saw a lot of bands, but I never saw any that displayed the generosity and kindness of the Grateful Dead. It changed after a while, of course, as the Dead became a bigger, richer corporate entity, and we all got older and some of the band members started to request their own rooms on the road. At this time, however, it was truly a communal thing between band and crew. There was no separation. Sometimes I'd room with

Jackson or Heard; other times I'd stay with Jerry or Phil. It didn't matter. It was like we were all on some great and mystical journey, the point of which was to get the music out to as many people as we possibly could. And nothing else mattered.

I was thinking all this as I hung out in Phil's room, smoking a joint, talking with my friends. I wasn't as upbeat as I usually was, and I guess Phil sensed something was wrong.

"You okay, man?" he asked.

"I'm just having a tough time with Quicksilver."

Phil smiled. "Dino?"

"Yeah, Dino. He's too much to handle."

Phil nodded, took a tug on a joint. "Screw it then. Come work for us."

Jesus . . . was it that simple? Could I really just walk away from Quicksilver and return to the Grateful Dead, as if I'd never left?

"Seriously, man," Phil added. "It's a lifestyle choice: good or bad."

"Uh-huh."

"All right then."

We shook hands. "Thanks," I said.

Chapter 9

The first time that Jerry Garcia and I had a conversation of any depth occurred in late December of 1970, when I was still working for free, trying to learn my craft, sleeping in the back of a green '51 Cadillac that Ramrod had sold me for a hundred bucks. I'd gotten to know Jerry a little bit just by hanging around the band and working with Ramrod, Jackson, and Heard. As I said, Jerry liked the fact that I came from New York and sort of balanced out the West Coast attitude that permeated the Grateful Dead scene, but we were far from friends. I was just another new kid who didn't get in the way and seemed not to be a jerk, which was really all that was necessary to be viewed favorably by Jerry—he was a good and gracious man who opened his arms to all kinds of different people.

At this time Jerry was an immensely vibrant and voracious artist, so fascinated with writing and playing music that he seemed always to have a guitar in his hands. From the time he woke up in the morning until the last joint had been smoked late at night, Jerry would sit there noodling. Sometimes he'd rehearse his own songs, sometimes he'd create new ones on the spot. Sometimes he'd play old bluegrass standards. And sometimes he would just jam endlessly. Don't get me wrong—Jerry loved to perform, but I always got the feeling that even if no one was around to listen, he would have played anyway. The music came from somewhere deep in his soul, and there was no separating the two.

In addition to fronting the Dead, Jerry used to feed his muse by playing gigs all over the city—sometimes solo, sometimes with other musicians. This was the genesis of the Jerry Garcia Band, for example, an eclectic and revolving cast of gifted musicians that always included bass player John Kahn. Around this same time Jerry's restlessness, and his interest in exploring other types of music, led to the formation of another ancillary project, the New Riders of the Purple Sage. Phil Lesh and Mickey Hart also played with the New Riders, whose sound was, perhaps inevitably, reminiscent of the Dead although with more of a country flavor. Jerry played pedal steel guitar for the New Riders, and I swear he was at his happiest when that band opened for the Grateful Dead, even though he would be compelled to spend the better part of five hours on stage.

In those glory days there seemed to be no limit to Jerry's stamina or creativity. Blues, rock 'n' roll, folk, country, bluegrass—he could perform and write in any genre. And he could find happiness and fulfillment in any of them. For Jerry it wasn't enough to simply be the genius behind the Grateful Dead, because to him it wasn't about money and fame. Not primarily, anyway, and especially not then. It was about art and music, the things he loved best. Jerry wanted to be free to play whenever and wherever the mood struck him, and to that end, despite his status as a rock 'n' roll superstar, he continued to play the role of a troubadour on the side, performing gigs at small clubs and coffeehouses throughout the Bay Area. Sometimes there would be no advance notice that he was going to play. He'd just make a call in the afternoon and be on stage with his guitar a few hours later, sitting in with other musicians, entertaining a few dozen or a few hundred lucky onlookers with a dazzling set—you know, the kind of show that would be referred to as "unplugged" a quarter century later, but which really wasn't unplugged at all. It was just more subdued, more dependent on the raw talent of the artist than the typical rock 'n' roll show.

Usually Jerry was accompanied on these forays by Ramrod, whose job was to carry and set up Jerry's favorite amplifier, a Fender twin reverb. After a while, however, Ramrod got tired of carting this thing around, especially after working in the studio all afternoon. So, one day, as we walked out of Alembic, Ramrod passed the responsibility on to me.

"I don't feel like staying in the city tonight," he said. "Can you help me out with Jerry?"

"What's involved?" I asked, although I didn't really care. Whatever was required, I was I was willing to do it if it meant I'd get to hang out and work with Jerry Garcia all night. It hadn't occurred to me that this brief conversation might represent a door opening, and that on the other side was a whole new career.

"It's easy," Ramrod said. "Just take the gear over and help him set up. He'll do the rest."

"Okay," I said. "No problem." So we put the amp and one of Jerry's guitars in the trunk of my Caddy and I drove across town to a club called the Matrix, where Jerry was scheduled to play a show that evening. When I arrived, at about 2 P.M., there were only two people at the Matrix: Jerry and the owner of the club.

"Steve," Jerry said with a smile. "What are you doing here?"

"Filling in for Ramrod . . . if that's okay with you."

He nodded and waved me in. "Absolutely. Come on."

As Ramrod predicted, Jerry was as patient and gracious as could be. We walked out onto the quiet, darkened stage, and he began explaining what sort of setup he preferred: where he wanted to sit or stand, where the amp should be positioned. It took only a short time to put everything in order, so by four o'clock we were ready for the show. That left us with several hours to kill. We walked down the street to a burger joint, where Jerry treated me to dinner, and then we went back to the Matrix, retreated to a back room, lit up a joint, and got to know each other.

One of the great things about pot was (and is, frankly) the way it gently broke down inhibitions and barriers, and allowed two people to express their feelings. The very act of sharing a joint was a communal experience that facilitated friendship and bonding in a way that no other drug could. One person rolled, the others watched. Then you lit it up and passed it around, and pretty soon you were all a bit looser. It was, to my way of thinking, the perfect party drug: not only was it cheap, easy to use, and comparatively harmless (to my way of thinking, marijuana, which has wonderful healing properties, is less a drug than a blessed herb, and does far less damage than many over-the-counter drugs, most notably alcohol), but it seemed designed for group use. Pot, LSD . . . those were social drugs. You wanted to be in groups when you did them. You didn't want to be alone. That was no fun. Heroin? You might as well have been hiding in a bathroom somewhere for hours and hours, with the door locked, the world just an irritant trying to invade your fantasy. Pot was about friendship, laughter, good times. Heroin, and to a lesser degree cocaine, was about isolation, darkness, damage.

Jerry wasn't into any of that shit at this time. He was never much of a drinker and hadn't yet been sucked into the blackness of the opiate powders. LSD? Pot? Nitrous? Sure. We all enjoyed a good psychedelic high now and then. Pot, in fact, was a major part of our daily diet, one of the fundamental building blocks in the great pyramid of nutrition.

We saw no harm in it whatsoever. It fostered friendship and creativity, and it was as much a part of the Grateful Dead scene as the music itself.

As we talked and toked that night at the Matrix, Jerry and I connected in a way that I hadn't anticipated at all. Although I was no longer starstruck when in the presence of the band or any of the other great musicians who traveled in their circle, I still looked up to them. Despite the Dead's egalitarian philosophy, I was aware that band members existed in one world, and crew members existed largely in another. They were the stars and we were the supporting cast. And it was equally true that among the stars, Jerry burned brightest. He was the creative force behind the Grateful Dead, an eclectic and innovative composer and guitar virtuoso of almost unparalleled skill and imagination. I considered him to be nothing less than a genius, and what I saw that day only served to reinforce my beliefs. More than that, though, I came to see what a genuinely decent man he was, what a gentle and compassionate soul. He believed there was an inherent goodness in people . . . in all people.

I was younger than Jerry and already more cynical and skeptical than he was (probably because I came from New York), but I shared with him a fascination with the lost souls of our society, with the weird and woebegone. For me it started when I was a kid, in an area called the Bowery, in lower Manhattan. I told Jerry about going down there with my father, and how these downtrodden men would come over to the car and hold out their hats or their dirty, calloused hands and beg for money. The more ambitious (and sober) would do the windshield thing: they'd jump out of the shadows and spritz the glass and start to work with the squeegee before you even had a chance to react. Didn't matter whether or not your car needed to be cleaned; didn't matter whether or not you wanted them to clean it. The point was, they did it. And then you'd feel obligated to give them something, anything. Not everyone gave, of course. Some people just honked their horn, cursed at these stinking, sorry men, and then drove off. But I remember feeling nothing so much as sadness for them, that their lives had been reduced to this. My father, hardened as he was, seemed sympathetic, too. He'd sit there in traffic, letting the men clean his window, and he'd explain to me who they were, that not all of them were alcoholics or drug addicts or escapees from mental asylums. Some of them, he said, were once great men, titans of industry—bankers, lawyers— winners who had become losers after the crash of twenty-nine. They'd become lost and rootless and never found their way back home. So now they lived on the streets.

While growing up I was always curious about these men, about how some people survived hard times and some people did not, and how society dealt with the homeless and the forgotten. Jerry nodded as I told him this story.

"I know how you feel," he said. And then he went on to tell me about his own upbringing, about what it was like to be a kid whose mother ran a saloon. Not a tavern or a pub or a restaurant, but an honest-to-God *bar,* one that catered primarily to hard-drinking sea-men and longshoremen, with a steady flow of bums intent on drinking away their public assistance checks or whatever they had accrued through handouts.

Like me, Jerry knew what it was like to be essentially homeless. He and his friend Robert Hunter, a brilliant poet who wrote the lyrics to many of the Dead's best songs, had spent some time in the early years living out of their cars, just as I had done more recently, and was in fact doing at that time. Jerry didn't think it was sad or pathetic that an old Caddy was my home; he seemed almost wistful about it, as if it reminded him of a simpler, quieter time in his own life. Not that he wanted to go back, really, but there was a romanticism to the wander-ing life, especially as seen through the eyes of Kerouac and Kesey and other writers Jerry admired. So, in addition to offering me a few bucks to help me out of my wretched situation, Jerry always offered a smile and a few words of wisdom.

"You're a big guy," he said. "Too big to sleep comfortably in the back of a car."

"Jesus," I said. "It's a Cadillac—they don't come any bigger."

"I know, so here's what you do. Take out the backseat, lay down on the floor, and stretch your feet into the trunk." He laughed. "Almost as good as a Hilton."

He told me other things, too, like how to extend a buck by using water, ketchup, salt and pepper—typically absconded from a diner— to make a suitable cup of tomato soup. He wasn't kidding, either. It was a sincere bit of advice from one who had been there. It was almost as if Jerry knew I wouldn't be living that poverty-stricken nomadic existence forever, that soon I'd be an official part of the Dead family and everything would be better. But it would also be different, and in some way he was trying to make me understand that it was okay to enjoy whatever weird things life brought my way. It was okay to have something in common with the Bowery bums and the waterfront drunks, because that connection made you more human, more complete. It made you a better person.

Deep down Jerry considered himself to be a bit of a freak. He knew he was different from other people, and not merely because of his musicianship. He saw things differently and he felt things differently. He believed he was an outcast, and so he was fascinated with the tortured souls of the world. People like Rondo Hattan, a giant of a man who suffered from a glandular disorder that gave him a thickened brow and a genuinely menacing appearance. The disease surely made his life miserable, but it also helped him build a career as a villain in a string of old Hollywood movies. Like me, Jerry loved old movies, and when I mentioned Hattan's name, he slapped his hands together and fell back in his chair. That had never happened before—I'd never met anyone who had heard of Rondo Hattan.

Less surprising, I guess, was the fact that Jerry knew all about Johnny Puleo and his Harmonica Gang, a strange and mostly forgotten combo of jazz-playing midgets. He wanted to know how I'd heard of them, and I explained that there was a bit of musical heritage in my family. I told him about my uncle, Mitchell Parish, who was a very successful lyricist who had composed more than five hundred major songs, including "Deep Purple," "The Stars Fell on Alabama," "Sophisticated Lady" (with Duke Ellington), "Moonlight Serenade" (with Glenn Miller), and, perhaps the most famous of all, "Stardust."

Jerry's jaw dropped. "Your uncle was Mitchell Parish?"

"Uh-huh."

"Holy shit," he said. "That's wild."

"Why?" I mean, it was wild, but I wasn't sure exactly what he was getting at.

"Because my mom's all-time favorite song was 'Stardust.'"

We both shuddered. I had always believed in fate, in the possibility of some cosmic force dictating our movements and decisions, and ultimately bringing us face-to-face with people we were destined to meet—people with whom we shared a common bond—and this sort of thing confirmed my belief. Many years later, with the help of my cousin, Jane Ross (who was a big Dead fan), Jerry and I went and found Mitch, who was living in Manhattan at the Dakota. I hadn't seen him since I was a kid, when he used to come to our house for family reunions, and although his knees had deteriorated so badly that he was confined to a wheelchair, he was as sharp and as pleasant as I remembered. Mitch wore an ascot and talked perfectly. He was very flamboyant, a real showbiz kind of character, and he and Jerry hit it off right away. He knew all about the Grateful Dead, of course, because he continued to follow popular culture, especially music. Over the next couple years Mitch came to several Dead shows at Madison Square Garden and oh, man, he was just incredible. He'd stay with me, right at the edge of the stage during the show, and afterward he'd hang out with me and Jerry and tell us these fantastic stories of the music business. We had so much fun with him, and he absolutely loved the music. Mitch and Jerry even talked about writing some songs together, which would have been a trip, a collaboration for the ages, and Jerry even mentioned the possibility of doing a documentary about the life and work of Mitchell Parish, but none of it ever came to fruition. Mitch passed away in 1993, right before we got to do anything like that. But what a great resource he was, and what a great man.

Jerry, I realized that night at the Matrix, was more than just a writer or a guitar player. He was a historian, a true student of music in all its myriad forms. At one point he asked me to retrieve his amp from the stage so that he could fool around with his guitar for a while. I'd see him do that often over the years, watch him fidget and fuss in a back room after the stage had been prepared, and wait for the inevitable moment when he called for the amp. See, that was Jerry: he was never completely comfortable unless he had a guitar in his hands. So I did as he requested, and pretty soon his fingers were flying, playing old songs like "Stardust."

"Name a tune," he said with a smile. I did, and instantly Jerry began playing the melody.

"Try again," he said.

And so it went, practically right up until the moment he walked out on stage to a full house at the Matrix. I don't know how many song titles I gave him. Maybe thirty. Some were pretty damn obscure, but Jerry knew every one, and he played each of them flawlessly. I couldn't stump him. Not that I cared. It wasn't a competition, really, but more like a private tutorial. And I couldn't have been a more grateful and eager student.

Chapter 10

Even in the peace-love-and-understanding climate of the late 1960s and early 1970s, it was not impossible to wear out your welcome. I was working like crazy in '70, '71, lugging Jerry's amp wherever and whenever he needed it, helping out the crew of the Grateful Dead, and trying to latch on with the New Riders, which I considered to be my best chance at a full-time paying gig. And, still, I relied on the kindness and generosity of friends and strangers alike when I wanted a clean mattress and a hot meal, when I simply couldn't stand sleeping in my car and eating ketchup soup any longer.

Rucka Rucka remained option number one, at least until late 1970, when I fucked up a couple times and gave Bobby, the most laid-back, thoughtful guy you'd ever want to meet, reason to question whether I was worth the trouble.

It began one night when I was driving back to Rucka Rucka in an old flatbed truck. It wasn't unusual for us to have mechanical problems, such as broken gas gauges, with our vehicles—we drove them long and hard and didn't exactly take care of them—and when I heard the engine sputter and cough, I knew I was in for a long night. I pulled over to the side of the road and waited for someone to stop and offer assistance. That person turned out to be Bob Weir, who was also on his way home.

Bobby was driving a brand-new orange BMW. Good Samaritan that he was, he offered to give me a lift back into town, so that I could get some gas (I figured from the sound of the engine that the problem was no more serious than that) for the truck. I thank him and jumped into the passenger seat.

We returned about a half hour later. I dumped five gallons of gas into the tank of the truck and tried to start it up. No luck. The alternator cranked, but the engine refused to turn over.

"Dry as a bone, huh?" Bobby said.

"Yeah. I'll have to prime it."

I popped the hood of the truck and dumped some gasoline onto the carburetor, an old gearhead's trick that usually works, but can be a bit dangerous under some circumstances. Unfortunately, this was one of those circumstances: hot night, hot engine, volatile fumes . . . a shitty vehicle. I jumped behind the wheel, turned the key and . . .

WHOOSH!

The engine burst into flames.

"Jesus Christ!" Bobby yelled. "Turn it off!"

I did, but the fire continued. Pretty soon the front of the truck was practically engulfed in flames. Bobby stood there on the side of this county two-lane, half laughing, half scared to death, expecting an explosion, as I ripped off my shirt and flailed away at the flames. Realizing that wasn't going to do the trick, I began scooping up big handfuls of dirt, which I tossed onto the engine block. Eventually the blaze diminished and the flames withered and died, leaving a smoking, soot-covered truck that looked as though it had just been charcoal-broiled.

As we wiped away the dirt and futilely tried to start the truck again, I saw another car off in the distance, coming toward us. As it drew near I could see the faint but unmistakable outline of a law enforcement vehicle. The car, a local sheriff's patrol, approached slowly, without lights or sirens. The driver stepped out, looked at the still-steaming truck, smelled the acrid air, and smiled.

"You boys trying to build a bonfire here?" he asked.

"No, sir," I said. "Just trying to get home."

He asked each of us for identification, then went back to his car. As he shut the door, I looked over at Bobby, who appeared to be nervous.

"What's wrong, man?" I asked. I knew the cop was just checking for outstanding warrants, making sure that neither of us was an escaped felon or something. I knew I was clean, and from everything I'd seen of Bobby, he had to be clean, too.

"Not good," he said, shaking his head. "Not good at all."

The cop returned after a few minutes. He handed my license back to me, but waved Bobby's ominously in the air, as if it held some terrible secret. "I'm afraid we've got a little problem here, Mr. Weir."

It turned out that Bobby was a serial scofflaw who had accumulated scores of traffic and parking violations over the years, and now owed hundreds of dollars in fines. I was allowed to make a phone call to a towing company and get a ride home; Bobby was handcuffed and taken to jail. He spent only a few hours there, of course, but if it hadn't been for me and the fucking truck, he wouldn't have been arrested. Not that night, anyway.

Bobby forgave me because that was his nature; unfortunately, just one week later, I really tested his generosity. I drove home late one night after a gig with the Garcia Band and parked the truck—the very same truck, which had somehow survived my attempts at resuscitation—in the driveway, not far from where Bobby kept his BMW. Now, this truck had kind of a strange emergency brake on it, like a toggle switch, and I guess I must have failed to set it properly, because the next morning I heard a knock at the door of the bunk house where I was sleeping. I rolled over to see Bobby standing in the doorway, a look of exasperation on his face.

"Man, what do you have against my car?"

"Huh?" I had no idea what he was talking about, but I found out soon enough. Bobby led me out to the driveway, where my truck was embedded in the driver's side of his BMW. Apparently the brake had released, allowing the truck to T-bone Bobby's beautiful car.

"You're a menace behind the wheel," Bobby said, shaking his head in disgust.

What could I say? I had no response, no reasonable excuse or explanation. *I got fucked by the brake?* Well, whose fault was that? I could have been more careful. I could have checked the brake. Hell, I could have just parked the truck a half-mile away, isolated it from any potential collision. Given its history, that would have been the smart thing to do. But I was still young . . . still learning.

Bobby was quick to forgive me—again. Nevertheless, I stayed away from Rucka Rucka for a while after that, and instead set up temporary digs at a big house in Kentfield, California, which served as sort of a headquarters for the New Riders of the Purple Sage. I had found something of a kindred spirit in David Nelson, a guitar player and vocalist who had formed the band with Jerry Garcia and John "Marmaduke" Dawson in 1969. I'd known Nelson for a while. A respected artist who had been a pivotal player in the whole Haight-Ashbury scene, he started out as a member of the Wildwood Boys with Jerry and Robert Hunter, and later appeared on a handful of Grateful Dead albums. Nelson was a talented and innovative musician; like Jerry, he was also a man of eclectic and sometimes bizarre interests, which naturally appealed to me. We'd sit around together and listen to country and bluegrass music and smoke weed and talk about underground comics (Nelson had one of the biggest collections I'd ever seen). Nelson was a historian, too, born and raised in the Bay Area, and he enjoyed taking Easterners such as myself on long drives along the coast, up and down the peninsula, explaining the history of the region. I liked Nelson right from the start. We quickly became friends, and we remain close friends to this day.

Not everyone in the Riders, however, was quite as smitten with me. Marmaduke, for example, was not my biggest fan. I was an interloper, in his eyes, a freeloader who brought nothing of substance to the band. Like Rucka Rucka, the Kentfield house was a communal place where people from diverse backgrounds lived together, worked together, partied together, and slept together. In general, no one seemed to care who was fucking whom. But on occasion I did notice a look of disapproval from Marmaduke when he'd see me opening the refrigerator and perusing its contents. Sometimes he'd accuse me of drinking his apple juice, and of course I was guilty, although I didn't think it was a serious offense. For whatever reason, our personalities clashed. Marmaduke didn't like the fact that I was hanging out at Kentfield, and he didn't like the idea of my working for the New Riders. In the end, it was Marmaduke's influence that prevented me from landing a full-time, paying position with the New Riders. Some sort of vote was taken, and a decision was made to recruit Johnny Hagen, who had been working for the Grateful Dead but was now on sabbatical back home in Pendleton. That left me out in the cold, which was fine as it turned out I soon became a paid member of the Grateful Dead crew. The salary was only seventy bucks a week, but it seemed like all the money in the world at the time.

Despite the fact that things didn't work out between me and the New Riders, I have nothing but fond memories of Kentfield. It was there that I met Annette, the band's smart and thoughtful secretary, a pretty woman with whom I fell in love. It took a while for that relationship to blossom, mainly because another resident of Kentfield was Truck Drivin' Sherry, who often walked around in the world's shortest miniskirt, emblazoned with the American flag. Sherry never wore underwear. I'd go for rides with her in her Volkswagen bug, and she'd drive up on the sidewalk and get pulled over, and when the cop would walk up to the car she'd give him a smile and a little glimpse of skin, and that would be the end of it. I never saw her get a ticket. She could sweet-talk anyone. Sherry loved sex, and she saw nothing wrong with acknowledging it. We'd be sitting around sometimes at night, drinking beer, and Sherry would play this game. If you opened a bottle of Olympia beer, the back of the label would have a certain number of dots on it, representing the bottling plant of origin. If you got a label with four dots on it—a "four-dotter," we called it, you were the grand-prize winner. A four-dotter was a voucher for a lay in Sherry's world. I was lucky enough to get a few four-dotters, and I was grateful each time it happened.

But it was all very innocent. Sex was just part of the lifestyle we led. Sometimes I slept with Sherry, sometimes I slept with Annette. There was no jealousy, no anger. Not for a while anyway.

It was through Sherry, indirectly, that I first got to know some of the guys in the Hells Angels. I came home to the Kentfield house one night and walked in on Sherry having sex with a giant of a man. They were naked, entwined on the floor, his back rising and falling on her. It seemed almost comical to me—he had long blond hair and a thick beard, and he must have weighed more than 300 pounds. He looked like a Viking, and my first thought was, *Jesus, he's going to crush her!* Sherry peeked out from beneath him after a few seconds, spotted me, and began to laugh out loud—she had a loud, high-pitched cackle—which prompted her partner to look back over his shoulder.

"Hey," he said with a smile, still thrusting with all his might. "How ya' doin'?"

"Fine," I said, and then I left the room. I wasn't upset, didn't think I had any claim to Sherry, and was hardly laboring under the illusion that she was in love with me. In fact, when they were through, Sherry introduced me to her friend, whose name was Badger. Badger was a member of the Richmond chapter of the Hells Angels, and although he did have a genuinely warm side, he was every bit as tough as you might expect. Through Badger I got to know the guys in the Richmond chapter, including Angelo, who would later become my dear friend. When we'd go to their clubhouse, especially in the early days, Badger would always be careful to remind me of the proper protocol.

"If you get in a fight with anyone, just make sure you're right," he'd say. "Because I'm the one who's going to have to back you up. I'm bringing you, I'm responsible for you."

"Got it," I'd say.

"Good, because if you're wrong, I'll kick your ass, too."

Badger's toughness extended naturally and genetically to his children. I was once with him (in the days before child seats) when he slammed on the brakes of his car to avoid an accident. The sudden stop catapulted Badger's son, Ivan, a little bruiser of a kid, from the back seat all the way into the windshield. The force of the collision cracked the windshield, but Ivan just rolled onto the floor and came up smiling.

"Now that," I said, "is a tough kid."

Badger laughed. "No shit."

Chapter 11

To understand and appreciate the unlikely and sometimes fragile bond that formed between the world's most notorious outlaw motorcycle club and the world's most laid-back hippie band, you have to go back a long ways—like, all the way to 1969, and Altamont, California, site of one of the saddest and most infamous events in rock 'n' roll history.

Altamont—the concert, I mean, not the tragedy—would not have happened if not for the efforts of Rock Scully, another in the long list of Grateful Dead managers. During a trip to London, Rock got to know the Beatles and the Rolling Stones, so he became the conduit between those venerable British bands and the American popular music scene, which at the time was headquartered in Northern California. Eventually Rock's relationship with the Stones—and in particular their road manager, Sam Cutler—led to the organization of a big free concert in the Bay Area, featuring the Rolling Stones, the Jefferson Airplane and the Grateful Dead. It was the right idea at the right time . . . in theory, anyway.

Unfortunately, somebody had the bad idea to hire the Hells Angels to do security at Altamont. The Angels were the last people you'd ever want to do security at a rock show, because they do not take "no" for an answer. The idea behind security is to prevent confrontations and violence, but it's tricky and sometimes dangerous work. If you tell people at a rock show to move . . . well, they don't always listen. They're having fun, they're partying, and as often as not their response is, "Who the hell are you to tell me what to do?" If you're doing rock 'n' roll security, you have to mean it. You have to be willing to put your body on the line. This was especially true thirty years ago, when many bands handled their own security and festival seating was the rule rather than the exception, and drug use among concertgoers was widespread. It was difficult, demanding work. I did a fair amount of it in my early years with the Dead, and I got pretty good at it, but it required putting on a different face and being willing to challenge the very people who were, indirectly, paying your salary: the kids who bought Grateful Dead records and went to Grateful Dead concerts. Somebody, though, had to keep the stage clear, to block and tackle the occasional psychotic who got some bad acid and wanted to run onto the stage naked and begin dry-humping an amplifier.

What happened at Altamont was a result of bad planning. The most famous incident, of course, involved a fan who was knifed as the Rolling Stones performed on stage. His death was captured on film in a documentary titled *Gimme Shelter*. But there were other, smaller, confrontations, some involving members of the bands' crews. My buddy Rex Jackson, for example, got beat up because he tried to come to the rescue of the Jefferson Airplane's lead singer,

Marty Balin, who was getting pushed around by some Angels. I was very new to the whole scene at the time, so I was merely an observer, but it made me understand what could happen when a crowd got out of control, and how important it was to have reliable security at a concert.

Altamont left a bad taste in the mouths of virtually everyone associated with the bands who performed there. It became one of the biggest news stories of the year, and, combined with the grotesque and evil work of Charles Manson, who gleefully proclaimed his allegiance to the Beatles, naturally provided ammunition for anyone who believed rock 'n' roll was a sure sign of the decline of Western Civilization. The fallout for some people was more immediate and pronounced than it was for others. Sam Cutler, for example, was fired by the Rolling Stones and ended up hanging out with us at Rucka Rucka. Their loss, it seemed, was our gain, for we soon hired Sam as road manager of the Grateful Dead. I'll tell you right now that I consider Sam to be the greatest road manager who ever lived, and back then I couldn't spend enough time with him. I loved sitting around talking with him about the music business, and the types of things he would see and experience from his corner of the world. Watching Sam work was like getting a lesson in real-life diplomacy: the way he would talk to people on the road, the way he would conduct business. With Sam, everything was always done with a hunk of money—at hotels, restaurants, airports, theaters. Wherever and whatever. That's how he got things done: with cash and a smile. Sam would slip twenty bucks to the right skycap and all our stuff would go on the plane free of charge, as excess baggage. If there was damage to a hotel room, Sam took care of it quietly and discreetly. He made things happen and he made things go away.

Sam looked the part of a somewhat eccentric but confident road manager, too, this Englishman with the Cockney accent who favored World War II British bomber jackets with fur collars. But there's no question that Altamont took a heavy toll on him. The Stones were pissed at him; the Angels were furious and held him largely responsible for what happened, to the point where Sam actually feared for his life. It was a terrible, tragic day, and Sam unfortunately caught the brunt of it. I didn't realize just how deeply he was affected by it until one night a few months later, when he stopped by Rucka Rucka. I had a knack for reading tarot cards back then, and for some reason I read Sam's cards that night, and they revealed just how heavily Altamont was weighing on his mind. The stabbing had become the most important event of his life, even though he had been reluctant to admit it. As I read the cards Sam expressed a sense of relief, as if he finally felt he'd been given permission to acknowledge how deeply he'd been hurt by the events at Altamont, and how terrible he felt about the whole thing. Sam trusted me after that, and we became very good friends.

It remained important to Sam, for reasons related to his own reputation and his desire to stay healthy and alive, to repair his relationship with the Hells Angels. That led to a handful of bizarre incidents, the first of which occurred in early 1971. Jerry had been jamming semi-regularly around San Francisco with Howard Wales, a gifted keyboard player who had spent much of the sixties working with such soulful musicians as the Four Tops and James Brown before eventually settling in the Bay Area and hooking up with Jerry. In 1970 Howard played on the Dead's *American Beauty* album, and in '71 he and Jerry teamed up to release an album of their own, *Hooteroll?* Although Jerry was busy as hell, he liked working with Howard, and together they decided to hit the road to promote their album. The idea was to go out and squeeze in a little tour between all the Dead work and the Jerry Garcia Band projects. Sam Cutler arranged the tour; the road crew would be small—just me and Joe Winslow, another cowboy from Pendleton.

This was my first time out on the road alone with Jerry—without the other guys from the Dead, and without Jackson, Heard, or Ramrod. Winslow was even greener than I, so I had no choice but to be a responsible, hardworking adult. But it was a baptism of fire, despite the fact that the tour began in Buffalo, New York, in the middle of winter. It was so cold that when Jerry stepped out on stage and strummed his "Alligator" (a gorgeous white Stratocaster that had been given to him by Graham Nash), the face plate on the guitar broke and all the guts popped out. That's how the show began. Jerry turned and looked at me, and though he didn't say a word, his face communicated this message: *Steve . . . what the fuck is going on?*

See, when you do a guy's equipment, there's a connection—a trust—between the two of you. I'd gotten pretty good at setting up Jerry's amps and tuning his guitars. Frankly, it really wasn't all that complicated. Ramrod had patiently tutored me on these matters, taught me how to hook up the equipment and how to troubleshoot problems. If something was wrong, you started from the guitar and worked your way back to the amp and finally to the electrical outlets. Usually you could solve the problem pretty quickly. But the face plate popping off? This was new to me, and from the looks of things it was new to Jerry. Nevertheless, it was my job to put it back together, to make everything right again so the show could go on. So I grabbed a roll of gaffer's tape—the "rock 'n' roll bandage" we called it because it saved our asses so many times—and ran out on stage and put the guitar back together. When I finished, Jerry strummed a chord, smiled, and resumed playing.

I should have known then that this would be no ordinary tour, and indeed it wasn't. For one thing we brought some great pot with us, as potent and pure as anything I'd ever smoked. Those of us in Jerry's camp could handle it—we were, after all, champions at this sort of thing—but others who joined us in our nightly parties had all kinds of problems. We had people fainting and suffering hallucinogenic nightmares; promoters would smoke with us backstage or at the hotel after the show, and then they'd just disappear, and no one would hear from them for days on end.

The weirdest thing, though, occurred one morning at the Navarro Hotel on Central Park South in New York, after the first of four consecutive shows. I stayed in a lot of hotels in New York with the Dead and with Jerry's band, but the Navarro, more than any other, became our home away from home. Usually they gave us the same suite and accouterments; they knew our routine, our likes and dislikes, and they went out of their way to take care of us. It was a great place, and not at all the type of hotel where you'd expect to find yourself staring down the barrel of a gun. But that's what happened.

It began around ten o'clock, with a phone call from Sam Cutler.

"Steve," he said. "I'm in Jerry's room, get down here right away. There's someone here with a gun."

I sat up in bed, rubbed the sleep from my eyes. "What?"

"Just get down here," he repeated, his voice clearly reflecting distress. "Now!"

I got dressed as fast as I could and hopped into the elevator. None of this made any sense at all. Although we weren't averse to a little target practice at Rucka Rucka, guns were not part of the Grateful Dead travel package. Drugs, yes. Guns? No fucking way. We didn't mess with anything like that. Life on the road was inherently wild and crazy— everyone shucked off their inhibitions and behaved in ways they would not have behaved at home. Throwing guns into the mix would have been the height of stupidity. And if anyone was least likely to break this unwritten rule, it was Jerry.

When I knocked on the door, Sam answered and invited me in. He seemed nervous, scared, and once I was inside the room I could see why. Seated in a chair by the window was Jerry. Directly in front of him, wearing a snap-brim hat, was a twitchy little guy with olive skin. In his hand was a gun, and it was pointed directly at Jerry's chest.

What the fuck is this?

As I came in, Sam sort of slipped out, which, oddly enough, didn't seem to bother Jerry's guest in the least. He looked like a little mafioso, circa 1940. He also seemed kind of nervous, like he wasn't exactly in control of the situation. So I engaged him in conversation, asked him why he was there and what he wanted, and he told me his whole sad story without ever once lowering his gun.

It turned out that this guy was a pimp whose stable included a girl who had recently, maybe a few months earlier, answered a call from a man claiming to be Jerry Garcia. I don't know exactly where it supposedly happened, but it wasn't the Navarro. The pimp said the man looked like Jerry and sounded like Jerry, and that he'd seemed friendly and nice while striking the deal. As the "date" went on, however, the customer revealed himself to be a dangerous and violent man with a seriously sadomasochistic taste in sex. "Rough sex" is one thing, the pimp said—all his girls understood that some customers liked that sort of thing. But what "Jerry" had done was totally inappropriate. He'd allegedly used some monstrous dildo on the girl, along with some other apparatus, and in the process had done irreparable damage to her vagina and internal organs.

This, of course, was not exactly the way the pimp told the story. He used street vernacular, and as he spoke it became apparent that what he felt was not merely anger at having lost a business investment, but something akin to a broken heart. The woman who had been assaulted was obviously his girlfriend.

"You fucked her up!" he shouted at Jerry. Then, with tears streaming down his cheeks, he added, "You hurt my lady . . . and I'm gonna hurt you, you mother-fucker!"

I realized then that he wasn't a high-ranking mobster, but merely a street hustler. He seemed like a sad, pathetic loner, an outsider, someone hopelessly disconnected from the real world. Maybe that's why Jerry didn't seem particularly nervous, even as the pimp waved the gun in his face. Jerry was intrigued by people such as this, he wanted to know more about them. I'm sure it seemed like some great irony to Jerry that someone had stolen his identity and used it to hurt this man and the woman he loved.

Nevertheless, it was a dangerous situation. The pimp believed Jerry had done something horrible and now he was here to exact his revenge. How he found out that we were staying at the Navarro, I don't know. Nor do I have any idea how he got Jerry's room number. All that mattered was that he was here now and he had a gun and he seemed distraught enough to use it. So I kept talking to him, trying to calm him down, trying to make him understand what had happened.

"Someone lied to you," I said. I pointed at Jerry. "I know this man, and he'd never hurt anyone."

"How do you know?" the pimp asked.

"Because I just do."

It went on like that for a while, me talking to the pimp, trying to keep him calm, trying to make him understand that some people get their kicks out of impersonating celebrities, and while most of them are harmless losers, a few of them are deluded and dangerous. His girl had apparently run into someone from the latter camp. Jerry, for the most part, said nothing. He just sat there with his hands folded on his lap, taking it all in, almost as if he found the entire experience fascinating on some level. I was at once awed and disturbed by his ability to remain calm while sniffing the muzzle of revolver.

Meanwhile Sam was out running around, frantically requesting help from the cavalry. And I'm not talking about the cops. No, no, no. This was not an incident Sam wanted to see publicized on the cover of the New York *Daily News*. A mutilated prostitute, a psychotic pimp, Jerry held hostage at gunpoint? It was all too sordid. That it really had nothing to do with Jerry or the Grateful Dead was irrelevant; the story would be ugly and terrible and nothing good would come of it. Better to keep it quiet, take care of it in a more efficient, clandestine manner. And who better to answer that call for help than the Hells Angels?

Sam welcomed this opportunity to mend fences with the Angels, to repair some of the damage that had been done at Altamont, and to get in the club's good graces once again. Two days earlier I had met Sandy Alexander, who was then president of the New York chapter of the Hells Angels, which none of us in the Grateful Dead really even knew existed, because we associated the Hells Angels exclusively with Oakland and the Bay Area. Unbeknownst to us, the club was expanding and moving all over the United States. I mean, I knew there were other charters, but I didn't think much of it . . . not until I met Sandy and a few of his brothers: Flash and Fuzzy and the infamous Big Vinnie. These guys *were* the New York chapter, and they were every bit as impressive as the Angels I'd come to know in Oakland. Sandy, in particular, seemed like a man of substance. He was tough but charismatic, and he wore his heart on his sleeve. To Sandy the club was all about friendship and loyalty, and it was hard not to be impressed by him and his friends. I've met enough Hells Angels and I've spent enough time in their universe to know that they're no different from any other group. What I mean is, you have to take each individual Hells Angel for who he is. Some you can't hang with. Some don't want to know you or talk to anyone who is not a Hells Angel or who doesn't ride a Harley-Davidson. But they're not all like that. Sandy certainly wasn't. At that time he was on a crusade to make the Hells Angels more acceptable to people in general and to celebrities in particular. The Angels had a terrible reputation in the wake of Altamont—a lot of people wanted nothing to do with them. Sandy was smart enough to realize that a bit of spin-doctoring was necessary, and he was the right man for the job. He was a natural leader.

In a sense, the Angels needed Sam Cutler, and at this moment Sam needed the Angels. Desperately. So when he slipped out of the room, Sam went directly to a pay phone and called Sandy. Within fifteen minutes there was a knock at the door, and in walked Sandy and Big Vinnie . . . and Jesus did they take control of the situation! Big Vinnie's sheer size (about 350 pounds), combined with his penchant for wearing nothing but a leather Hells Angels vest over his massive shirtless torso, was enough to give the pimp cause for concern. He froze as Big Vinnie and Sandy walked toward him without saying a word. Then Vinnie slapped the gun out of the guy's hand and Sandy said, "Let's see some ID." At first the guy refused and tried to act tough, but that charade ended when Vinnie picked him up by his feet—as easily as you'd pick up a bundle of carrots—and dangled him out the window of the hotel room. Considering we were on the nineteenth floor, this was no small threat. It was the kind of thing that was bound to get your attention.

The pimp began screaming, wailing, begging for mercy, so Vinnie yanked him back in with a laugh and dropped him on the floor.

"You ready to talk now, asshole?" Vinnie said.

The pimp struggled to his feet, nodded, and proceeded to tell the whole story again to Sandy and Vinnie. To me, a kid barely out of his teens, this was shocking and brutal behavior, but it was undeniably effective. The pimp calmed down and became extremely cooperative. As it turned out, he was telling the truth. This girl really had been badly hurt by someone who called himself Jerry Garcia, which didn't sit well with Sandy and Big Vinnie and the rest of the Hells Angels. They didn't like the fact that some sick bastard had brutalized a woman, and they really didn't like the fact that he had committed the act while impersonating the leader of the Grateful Dead. The Angels genuinely loved Jerry and the band, and they considered this to be a serious transgression, so they began working with the pimp in an effort to catch the imposter. (They failed, unfortunately, and the culprit never was apprehended). But what impressed me was the loyalty and devotion displayed by Sandy and the rest of the Hells Angels. They genuinely wanted to help us.

After that incident the Hells Angels started to become more of a presence at Grateful Dead shows. They would do anything for us. If one of our trucks got impounded, which happened all the time, they'd help us get it back. And, you know, when we were on the road back then, in the early days, we had no protection, no real security. Hiring the police was not an option; we didn't believe in that. So, whenever we could, we handled our own security. But there were times when it was nice to know that we could rely on the Hells Angels to watch our backs. While it may sound somewhat barbaric, there was a certain comfort in knowing that when confronted by a madman with a pistol, we could always rely on the Angels to stop by and teach the guy a lesson in gravity and in good manners.

Chapter 12

The mysticism of the road was something that sustained us in weary times. Being on the road was not just about making music and entertaining crowds, although it was certainly that. And it wasn't just about having lots of sex with unfamiliar but pliant women and smoking tons of great dope, although it was certainly that, too. I looked for magic on the road, for events serendipitous and fateful and potentially karmic.

A lot of people don't realize the true meaning of the term "grateful dead," but its roots can be traced back to European folklore, and the tradition of stumbling across people in need and helping them without question or judgment or any concern for remuneration. Of particular importance was the willingness to help people searching for a decent and dignified end to their lives. For example, if you passed through a village and came upon someone burying a friend or family member you were obligated to help with the burial, to aid that person on the final leg of his journey to the afterlife. Once there, the legend holds, that person will remember you and be forever grateful, and provide you with guidance and assistance from beyond.

Hogwash or not, this was a philosophy that most of us with the band embraced: the belief that the downtrodden and forgotten of the world deserved our sympathy and compassion, rather than our contempt; that in time we'd be rewarded for good deeds, and that part of our mission was to embrace the weirdness of the road and to lend a hand to the lost souls we encountered.

As I said, Jerry was fascinated by these souls, and that was one reason he enjoyed making excursions to New York, where there was never any shortage of street people. For instance, one night at the Navarro we came home from a gig with the Garcia Band around three in the morning, and I looked out and saw this guy with a scraggly beard and tattered clothes sneaking around, acting like a spy or something. There was a statue of Simon Bolivar on Central Park South, and the guy was hiding behind the statue. He stood there for a while, peeking out, trying to see if anyone was watching, then suddenly he bolted to a nearby garbage can, flipped it over, dumped the contents all over the street, and then ran back behind the statue. Five minutes would pass, then he'd sneak out again, bent low at the waist, his head on a swivel, as if he expected a sniper to take a shot at him. He ran to the garbage can and began quickly picking through the mess he'd made. I figured he was hungry or thirsty and looking for something to put in his belly, especially when he picked up what appeared to be a bottle and raised it to eye level. Instead of drinking from it, though, the guy heaved the bottle at a street sign. As the bottle shattered into a thousand pieces he jumped up and down and clapped his hands and howled with delight. Then he ducked back behind the statue. Five more minutes passed before he emerged again. This time he crouched in the middle of the street, as if protecting his pile of garbage, and began scooping things up and chucking them at a traffic light.

I watched this guy for nearly an hour. The next morning, when I saw Jerry and John Kahn, who was out on tour with us, I began to tell them what I'd seen. Jerry just started laughing. So did John. They'd both watched the show, too, and had been as mesmerized as I'd been.

We saw the guy again the next time we returned . . . and the time after that. His routine was always the same. It became our joke that this homeless man must have been a municipal employee at one time, and now he was at war with the city.

Another character we'd see all the time hung out on Forty-eighth Street, home of some of the greatest music stores in the world. We'd go there to buy supplies whenever we were in New York, and everyone treated us like royalty. Jerry was always remarkably gracious in these settings. He'd sign autographs, shake hands, chat up the customers and staff, and invariably wind up playing a little impromptu concert. Jerry wasn't the only one who liked to jam in this neighborhood. Every time we visited we saw a black guy in a long trench coat who would walk down the middle of the street and drum on the blacktop with a pair of beat-up sticks. And he was amazing. I mean, the guy had talent. Not far from him was another drummer, this one wearing a bow tie and jacket, hammering away at a snare, playing rudimentary stuff, yelling out "paradiddle!" and "flamadiddle!" The guy later appeared in the Martin Scorsese film *Taxi Driver*, looking every bit as strange and distant as I remembered. He'd stare off into space, never acknowledging anyone or anything, even as people passed by and dumped change at his feet.

We were drawn to these people rather than be repulsed by them. I remember getting out of a limo with Jerry and being approached by a bum. This guy was a stew, completely drunk and reeking of feces and vomit . . . the kind of creature most people would run from. Not us, and especially not Jerry. The drunk latched onto Jerry, put an arm around his shoulder, and began talking to him, or at least trying to talk to him. Really it was just gin-soaked gibberish, but Jerry didn't care. He pulled out a cigarette, lit it, and handed it to his new friend. The drunk smiled, put the cigarette in his mouth, took a deep breath, and . . . suddenly began pissing his pants! As a sour puddle formed at his feet, the bum seemed not to even notice. Personally, I was a bit grossed out by it, but not Jerry. He just smiled at the guy and gave him a pat on the back. His reaction betrayed not a trace of disgust or anger, but merely sympathy. It was fashionable in the sixties and early seventies to express kinship with the poor huddled masses. For most people it was nothing but lip service, a half-assed attempt to seem cool and compassionate. In Jerry's case, though, it was utterly real. He and Robert Hunter even wrote a song around this time called "Wharf Rat," which was essentially a paean to people such as this, the bums and beggars and besotted wretches who couldn't control their bodily functions, and who could be found on every corner of every street in America, yet somehow seemed invisible.

We talked about this a lot, about how important it was to appreciate any comfort we had in life. "Don't take it for granted," Jerry often said to me. "It's a gift." I knew that, of course. We all did. With few exceptions we'd come from modest backgrounds, especially those of us on the crew, and we understood how quickly it could all slip away—the fame, the money, the sex, and the drugs. As much as we saw the top shelf of society—the movie stars, the politicians, the society bimbos who liked to hang out with us in hotel rooms—we still took notice of all the other people who existed quietly and sadly at the bottom. I can't really explain why we were fascinated by them, but we were. It wasn't morbid, it was just something we couldn't help noticing. And we felt for them.

To me there's something wonderful and life-affirming about slapping ten bucks into the palm of a homeless man, and it's something I do to this day. Maybe he'll spend it on a bottle of Mad Dog. Probably he will. So what? At least he has an opportunity to do something else with it, and it makes me feel good; it makes me feel connected in some way that's difficult to put into words. We all did this at times, from Jerry right on down to the lowliest member of the crew. It was part of who we were: the Grateful Dead. I remember being keenly aware of the band's success, and how it trickled down to every one of us, and how fortunate we were to be living something akin to a fantasy life. Through all the drugs and sex and self-destructive behavior, two things remained constant: the music and the desire to help people. Trite as it may sound, we believed in random acts of kindness.

Strange people were always around; they seemed to be drawn to us, just as we were drawn to them. I can remember distinctly a withered old lady coming up to me and Jerry in front of the Navarro and shouting, "Who are you, Johnny Carson?" Then she took a crab apple out of her purse and put it in front of my face. She kept waving and shaking it, like she expected it to talk. Finally she stopped and yelled, "Did you see the seahorse?"

I looked at Jerry. He looked at me. We both shrugged.

"Uh, no."

She rolled her eyes, as if we were the stupidest people she'd ever met. "It's a secret television in Dallas. That's where they keep track of you guys, you know."

Jerry burst out laughing. "Okay, thanks for the warning,"

That very same day, I shit you not, a car pulled up and a man jumped out—he must have been a Deadhead, because he knew exactly who we were—and he handed Jerry a shoebox. "Take care of this, man," he said. "Please, whatever you do, don't lose it." Then he split, leaving Jerry holding the box, as it were.

Now, if that happened today, to just about any celebrity, he'd heave the box as far as he could and duck for cover while waiting for the inevitable explosion. But Jerry just stood there staring at the box, on the cover of which was a small, handwritten note:

THIS IS THE LIZARD GOD, CHONGA-BONGA. DON'T LET HIM DIE

So we opened the shoebox, and indeed there was a lizard—an iguana—resting peacefully on a bed of grass. Just about anyone else would have flipped the box over and let the lizard crawl into traffic or out into a field to be eaten by a hawk or something. But not Jerry.

"Let's go," he said. "We have our orders."

For the next several weeks Chonga-Bonga became part of our entourage. He went everywhere with us. We bought books that taught us what and how to feed him. We learned from a guy at a pet store how important it was to keep his environment warm. To that end we'd put Chonga-Bonga in a tub and drip warm water on him and let the room get good and steamy, and that did seem to make him happy. One night, though, we got into a city late and I handed him off to Sam Cutler with only the briefest of instructions. Sam, unfortunately, cranked the faucet as high and hot as it would go accidentally, scalding and killing the lizard in a matter of seconds.

And that was the end of Chonga-Bonga—the one and only lizard god.

Chapter 13

In 1972 the Hells Angels asked the Jerry Garcia Band to do a show for them. Now, my personal friendship with several of the club members notwithstanding, I have to admit that working with the Hells Angels was a complicated matter even under the best of circumstances. For one thing, when you mixed the Hells Angels with regular civilians, and threw in copious amounts of drugs and alcohol, there was bound to be trouble. It just didn't work, unless the civilians were friends of the Angels.

Several people associated with the Grateful Dead recognized this problem and refused to be a part of any venture involving the Angels. Bob Weir, gentle soul that he was, had a deep and abiding dislike for the Hells Angels and the way they sometimes behaved. The Angels were hard folks; they liked to fight. Sometimes they could be bullies, and Bobby didn't like bullies. Bobby was somewhat refined, too—he was one of the few people in our world who had been raised in affluence—and I think there was a callousness to the Angels that bothered him. Not that he lacked compassion and understanding—Bobby would have given the shirt off his back to anyone he met on the street—but he had a difficult time accepting the Angels for what they were: men who lived by their own rules and didn't give a rat's ass about decorum and civility. Not all of them, mind you—there were poets and artists among the Angels, too, but they were the exception, not the rule.

I remember once sitting backstage with Bobby and John McIntire, getting a lesson from them on the finer points of French wine: how to choose the right vintage, how to open a bottle and let it breathe, how to choose just the right glass, and how to enjoy that first glorious sip. All of a sudden in walked a guy named Bert, a member of the New York Hells Angels who was visiting some friends in the Bay Area. Bert was a great guy—funny, interesting and full of energy—but he was rough around the edges, no question about it.

"Hey, Steve," he yelled as he entered the room. "How ya' doin'?"

I stood up, said hello, and gave him a hug. Bobby and John said nothing, acting as if he wasn't even in the room. Bert didn't care. He just marched over to the catering table, grabbed a plastic cup and filled it with ice cubes, then splashed it with some of McIntire's fine French wine. Bert downed the glass in one gulp, like it was Dr. Pepper, wiped his mouth with his sleeve, said "Thanks," and walked out of the room, leaving John and Bobby speechless. I saw things like this all the time, and I saw the animosity from people like John and Bobby build to the point where the Grateful Dead wanted absolutely nothing to do with the club. And yet, the Angels were swarming all over us. They loved Jerry and the Grateful Dead and just about everyone associated with the band. It was, to say the least, an awkward time.

Another stumbling block to working with the Hells Angels was Bill Graham, whose resentment of them dated back several years, to a time when club members would routinely show up at the Fillmore West and make life difficult for both the promoter and some of his more tranquil customers. The Angels were paying customers like everyone else. They just wanted to enjoy a show and have a few drinks. But they were, undeniably, more inclined to get rowdy. Shit, they were Hells Angels. Anyway, Bill felt they were just a little too hardcore for the hippies, the peace and love crowd that comprised the majority of his audience at the Fillmore, and so he continually had problems and disagreements with the Hells Angels, to the point where when I first came around, Bill was still trying to recover from the humiliation of having recently had his head stuffed into a toilet by several members of the club. Shortly thereafter, at a Fillmore East show, while Bill stood at the microphone and introduced the band, as he always did, Big Vinnie walked up behind him and poured a pitcher of beer over Bill's head.

Well, Bill was not a man who was easily frightened or intimidated. He was a rock 'n' roll promoter at a time when the business was as cutthroat as it could possibly be, and he dominated it like no one before or since. He didn't achieve that success by being a pussy, but when Bill turned around and saw Big Vinnie standing there, holding an empty pitcher upside down, laughing along with the crowd, Bill just froze. Had it been anyone else I'm sure he would have gone crazy and tried to rip the guy's throat out. You just didn't do this sort of thing to Bill—not in his backyard. But this was Big Vinnie, a mountain of a man who would wander through the audience at our shows wearing razor-sharp wristlets on both arms, a foot-long Bowie knife sticking out of his belt. The first time I met him, Vinnie said, "Hey, did you know that if you have three tattoos, it usually means you're a felon?"

I looked at Big Vinnie's massive chest and arms, which were covered with ink, and shook my head.

"I've got seventy-three tattoos," he said. "What do you suppose that makes me?"

Scary, I thought to myself. *It makes you real fucking scary.* And it did, too. Standing out among Vinnie's many tattoos was a vivid and detailed image of a demon. I've been through a lot in my life and I'm not afraid of many things, but I'll tell you . . . to look at that demon was frightening. But it was a perfectly appropriate symbol for Big Vinnie. He was the kind of guy who would stand out in front of a building in the middle of the day and say, for no particular reason, "You know, somebody could have us in the scope of a high-powered rifle right now."

And I'd say, "Yeah, that's something to think about. I hope you're wrong."

"Probably so," Vinnie said, and then he'd toss his head back and laugh.

When Vinnie attended a show it was a sight to behold. He'd hit up everybody in the club for whatever type of drugs they had—who was going to refuse his overtures?—and then he'd come back with a handful of pills and swallow every one. I saw him ingest staggering amounts of liquid LSD, just squeeze the whole bottle into his mouth—the way an athlete might drink Gatorade—and then toss the empty container into the crowd. Big Vinnie was way, way out there. Strangely enough, though, he was rarely a problem, at least not to anyone but Bill Graham.

In the past the Dead had performed numerous benefits concerts, including one just a few months earlier for my friend Badger, who was in need of some rather expert and expensive legal counsel. You see, one evening in early 1972, shortly after I'd moved in with Annette, Badger showed up at our place, looking for all the world like a man in deep shit.

"I gotta hide out for a little while," he said, and I didn't ask why—not until later that night when I was watching the eleven o'clock news, and the lead story was about a double homicide in which Badger had been implicated: When the reporter said his name—"Paul F. Mumm"—I practically fell off my chair. Badger just shrugged, said it was all a big mistake, that he hadn't killed anyone. (I guess that turned out to be true, for he wound up spending only about a year in jail on a conspiracy charge.) So the Grateful Dead agreed to do a show, the proceeds from which would benefit Badger's legal defense fund.

Now, however, things had changed. The Grateful Dead had no interest in supporting the Hells Angels, so the Jerry Garcia Band stepped in. The idea was to perform at a concert in New York; specifically, we were to play for the New York chapter of the Hells Angels. It was a strange and memorable show, staged on a rented boat in New York Harbor. Kid was working with me on this one, and together we got up real early in the morning and headed down to the waterfront to put the gear on board. The captain and crew were true sea dogs, completely oblivious to who we were or what we were doing. Their boat had been rented and they had a job to do, and all they really cared about was getting paid. It didn't matter that Jerry Garcia was playing or that the Hells Angels would be on board. To them, it was just another charter.

Of course, nothing could have been further from the truth. This was one of those concerts at which civilians mixed with Hells Angels, and it was a typically volatile combination. Sandy Alexander had assigned one of the Angels, a guy named John-John, to stay with us while we set up for the show. It was John-John's job to make sure no one gave us any trouble, and he took his role quite seriously. He stood there on the deck of the boat, close to the where the stage would be, with a bottle of whiskey in one hand and a .38 special in his waistband. We had subcontracted some of the equipment, and with that agreement came a handful of technicians. Now, whenever we were faced with that type of situation we always watched the technicians carefully, to make sure they were doing things right and didn't damage any of our gear. Well, at one point during the setup I saw a guy lazily drop a bunch of microphones on top of our B-3 Leslie, which is a nice hardwood speaker cabinet, very expensive and, in our hands, well maintained. So I yelled at the guy: "Hey! Watch what you're doing, buddy."

He nodded and went about his business, and I figured that was the end of it. After running some wires, though, I turned back around, just in time to see John-John throwing a noose around the guy's neck.

Jesus!

John-John tightened the noose with all the expertise of an executioner and tossed the poor bastard overboard. As he kicked and screamed and clutched at his throat, John-John just stood there, holding the other end of the rope, watching the guy dangle like a fish on the end of a line.

"John-John!" I yelled. "Get him back in the boat. We need him."

John-John cocked his head, as if confused. "I thought you were mad at him, man. I was just trying to help."

What could I say? On some level it was impossible not to appreciate the sentiment, although judging from the look on the guy's face as he was reeled back onto the deck, I'm not sure he would have agreed.

Disturbing as it was, that incident was merely a prelude to one of the wildest shows I've ever experienced. There was endless bad judgment on display that night, starting with the decision to put a nitrous tank on the upper deck. People were taking hits and diving into the water or falling into the water, or, in one case, getting tossed into the water. It happened when some guy got into an argument with one of the Angels—I have no clue as to the origin of their disagreement. All I know is that from the main deck I could see the guy flying out over the water and landing with a tremendous splash. Then, as he bobbed in the harbor, cursing and shouting, "Hey, man, that's my fucking tank!" I saw the Angel rip the tank from its base, hoist it over his head—we're talking about a 200-pound steel tank—and chuck it into the water. It broke the surface not three feet from where its alleged owner was treading water, and for a moment he was enveloped in a wall of foam. I thought perhaps he'd drowned, but soon he was climbing back on board, presumably smart enough to keep his mouth shut for the rest of the night.

Later I watched Jerry singing sweetly and softly as Big Vinnie strutted around, working the room, telling stories in his usual animated fashion, his wristlets whirring like miniature buzzsaws. There were other Angels there, too, not just representatives of the New York chapter. Big Albert from Oakland was in attendance, which wasn't a great surprise, considering how much Albert loved the Grateful Dead. Albert once told me that he started every day with a routine: he'd wake up, put on a song from the Dead's first album, a song called "Viola Lee Blues," and then take a big hit of DMT, which was a smokable psychedelic that usually gave the user a huge instantaneous flash that lasted about fifteen minutes, maybe a half hour. (DMT was pretty popular among the Dead and its crew for a while, until we got the sense that there was some bad karma surrounding its use; specifically, it seemed like whenever we smoked it around the stage, something weird would happen to our equipment. Amps would go out and things would explode whenever we messed with it during a show, so we became very wary of it. It was potent, scary shit, which was probably one of the reasons Albert liked it so much.)

A highlight of that night was watching Big Albert and Big Vinnie, two of the baddest mother-fuckers ever to wear the patch of the Hells Angels (and that, it goes without saying, made them two of the baddest mother-fuckers on the planet), dancing together by the stage, doing this weird little macho shuffle. They were huge men, well over six feet tall and weighing at least three hundred fifty pounds each, so it wasn't like they were light on their feet. But they were dancing. Kind of. Actually, they were just sort of sliding around, staring at each other, improvising as Jerry played his guitar. All of a sudden Vinnie pulled a ball peen hammer out of his waistband and slammed it down on the organ. Albert looked at him, smiled, reached into his back pocket or his waistband (I'm not sure which), and withdrew a little sledgehammer with the handle sawed off—a lethal weapon that fit neatly in the palm of his hand. And Albert slapped that down on the organ. They kept moving, dancing, circling . . . and then Vinnie pulled out one of those Filipino butterfly knives and with a single motion unfurled it like a fan—*Whap! Whap! Whap!*—exposing a huge, glistening steel blade. Not to be outdone, Albert presented a big Bowie knife, a real Arkansas toothpick, as it's sometimes called, and laid that out for all to see.

The stakes were rising now, and the crowd was growing, just like the pile of weapons on the top of the organ.

Brass knuckles . . .

Nunchucks . . .

Switchblades . . .

Finally, Vinnie bent over and withdrew a little .32-caliber pistol from an ankle holster and held it out for Albert to see. Albert smiled, reached into his back pocket . . . and also pulled out a .32.

Game over. Tie score.

They laughed, embraced, and spent the better part of the next half hour reassembling their arsenals.

Appropriately enough, the Jolly Roger flew from a mast high above the boat, a signal to all that this was no ordinary harbor cruise. One of the Hells Angels, a guy named Flash, actually got married that night, right there on the boat as the band played. Drugs were everywhere, but it was the booze that caused the most problems. I knew early in the day, when I saw cases of whiskey and vodka and gin being loaded on board, and I saw the amazed looks on the faces of the ship's crew that this would be a show to remember. Indeed, it wasn't long before the boat was spinning around in circles. When I poked my head in the engine house, to see if everything was all right, I saw the captain out cold in his chair. Just to his right, standing at the helm, spinning the wheel as hard as he could, like someone running a game of roulette, was one of the Hells Angels. I didn't try to stop him. I just went out on deck and watched the show . . . or should I say shows? The one on stage and the one in the harbor, where a crowd of speedboats from the New York Police Department was moving in on us, forming a barricade. They kept waving, shouting over their loudspeakers, doing anything to try to get our attention.

Meanwhile, the band kept playing and the party roared on, with the occasional fight breaking out and the occasional passenger falling overboard. It was about as close to anarchy as you can get.

Later that night when I returned to the Navarro, I parked a truck filled with gear out on the street. You could do that then, so long as you parked on the side of the street closest to Central Park. I knew from experience that the cops wouldn't tow me right away in the morning, when the spot suddenly became illegal. They'd wait a few hours, give everyone a chance to move their vehicles and avoid fines and towing. It was all a big game, of course, and everyone understood the rules. The cops would cut you some slack on these matters . . . so long as you didn't try to embarrass them.

My only rule when transporting equipment in this fashion was to make sure that the guitars were never left in the truck. That way, even if everything else got stolen or the truck was towed, we could still put on a show. Amps, speakers, cables—these could all be rented or purchased on short notice. But not the guitars. These were precious to Jerry, and I took no chances with them. So when I got back to the Navarro around two in the morning, accompanied by a pair of Hells Angels, I parked the truck, removed two guitars, and then locked everything up. Then I went up to my room and fell asleep.

About six hours later I got a call from one of Jerry's girlfriends, who was traveling with us on this particular tour.

"Parish," she said with a laugh. "I think you'd better go outside."

"Why?"

"Because there's a bunch of cops all around your truck."

I threw open the curtains and recoiled from the morning light (when you travel with a rock 'n' roll band, you can't help but develop the sensibilities of a vampire). When my eyes adjusted I could see three NYPD cruisers and close to a dozen officers swarming around my truck. My first thought was, *Does it take this many cops to ticket and tow one vehicle?* As my head cleared, though, I realized something more serious was happening. So I threw on my clothes and went outside.

"What's wrong, officer?" I said to the person who appeared to be in charge.

He looked me up and down. "This your truck?"

"Yes, sir. Why? Is there a problem?"

"Could be," he said. "We received a report that this vehicle contains stolen equipment."

What happened was this: one of the bellmen at another hotel had apparently witnessed our late arrival, and when he saw the Hells Angels patches, and guitars being removed under the cover of night, he leaped to the erroneous conclusion that he was witnessing some sort of crime—or, perhaps, the aftermath of a crime, during which the stolen merchandise is removed from the getaway car and taken to some other undisclosed location . . . in this case, my hotel room. Why he had waited until the next morning to call the police, I have no idea.

"No, no, no," I said. "This is my truck and those guys were helping me out."

"What else is in here?" one of the cops asked.

"Rock 'n' roll equipment." I unlocked the door so they could look around. They seemed about ready to let the whole thing slide when another cop climbed out of his cruiser and approached us.

"Hang on," he said. "We have another problem."

"What?"

"I just did a check on those plates."

"So?"

"So . . . it's been impounded. It's not supposed to be on the road."

This couldn't be happening. It was true that the truck had been towed a few day earlier, but I paid the fine and got it back. I told the cops I even had the paperwork in my room to prove it.

"Fine," they said. "We'll follow you."

It wasn't until I inserted the key into my door and caught the faintest whiff of stale pot that I realized this might not be the greatest idea. See, I'd left a big roach sitting on my nightstand. If the cops wanted to break my balls, they could do it. They could jack me up on some type of possession charge. It wouldn't amount to anything, but it would make my life miserable for a few hours. I didn't really care, though. I was more concerned with getting the paperwork on the truck and proving to them that I wasn't a thief, so I led them into the room and quickly found the receipt on the truck.

"Satisfied?" I said as I showed them the paperwork.

They barely seemed to notice. They were too busy looking around my hotel room, and it wasn't the roach that captured their attention. It was the guitars, both of which were emblazoned with Grateful Dead stickers—the wordless kind, just a lightning bolt through a skull.

"What band are you with?" one of the cops asked.

"The Jerry Garcia Band."

His eyes lit up and he took a reverential step backward. "Jerry Garcia? Oh, man, you're kidding."

"Uh, no . . . I'm not."

"Look, I am so sorry," he said. "Don't worry about anything, okay? Just go move the truck to a legal spot."

The other cops nodded. And then it hit me: *Deadhead cops! Unbelievable!* They walked back outside with me and helped me find a new spot for the truck. Before leaving they told me to have a good day and please send their regards to Jerry. Oh, and one other thing:

"Any chance we can get some tickets to tonight's show?"

I laughed. "Let me see what I can do."

Chapter 14

It was axiomatic of road life that bad things could and would happen. In the early years, especially, we worked ridiculously long hours, often went days on end with practically no sleep, and thought nothing of driving hundreds of miles in the middle of the night in overloaded trucks that probably shouldn't have been on the highway in the first place. We understood that once we left the Bay Area cocoon, our lives were out of control, and we were basically a tabloid headline waiting to happen.

I'll give you a few examples. In the late 1970s there was a strange thing happening in the Midwest, a series of cattle mutilations that no one could figure out. Ranchers in Nebraska, Wyoming, Iowa,

Colorado—they'd come out in the morning and discover that some of their herd had been brutalized in the most bizarre fashion: lips and genitals surgically removed, things like that. Several of the guys on the crew and in the band were familiar with this phenomenon because we were UFO buffs, and many of the newspaper accounts of the cattle mutilations included supposed sightings of flying saucers and speculation from residents in the area that perhaps this was the work of extraterrestrials. Not only that, but it had actually happened to one of our friends, John Barlow, who had grown up with Bob Weir and was a lyricist for the Grateful Dead. John owned a ranch and had in fact been victimized by the mysterious cattle mutilators, whoever they were.

I didn't really know what to think, but it was fun to talk about it and to throw out conspiracy theories. Maybe the government was behind it, we joked, conducting strange experiments for God knows what reason. I bring this up because Kid and I drove through the Heartland around this time, in the middle of a crazy cross-country trip in a van owned by the Jerry Garcia Band. The plan was to drive straight from San Francisco to New York, nonstop, and kick off a tour with Jerry. I could be a pretty stubborn guy on trips such as this, often refusing to give up the wheel to my co-pilot, even when I was exhausted. Twenty-four hours after we left San Francisco I was still driving, much to Kid's chagrin. I pulled into a gas station near Rawlins, Wyoming, and Kid demanded that I take a nap and let him drive for a while, but I was stoked on speed and full of youthful swagger, so I refused. Well, Kid was a feisty guy himself, so we wound up having a pretty good fight—not a fistfight or anything, but a fairly serious and loud, profanity-laced argument. Eventually I relented and threw the keys to Kid. Then I curled up between the driver's seat and the pile of equipment that was stacked in the back, and tried to get some sleep.

For some reason, though, Kid pulled over to the side of the highway less than a minute after we'd left the gas station.

"Come on!" I shouted, pounding the seat in front of me. "Let's get going!"

Kid said nothing, just sat there quietly with his hands on the steering wheel.

Suddenly I heard voices outside and I knew something was wrong. I sat up and felt the warm glow of police lights.

"Oh, great," I said. "What is this about?"

"I don't know," Kid said. "Just be cool."

"Always, man."

The cops took us out of the car at gunpoint and made us kneel by the side of the road with our hands locked behind our heads. They asked us for identification and then instructed us to open each and every box and case in the van.

"May I ask what this is all about?" I said, as politely as I could.

"Shut the fuck up and do as you're told!" one of the cops barked.

We were a very long way from home, on a dark and lonely road, surrounded by uniformed officers. It didn't seem like the right time to ask for a warrant. So Kid and I helped them search every piece of equipment in the van. One by one. It went on for the longest time, and reached a peak of excitement when one of the cops found a cowskin blanket on the floor of the van.

"What's this?"

"Just a blanket, sir. We sleep on it."

He turned it over several times, as if looking for blood, and even gave it a good sniff. Then he tossed it back into the van. When they were finally done, after they'd inspected everything and checked out our IDs, the police let us go.

"Thanks for your cooperation," the cop in charge said as he handed me my driver's license. "You boys have a nice night . . . and take it slow out there."

I stuffed the ID into my wallet and started to walk away. But curiosity and indignation wouldn't let me leave.

"Officer," I said. "Would you please tell me why you stopped us?"

He smiled. "Suspicious-looking vehicle." Then he tipped his hat.

It wasn't until several days later that I read a story on the latest cattle mutilations in the Midwest, in which law enforcement officials announced they had no new leads, except for this: several of the incidents had been accompanied not only by supposed UFO sightings, but by sightings of a white van. Someone at the gas station must have called the cops and said there were two crazy men fighting in his parking lot. I could almost hear him:

"Get out here fast! They look like cattle mutilators!"

And we probably did.

Another time—this was all in the early seventies—Kid and I were driving a rental car from New York City to Albany for a Garcia Band show, when we got nabbed by a speed trap set up by the New York State Police. Typical of that period, I wasn't just speeding; I was smoking up a storm at the same time, so the car reeked of marijuana. When the state trooper poked his head into the car and asked for my driver's license, his eyes practically started watering.

"Out of the car," he said. "Right now."

This was fairly early in the tour, so I had a significant stash of pot that I carried with me most of the time. How much? Well, at that very moment my luggage contained about a quarter of a pound of Colombian pot and a couple ounces of Thai stick. Kid had some Thai stick, too. The trooper went through our bags and naturally found the weed and had to arrest us. Actually, he only arrested me—I took the rap for both of us so that Kid could go to the show. That was the deal on the road: if you were stupid enough to get caught you did it on your own, so the show could go on. Ninety-eight percent of our stash belonged to me, so it was only right that I took the heat. After we explained that we were with the Jerry Garcia Band and we had a show that night in Albany, they let Kid go. He drove off in the rental car and I was taken to a nearby state police barracks, where they put me in a cell and held me for an hour or so. It was the strangest thing, though: after a while one of the troopers walked over and said, "You know what? I never searched you, did I?"

I realized then that he hadn't. Despite finding all that pot in the car, the cop hadn't even patted me down. I guess that says something about the prevailing attitude toward drugs in general and marijuana in particular in the early 1970s. No one—not even the cops—considered possession to be that big a deal. Especially possession of pot. There was, however, one little problem. As the trooper asked me to turn around and spread my arms and legs so that he could do a basic search, I remembered something. Something very important. Before leaving the hotel in New York, a West Coast Hells Angel named Jeff, who was out on tour with us, offered me some cocaine for the ride. I wasn't a big coke user, although I didn't mind taking a snort once in a while, and I certainly understood the difference between getting caught with pot and getting caught with cocaine. So at first I refused his offer, generous though it may have been. But Jeff laughed and took out a little plastic bag filled with a small amount of white powder.

"Here," he said. "Just in case you get tired." Then he stuck the bag into my shirt pocket.

And now the cop was running his hands over me, patting my arms, my legs, my chest . . .

"Hey, hey, what have were here?" He stopped patting, reached into my pocket, and withdrew the clear plastic bag.

I shrugged. "I don't know, officer."

"Oh, yeah? Guess it must have just jumped in there, huh?"

He tapped the bag, gave it a good look, then called out to another officer. "Hey, Harry, come on over here."

Harry walked over.

"What do you make of this?" asked the first trooper.

Harry took the bag from him, rolled it across his palm, squinted, and said, "That's cocaine. Book him." Then he tossed the bag on a table.

"Wait a minute, man," I said. "That's your scientific assessment?"

Harry nodded. "Uh-huh."

For the next few hours, until just about nightfall, they let me stew in my cell, stopping by only occasionally to inquire about my role within the band. I kept telling them I was just a roadie, that I helped set up the band's equipment, in this case Jerry's guitars, but they didn't believe me. One of them, a real straight-looking guy with Coke-bottle glasses, kept shaking his head and saying, "I know you're a musician— you've got that look."

That look?

He paused, as if something suddenly dawned on him. "Hey, do you know Crystal Gayle?"

Crystal was a real popular country singer at the time. "Sure," I lied. "We've met."

The cop nodded approvingly, then walked away.

Finally, less than an hour before the show was scheduled to begin, they brought in a judge and set up some makeshift courtroom and prepared for the business of arraignment. By now I'd had a lot of time to assess the potential fallout of my actions. Although my juvenile record was sealed, I still had some prior convictions for fighting, possession, that sort of thing. Nothing major, but enough to merit consideration when passing sentence for this particular transgression, especially since I was in New York, where the notoriously stiff Rockefeller Laws had recently been put into effect. As I watched the judge, a dour little man who didn't seem the least bit happy about being dragged out to the hinterlands on a Sunday night, I started to sweat. I realized then that things could get ugly, that there could be serious consequences.

Or so I thought.

Instead the judge read the police report, gave me a quick look, and said, with a big smile, "Okay, Mr. Parish, let's get this over with as quickly as possible. I don't want you to miss the show."

I was too stunned to respond. So were the state troopers.

"Well?" the judge said. "I'm waiting."

The evidence was laid out—the pot, the Thai sticks, *the fucking cocaine!*—and I have to admit, it looked pretty bad. But the judge was as compassionate as could be. He let me off with a fine of $350 and sent me on way. "Case closed," he said, banging his gavel for emphasis. "Now get out of here. My daughter is a big fan of the Grateful Dead, and she'll kill me if she finds out I made you late."

I drained my wallet, paid the fine, and—honest to God—got a ride to the show from one of the troopers!

The next morning I got a call from my mother, because the news services had picked up the story of my arrest and, perhaps inevitably, screwed up the details. The headline in my mother's paper read, GRATEFUL DEAD GUITAR PLAYER ARRESTED FOR DRUG POSSESSION. The name of the guitar player was Steve Parish.

"What's going on, Steve?" my mother asked. "Is this true?"

"You mean that I got arrested?"

"No . . . that you've been promoted."

"Not exactly, Mom."

As spooky and mystical as it could be, the road also sometimes filled you with a false sense of security, as if the usual rules didn't apply (and many of them did not) and you could do almost anything you wanted to do. There was a time in 1973 when Kid and I were driving all around the country with the Garcia Band, working hard to keep Jerry happy during those many interludes between Grateful Dead concerts and studio sessions. Jerry couldn't sit still and relax, and as long as he wanted to work, we were there to help him.

We drove equipment all across America that summer, from New York to California, from Nebraska to Texas. As sometimes happens when you're spending so much time in close quarters with another human being, especially a good friend, Kid and I got into a fight about something one morning. We were in the middle of a long drive from Houston to Kansas City, and hours went by without a word passing between us. (In all honesty I have to say that I can't recall the cause of the argument—I'm sure it began with something utterly trivial.) The fight ended the way most of fights ended, with Kid rolling a big joint and offering me a hit off the peace pipe. I laughed, took a big toke, and suddenly the world seemed like a friendlier, warmer place. The interstates in this part of the country, along Tornado Alley, were as flat and open and desolate as could be; you could practically drive with your hands behind your head.

We were on this one particular straightaway for the longest time, just cruising along, smoking and laughing and enjoying the stark beauty of the Heartland, when suddenly I heard something over the CB. We usually kept the radio on so that we could monitor the conversations of truck drivers, who always relayed information on speed traps and that sort of thing. We'd been in such a remote area that we'd been able to pick up nothing but static for several hours, but now there was conversation, apparently between two truck drivers in the vicinity.

"What the hell is wrong with this boy?" one of them said, laughing loudly. "Don't he see?"

"Guess not," came the reply. "He's gonna be in deep shit, though."

With that I looked out the window, expecting to see . . . well, I'm not sure exactly what I expected, but what I saw was a cop car with its lights flashing, and the driver screaming at me, waving at me and demanding that I pull over.

I looked down at the speedometer. The needle was quivering just above the 80-mph mark. "Oh, shit. We're in trouble."

Kid laughed, took a final tug on his joint, and then crushed it beneath his shoe. "Relax, man. It'll be okay."

The cop ordered us to follow him to a gas station in town, which was some godforsaken little place that didn't appear on any map that I'd ever seen.

"What are we doing here?" I asked.

Pigpen on the balcony of the Grand Hotel. Even though Pigpen was ill he made it through what I consider one of our best and most enjoyable tours. Paris 1972.
(JOE WINSLOW)

Phil and me, also during the Europe in '72 tour. Later that afternoon the two of us had a psychedelic time at Notre Dame.
(JOE WINSLOW)

Badger with his Knucklehead chopper, 1969. (Author's collection)

Jackson, 1972.
(Mary Ann Mayer)

Sonny Heard,
circa 1973.
(Joe Winslow)

Joe Winslow (left) and
Dan Healy (right), circa
1972. (Joe Winslow)

Johnny Hagen, circa 1973.
(Joe Winslow)

A crew's-eye-view of Jerry and Phil at Kezar Stadium in 1974. (Joe Winslow)

Joking around with Bobby and Jerry at the Greek Theater in Berkeley, circa 1978.
(CLAYTON CALL)

A moment backstage at Winterland, New Year's Eve, 1977, with Bill Graham, Ken Kesey, and drummers Bill Kreutzmann and Mickey Hart.
(ED PERLSTEIN)

Friendly police escort? St. Louis, Missouri, circa 1977. (BETTY CANTOR JACKSON)

Egypt, 1978. A camel ride behind the pyramids with my guide, Abdul. The unbelievable opportunity to play at the pyramids during a full eclipse will probably never be repeated and is an experience that will stay with us forever. (AUTHOR'S COLLECTION)

That's me in front of the Front Street Studio with my bike in 1978—the greatest rehearsal hall/boy's club ever. It wasn't uncommon to see ten bikes rolling up to the studio. What a feeling of freedom it was to cruise the Bay Area with my brothers.
(AUTHOR'S COLLECTION)

Keeping an eye on Mickey. We were two wild men who had our differences, but Mickey was a guy who understood the crew and treated us as members of the same family. Santa Barbara, June 4, 1978.
(ED PERLSTEIN)

Bobby and me goofing around in the White House Press Room in the early '80s. We have always shared the same irreverent sense of humor. (AUTHOR'S COLLECTION)

The crew dressed up and cleaned up at the Bammy Awards. Left to right: Ramrod, Billy Grillo, Kid, and me. (AUTHOR'S COLLECTION)

Jerry and me in 1986. What a pleasure it was to work for a man who brought so much joy to so many people. (JOHN WERNER)

Jerry, my daughter Lauren, me, and Robby Taylor at Kailua Harbor, Hawaii, in July 1989. (AUTHOR'S COLLECTION)

Lauren Parish with Jerry at the volcanoes in Hawaii, August 1988. (AUTHOR'S COLLECTION)

My dear friend Bill Graham, circa 1989. His untimely death was devastating to the band and to the entire San Francisco music scene. (KIM PETERSON)

Doing my thing. Frost Amphitheater, April 30, 1988. (JON SIEVERT)

Jerry as we sometimes saw him—waking up after a nap on the airplane.
(RAMROD)

Me, Ramrod, and Jerry scuba diving in Hawaii. Three good friends having as good a time forty feet below sea level as we did on land. (VICKI JENSON)

Our dive master and buddy Jeff Leischer, me, and Jerry at my fortieth birthday party in Kona, Hawaii, May 1990. (AUTHOR'S COLLECTION)

My uncle Mitchell Parish, Jerry, cousin Jane Ross, and me, backstage at Madison Square Garden, 1992. (AUTHOR'S COLLECTION)

Backstage at the Shoreline in 1993. Left to right: Vince Welnick, Bobby, Jerry Ramrod, Bill Walton, and me. (AUTHOR'S COLLECTION)

"Marilyn Monroe" backstage at her first Dead show with Bobby and Jerry. Fall tour, 1994. (AUTHOR'S COLLECTION)

"Just follow me inside and keep your mouth shut," he said.

As we walked past the garage, a big, beefy woman in greasy coveralls rolled out from beneath a car.

"Hey, Meg!" the cop said, tipping his hat.

"Hey, Stan," she replied, wiping her face with the back of her hand. "Looks like you got one, huh?"

Stan laughed. "Yup. See you inside."

A few minutes later Meg walked into the station's only room, unzipped her coveralls to reveal a clean blouse and trousers, and then took a seat at a desk. From a drawer she withdrew a small placard—JUSTICE OF THE PEACE—and placed it on the desk.

"Okay," she said. "What have we got?"

I looked at Kid. He looked at me. We'd been through a lot of strange things in our time on the road, but this one of the strangest. It was like getting arrested in Mayberry.

"Speeding, Meg," Stan said. "Clocked him doing eighty in a fifty-five."

Meg wrote something on a pad, then hit me with a twenty-dollar fine.

"That's it?" I asked.

"Unless you'd like to leave a tip," Meg said, a response that left Stan in stitches.

"No, Ma'am." I dug a twenty-dollar bill out of my wallet, handed it to Meg, and got out of there as fast as I could. As I pulled out of the parking lot I could see Meg zipping up her coveralls. She grabbed a wrench, fell back on the board, and rolled out of sight.

One more story, this one from New York City, an illustration of how and why those of us on the crew felt so attached to our equipment and our vehicles, and to the people and things we knew and trusted.

This was the mid-1970s, when Kid and I were out on the road with the Garcia Band. We were in New York for a few winter nights at a club called the Bottom Line. Typically, on a night like this, we'd leave most of the gear, since we were going to be back for another show the next night. We'd take the guitars, a few other things, and get out of there pretty quickly. More often than not we relied on a limo and a private driver to escort us back to the hotel. The limo would take the guys in the band while we picked up, and then return for the crew a short time later. But on this night Kid and I left with an acquaintance of ours named Tommy who lived in New York. Tommy had come to the show and we all planned to go back to our hotel and party for a while afterward. So we went outside in our heavy coats and piled into Tommy's black Chrysler New Yorker. I put the guitars in the back seat, next to Kid and a girl he had picked up. Tommy drove and I rode shotgun. Before we pulled away, Tommy produced a wedge of hash and handed it to me for preparation.

So there we were, cruising through Manhattan at three in the morning, a cloud of smoke filling the car. Not three blocks from the Bottom Line Tommy stopped at a red light. Parked at the curb was an NYPD patrol car, with two cops fighting sleep in the front seat. One of them opened an eye and looked at us. Suddenly he bolted up in his seat and began shaking his partner and pointing out the window.

"Uh, Tommy?" I said.

"Yeah?"

"Is this car hot or something?"

"No, of course not. Why?"

I looked at the cops again. They were on the radio now, clearly interested in us and our vehicle.

"Because those cops are acting funny."

"Oh, shit!" Tommy said as he drove the car through the intersection. And with that the lights came on and the siren blared and they were on us in a heartbeat. Tommy slowly directed the car to the side of the street. He kept his hands on the steering wheel. We all sat stiffly, nervously, wondering what was about to happen. As we waited, more patrol cars showed up, along with unmarked police cars bearing New Jersey and New York plates. Pretty soon more than a dozen cop cars had arrived on the scene, along with a couple ambulances. The street was sealed off.

"What do we do?" I asked Tommy.

Before he could say anything, a voice bellowed over a loudspeaker from one of the patrol cars.

"DO NOT GET OUT OF THE CAR!"

We sat there for a few minutes, trying to not to make any movements that could possibly be construed as "threatening." Finally a red-headed cop showed up at the side of the car and instructed Tommy to roll down the window. Behind him were several other cops.

"Yes, officer?"

"This car matches the description of a car used in an armed robbery in Brooklyn," he began in an icy voice. "Two police officers were killed. Now step out of the car."

This guy was all business. If what he was saying was true, we were in deep fucking trouble. And even if he was lying, or if some mistake had been made, it was still a very dangerous situation that had to be defused. I tried to maintain eye contact with the cop, mainly because I was scared shitless that he was going to shoot me.

"I don't have a gun," I said. "I don't have a weapon of any kind."

"Shut up!" he yelled. Then he pushed me against the side of the car and patted me down. Kid and Tommy and the girl received the same treatment. Fortunately, none of us was carrying anything. Except, of course, the hash. I mean, the whole car reeked. But they didn't seem to care. They were looking for weapons, for some evidence that we'd really been involved in the murder of a police officer.

"What are you doing here?" the red-headed cop finally asked.

I responded carefully, calmly, with a tone of respect. I told him about our show at the Bottom Line with the Garcia Band. The cop at first wasn't convinced.

"Yeah?" he said. "Who owns that club?"

This was one of those occasions when I was thankful that I paid attention to details. "Stan Sadowski," I answered correctly.

The cop nodded. "Okay, but we're gonna have a little peek at your car here, if you don't mind."

I just nodded, but I noticed Tommy stiffening. I wasn't sure why. They obviously weren't going to bust him for carrying a small amount of hash—hell, they'd already found a couple ounces of Thai stick on me and didn't even say a word about it. The cop just squeezed the bag and tossed it aside. Now, if they found a single bullet or a gun of any kind, that would be a different story. If that happened, we were going straight to jail.

But they found nothing, of course. They looked in the glove compartment, beneath the seats—they even ripped out the backseat! When they finally realized that we clearly weren't cop killers, they just sent us on our way with a soft warning: "Try not to smoke anymore until you get back to the hotel. Driving this car, you might get stopped again."

Kid and I laughed all the way to Fifty-ninth Street, but Tommy said nothing. His face was blank, like he was in shock.

When we got back to the hotel, I asked him what was wrong. "It's okay, man," I said. "It's over."

Tommy shook his head. "They never looked in the trunk."

"Huh?"

He stared at me, his eyes wide, his jaw slack.

"They never looked in the fucking trunk."

I searched my memory banks and realized he was right. The cops had taken the car apart but had somehow neglected to pop the trunk of the car. A terrible thought crossed my mind.

"Tommy . . . what was in the trunk?"

A thin smile crossed his face. He seemed embarrassed and relieved. "Oh, nothing."

"Tommy . . . what's in the trunk?" I repeated.

"Just a big duffel bag," he said. Then Tommy—the drug dealer we really didn't know that well at all—paused and shrugged his shoulders. "Filled with twenty pounds of marijuana."

Kid and I made a vow that night to never take a ride from anyone. Stick to the band's transportation.

Chapter 15

1971-

*R*amrod and I are driving quietly through a remote section of Napa Valley, *following Phil Lesh in his BMW on a crystal-blue Northern California morning. Phil's father recently passed away, and we're here to help him clean out the family's summer home so that it can be put on the market. We aren't talking much because it's one of those melancholy, reflective kind of moments, the kind we experienced with some frequency in the Dead, as people came and went, and lives unraveled and withered away. Phil is a good and sensitive man, and this is a hard time for him. Ramrod and I just want to lend a hand.*

Suddenly we round a corner and enter a semisuburban neighborhood, and Phil slows down and begins to honk his horn. His arm extends out the window and he points to a sign: SHURTLIFF STREET.

That's Ramrod's real surname, so we both laugh at the coincidence. But Phil is still honking his horn, pointing and waving, and when I see the very next sign, at the corner of the very next street, I understand why.

PARISH STREET.

Suddenly there is silence in the car. Ramrod and I exchange glances. It's too weird for words. Phil pulls into a convenience store parking lot at the next major intersection, and the three of us get out of our cars and stand there scratching our heads. Phil walks inside, buys a six-pack of Heineken—he knows Ramrod likes beer and thinks this is an occasion worth acknowledging—and comes back out. We each crack open a beer, tap our bottles together, and drink to the strangeness of life.

There never was a crew like ours, and there never will be again. We weren't merely hired hands; we were band members who didn't play instruments. We were family. (Incidentally, when I say "band" I'm speaking primarily of the Grateful Dead—although I took my work with the Garcia Band just as seriously, there were fewer complications involved when touring only with Jerry and a handful of his friends. The shows were smaller, quieter, the setup less involved.) And we protected each other and supported each other accordingly. Over the years people have accused the Grateful Dead crew of having too much power, of sometimes usurping the authority of the band and its management. To me, that seems like just another way of saying we didn't know our place. Rock 'n' roll crews weren't supposed to have any authority at all. They were supposed to drive the trucks, unload the gear, set up the stage, and then sit back and let the band entertain. The crew was supposed to be invisible. But our situation was more complicated than that. Our traveling circus was like none before it, with a giant PA (known affectionately and reverently as the Wall of Sound) that by the end required scaffolding thirty feet high just to set it up. We had more equipment than other bands, and we had some of the most devoted fans in the world. So we took control of everything: security, setup, and sound. From the moment we arrived in town, the crew was in charge.

It had to be that way, and in truth the band wanted it that way. There were so many things that simply couldn't have been accomplished if we didn't seize that power. We had a meeting with the band in San Rafael in 1971, during which the primary topic of conversation was stage security. Our fans were hippies. They were typically kind and gentle kids who liked to smoke dope and sway to the music and not cause any trouble for anyone. But the prevalence of drugs at our shows invariably led to security problems—tripped-out kids storming the stage, often stripped of their clothes, wanting nothing more than to give Jerry or Bobby a big hug, which, of course, was something that couldn't be tolerated, because you never knew what might happen if you lost control, if you let anyone cross that boundary between band and audience, between stage and seats. Once, during a show at the College of William & Mary in Virginia, I was standing by the side of the stage when I saw something out of the corner of my eye, a kid running down the aisle, full-tilt, totally naked, screaming at the top of his lungs. This kid was so fucked up, and had such a head start, that nothing was going to stop him from getting to the stage. He sprinted up the stairs and began running toward Jerry, at which I point I intercepted him. We both tumbled across the stage, nearly toppling Jerry's stack in the process. Not that he noticed—Jerry just kept on playing as we wrestled across the floor. I was much bigger than this kid, but he was wild and sweaty and impossible to restrain—sort of like a greased pig—and as he slid away from me on all fours, the kid let go of his bodily functions! Right in front of me, just started pissing and shitting all over the stage. It was totally weird and disgusting, and understandably led me to turn matters over to the theater security staff, which pulled him down off the stage and dragged him away, leaving a trail of shit in his wake. It was one of those moments that left me thinking, *What kind of world am I living in?*

The answer, of course, was . . . the world of the Grateful Dead.

We talked a lot about how to control the crowds, how to put on a show that the fans would love while at the same time making sure that the stage remained a sanctuary. At some point during that meeting Jerry said to the crew, "It's simple. We'll take care of everything in front of the amps. You guys take care of everything behind the amps." What he meant was this: *The band plays. Everything else is up to you.* At least that's the way we interpreted it. And you have to understand that when something was said at these meetings, especially if it came from Jerry, it immediately became law. We took it upon ourselves after that to control the crowd around the stage, despite the fact that our zealousness led to friction with the guys in the band. I don't know how many times I got phone calls at three in the morning from a band member saying, "Hey, man, you threw my friend off the stage." More often than not it wasn't really a friend, but rather an acquaintance. A real friend—or family member—would have been known to us and thus immune from such manhandling.

Maybe we got overamped sometime, but we took our responsibilities seriously. We felt we owed it to the band, to the equipment, and, yes, to the fans, to maintain a sense of order around the stage (although we never hurt anyone). The stage was nothing less than our altar, and it was our sacred duty to protect it. That equipment—the Wall of Sound and everything that went with it—was our lifeblood. We built it with out own hands and therefore felt a personal connection to it.

You have to understand, too, that in those early years we were quite literally trying to create an industry. Along the way we met a lot of opposition—from law enforcement officials, theater owners, union representatives, and from stagehands who knew nothing but legitimate theater and naturally resented dealing with us. Often we'd come into town and start unloading our trucks, and immediately be confronted by union employees who were supposed to be working with us, and who hated the fact that we were touching our own equipment.

It wasn't just a union issue, though. It was a generational problem, too. Most of the stage hands were older, conservative guys, World War II vets who didn't like anything about our music and the people who came to our shows. To them, we were representative of everything that was wrong with American culture at that time. Most of the time we'd get along with them just barely well enough to get the job done, but it rarely went smoothly. What they wanted was for us to stand there and tell them what to do—to simply point and direct, and then get out of the way while they did their jobs at their own leisurely union pace. Well, that just wasn't practical, or even possible, with our gear and our setup. All we wanted was for them to help us unload the truck and move everything from the door to the stage. We could handle everything else on our own. If they wanted to do more, that was fine, so long as they took direction from us. But they wanted to exert themselves, to do things the way they did when a play came to town. But we were an entirely different ballgame.

I'm sure our condescending attitude didn't help. We didn't give a shit about unions. We just wanted to work hard and fast and get the job done so that the band could play. The most efficient way to do that was for us to take charge and simply tell the union employees what we needed, while working alongside them. That was not the way they were accustomed to doing business, which predictably led to some serious friction between the Grateful Dead and the International Theatrical and Stage Employees Union. The tension boiled over one night after a show at the Cleveland Municipal Auditorium in 1973. Cleveland was a hardcore union town, typical of Rust Belt cities at that time. Whenever we played there, we ran into trouble with the union. Usually we just bullied our way through it, and in fact that's what we had done during setup. But the load-out was different.

The stagehands kept yelling at us, telling us not to touch our own gear. They wanted to move the equipment from the stage to the trucks, as stipulated in their union contract. From there, the Teamsters would take over and load the gear into the trucks. We didn't listen. We just kept breaking things down and moving them out. That's what we always did when we ran into opposition: we ignored it. This time, however, the Teamsters got into the act. There were several of them down by the loading dock, and they were trying to tell us the same thing: *We'll load the trucks, you just point.*

To which we not-so-politely responded, "Bullshit!"

Well, one of them put out a call, and as we were loading the trucks more than 150 Teamsters showed up with baseball bats. We knew they meant business, mainly because we'd recently heard about the Teamsters putting a beat-down on some roadies from a Canadian band called the Guess Who. And I knew firsthand just how tough and nasty the Teamsters could be. My father had been a Teamster most of his adult life. I'd walked picket lines with him. I'd seen people battered and beaten for standing up to the Teamsters. So I had a healthy respect for their ability to do damage in situations such as these.

I also knew how to talk to them. Or so I thought. As the standoff went on, I sought out one of the union guys and began trying to reason with him.

"We're just trying to do our jobs here," I said. "We respect you and your union, and we want to work with your men. How can we make that happen? I mean, it's silly that you don't want us to touch our own equipment."

This man was probably fifty years old and not physically impressive. I almost felt like I was in control of the situation, despite my age and inexperience. But I was wrong. The man put an arm around my shoulder—he had to reach up to do it—and pulled me close. Then he took out a .38 revolver and just sort of let it roll around in his palm.

"You know, you seem like a nice enough kid to me," he said. "I don't have anything against you. I don't even have anything against your band. But we mean business here, son. And if you boys continue to insist on doing things your way, someone is going to get hurt."

No sooner had those words passed his lips than I saw Jackson heave a beer can at one of the Teamsters. Jackson had a temper and he often lacked patience, but this was neither the time nor the place for him to lose his cool. The beer can just missed the Teamster, which was fortunate, because I'm not sure Jackson would have gotten out of there alive if it had found its mark. As it was, the Teamster lunged at Jackson and the two of them began to wrestle. I immediately jumped in and pulled Jackson away before the fight escalated into something we surely would have regretted.

"Rex," I said, holding him tight. "We're slightly outnumbered here."

Jackson told me to fuck off, then he told the Teamsters to fuck off, but I was able to keep him from instigating any more trouble. Under the circumstances we decided the prudent thing to do was acquiesce to the unions' demands.

The next day I called my father and asked if he could help. He made a couple of phone calls, and soon we were issued traveling road cards by the International Alliance of Theatrical Stage Employees. The guys in the band thought that was pretty funny, because we'd always had such a nonunion attitude. And now we were effectively part of the union. As I said . . . life is strange.

Chapter 16

*Hey honey—want to meet
Jerry Garcia and suck my
dick?*

—Clifford Dale Heard

I've often been asked, "Did you guys ever leverage your position with the band to pick up women?" It's a silly question. Of course we did. In our minds, this was one of the perks of the road. And it wasn't like anyone in the band resented us for using them to unlock doors.

If this sounds hedonistic and more than slightly unchivalrous, well, you have to consider the time and circumstances. What a different world it was then, in the late sixties, early seventies. It was a time when you could get a cheap set of wheels, smoke pot, drive on the sidewalk, not bother with insurance, and no one really seemed to mind. The

Dead (and the Garcia Band) would play all over the country, sometimes for free, and almost always for several hours at a time. We'd go as long as we could, until the cops came along, reminded us we were breaking curfew, and shut us down. As the band's popularity soared, touring became a way of life, the road became our home. It was an almost unimaginably self-indulgent existence, and naturally it took its toll. Some of the guys would try to squeeze in a "normal" life between trips on the road, but that was hopeless. If you had two people on the crew who were trying to be good and loyal and mature, you'd have five others running around, doing drugs, having sex with anything that moved.

The guys in the band were more reserved, but only slightly so. They partied, too. They went through long lines of women and ingested large amounts of drugs. Sometimes, in the spirit of democracy and camaraderie, the same women and drugs would go through the band *and* the crew. Whatever was accessible was accessible to everyone. We had no rules, no line of demarcation. And the hardness of road life, the way we worked and fought and played, extended to the way we treated women. They became toys to us.

To my chagrin, I discovered this incredible sexual amusement park shortly after I moved in with Annette. I was young and dead broke and truly appreciative of what she had done for me, the way she had befriended me and opened her house and heart. I loved her— although I don't know if I was ever really *in love* with her—and I had some vague aspiration to be a loyal, responsible man. But once the road life started in earnest, there was no chance of that happening. I thought I could be a normal man in a normal relationship, in part because I had great affection not only for Annette, but for her son, Johnny. (Actually, his real name was Che, as in Che Guevara, but whenever he told people his name, they'd invariably say, "Jay?" After a while he got sick of correcting them and explaining the origin of his name, so he started calling himself Johnny.) Annette doubted me, of course, and rightly so, but she liked me at least as much as I liked her, so we decided to give it a shot. We lived together under one roof, taking care of her son and pretending to be a grown-up couple. Our parents even met once, and they liked each other. I think they probably thought we'd get married eventually and leave the rock 'n' roll life behind.

But I had no idea what I was up against, no idea what commitment really was. The instant I went out on the road I discovered that temptation was everywhere, and I was about as weak and impulsive as a man could be. There were girls everywhere. We'd screw in the back rooms of clubs, get blow jobs at the stage door . . . and that was merely a prelude to the long nights of wild sex in hotel rooms. It wasn't like this happened just once in a while, like we were ugly-ass roadies who happened to land a pity fuck once a month. This was almost a nightly occurrence.

I'd never tell Annette that, of course, although I'm sure she suspected that I was behaving like a complete tramp whenever I wasn't with her. In a way it was kind of interesting to watch our relationship evolve and devolve, the way it went from being based on sex and communal love, to one of greater intimacy and respect, and then fall apart completely because of my infidelity and immaturity. The expectations changed when Annette got her own house and I moved in with her. Suddenly it wasn't cool to have multiple partners, not with a kid around, and not with at least one of us making an emotional investment in the relationship. Say all you want about free love and sexual experimentation, but it's a rare couple that places no boundaries on such activity. When the heart gets involved, everything changes.

Even worse was my adherence to a ridiculous double standard: as our family was growing, taking root, and our lives were becoming intertwined, and I was out on the road trying to set some sort of record for sexual conquest, Annette was back home taking care of business—and I expected that of her! I expected her to be faithful to me, regardless of where I was putting my dick. Makes no sense, I know, but that's the way I felt, although I'm not sure that it really would have mattered much to me had I discovered she was sleeping around. I just presumed she wouldn't.

I checked in with Annette most nights, as soon as the show was over, but it was strictly a perfunctory gesture. Usually by that time I'd already met a few girls and invited them back to the hotel. Before they arrived I'd make a quick call to Annette, profess my love, and then get down to the business of serious partying. After about a year of getting away with that ruse (or so I thought), I got caught with my dick in the cookie jar. It happened when a hotel operator interrupted my conversation with Annette and patched through a call from a girl I'd met at the show who was hanging out in the lobby waiting to come on up. Somehow—I've always suspected it was the work of a sadistic operator—we all ended up on the phone together. For a few seconds, anyway, until Annette slammed down the receiver. That was the beginning of the bubble popping, and though we remained together for a couple more years, our relationship was never the same. It became tenuous at best, and even when we were together at home, we fought in a way that we never had before. I'm not sure why I let it go on like that—weakness and selfishness, I guess—but I did. I couldn't let go of the relationship, and yet I had no respect for it either, which is, of course, reprehensible.

It's hard to convey exactly what it was like to be a true road warrior, in love with the freedom and the insanity, and yet somehow reliant on the idea that someone was back home waiting for you. There were moments of extreme loneliness on the road, where you were far away from home, in your hotel room, all by yourself, trying to find something to watch on the television—no small task in the pre-cable era. As badly as you often behaved, you'd still miss your family. Boredom was often a nemesis. We had to amuse ourselves after the show, or on those thousand-mile drives, and we did it by hoping that we could find other people to bounce off, instead of just bouncing off ourselves. We drove everywhere, we were constantly sleep-deprived, crusty, pissed off, brimming with postadolescent testosterone. We looked for sex to take the edge off, and if we didn't find it, we got on each other's nerves. We were constantly looking for girls to fuck or guys to fight. That was our attitude, that was our mission.

It was a natural outgrowth of the way we lived in the early days—1969, 1970—when we weren't traveling quite as much but rather living together in true hippie style. The Grateful Dead family was so large, and there was so much experimentation. Men and women were living together, primarily as friends, but the prevailing attitude toward sex and drugs was . . . *anything goes.* When you're friends with a woman, living under those conditions, it's only a short jump from platonic to sexual. That prelude made it difficult for any of us to try to carry on a "normal" relationship. At one time or another we all tried, but inevitably you wound up in that situation where you were on the road and your old lady was back home, and she thought you were screwing around, which you certainly were, and so she went out looking for a little party herself. This sometimes led to very bad decisions and compromises, such as inviting your wife or girlfriend out on the road. We all tried that, too, more often than not with disastrous consequences. Keith Godchaux joined the band as a keyboard player in 1971, when Pigpen's drinking led to such severe health problems that he was unable to function much of the time. Before long Keith's wife, Donna, was out on the road with us, and the two of them were fighting like crazy. They'd have screaming matches in hotel lobbies, restaurants, backstage, anywhere. I saw them destroy a hotel room during one of their wilder confrontations, just splinter every piece of furniture. That's how intense it could get when you tried to pack up your life at home and take it on the road with you. There was just no way it could be done. The way we traveled, the way we lived, it was just too grueling and, quite frankly, too embarrassing to have someone's old lady in our midst. One woman wasn't going to civilize or tame the entire zoo; to be honest, no one wanted to be tamed. We were having too much fun.

I don't mean to come off as an inveterate sleazeball, but there's no point in lying about the way we lived, the crudeness and craziness of our existence at that time. The truth is, we were on a quest. We lived every day in a tough, macho world; there was hardly a soft spot. Sometimes the sex was less about physical release than it was about simply sharing time with a woman. There were moments on the road when a woman's touch really meant something, when it brought you back to civilization and made you feel, at least for a little while, as if you weren't a complete neanderthal. Sometimes you just wanted to touch and talk, not fight and fuck.

Sometimes . . .

Most of the time, I have to admit, we reveled in the baseness and carnality. It was like another drug, maybe the best drug. The downside is that, as with almost any drug, after a while, if you have any soul at all, you start to feel a little strange about imbibing so heavily, and you begin to wonder . . . *Am I becoming a sexual addict here?*

The answer comes quickly, as it almost does when an addict first looks in the mirror:

Naaaaaah.

There was a place in Los Angeles called the Continental Hyatt House that was like no other hotel in the world. If you saw the movie *Almost Famous,* then you saw the Continental, and the depiction was just about right. In the early seventies it seemed like every band that passed through Los Angeles stayed at the Hyatt House, which we called the Riot House because the hotel was basically one big party from the lobby to the rooftop. Celebrities—rock stars, mostly—were always coming and going, so there was never a shortage of groupies hanging out. And in the grand Southern California tradition, many of them were drop-dead gorgeous.

We stayed at the Continental in '72, and while hanging out on a day off I went downstairs to get something to eat. On the way back up from the lobby I shared an elevator with a willowy blonde girl wearing a one-piece velvet minidress. She was tall and thin and pretty, and probably barely out of high school (which would sound bad except that I was only a couple years older than her). By this time I'd gotten pretty good at picking up women—it was simply a matter of throwing the band's name around a little—and in this setting, where virtually all of the girls were looking to party, it was like shooting fish in a barrel. I introduced myself shortly after the elevator doors closed. By the time we reached the tenth floor, she had accepted my invitation to hang out for a little while.

Heard and Joe Winslow were rooming together across the hall, but when I got back with this girl, they were in my room, along with Bobby Weir, who sat on the bed and lazily strummed a guitar, which of course my new friend found absolutely breathtaking. But there's honor among thieves, right, and there are rules of decorum even on the road. I'd brought this young lady upstairs and she was now sitting on the bed next to me; protocol dictated that the others drift off in due course and leave me and my new friend all alone. Bobby left first, then Joe, and finally Heard. When the door clicked behind him, I thought it was safe to make my move. What I didn't know then was that Heard hadn't really shut the door all the way. He'd pushed it back open just a crack.

Now, I'm not saying I knew everything about girls. Hell, I was still a kid. But I'd learned a thing or two since joining the crew. I knew enough to be shocked when I put my hand on her thigh and it started vibrating like an engine. I had pretty good hands—the big, strong hands of a working man—but my touch had never elicited that sort of a reaction before. For a moment I was concerned that perhaps I'd frightened her, that maybe she wasn't quite as experienced or lustful as I'd imagined. My anxiety was quickly laid to rest, though, as she slipped off her dress in one single, graceful motion and leapt on top of me, pulling me inside her and taking control of the situation like a pro. And that was only the beginning. Within a few seconds after we'd started intercourse, she threw her head back and began moaning like a wounded animal. Then she started jumping up and down on me and screaming at the top of her lungs.

"Jesus!" I said between thrusts. "Are you all right?"

"Shut up and fuck!"

Ooooookay . . .

I didn't have to be told twice. I kept banging away, holding out as long as I could, but I wasn't even remotely capable of satisfying her. She was, it soon became apparent, a textbook example of a nymphomaniac. I'd never met anyone like her before, and never did again. All she wanted was sex—as much as she could possibly get.

Fortunately, she'd come to the right place.

Heard, who had been out in the hall listening, slipped back into the room just as I was finishing up and wasted no time in taking my place. The girl barely seemed to notice the substitution. Heard gave it his best shot, and then I took another turn. Then it was Heard again. Twice each, and this girl was just getting warmed up. By that time word had spread that something interesting was happening in my room, and the line was beginning to form. It went on for the better part of a day and a half, a tireless gang bang in which almost every member of the crew and a few guys from the band took a ride. It became the equivalent of a porno flick, with guys putting on a show for each other, tag teaming, and working this girl in every way imaginable . . . and a crowd applauding the sturdiest efforts.

She said almost nothing throughout the whole experience, just, moaned and wailed and occasionally asked if that was the best we could do, which I thought was pretty funny. It's a hard thing to explain in the cold light of day, especially thirty years later, now that we're all grown up and married and have children of our own—including a teenage daughter, in my case. But it was a beautiful thing in a funny sort of way. We were playing, and everyone enjoyed the game. No one got hurt, no one was coerced into anything. At the end of it we got to talking a bit, and I liked her. She was a spunky gal. Maybe it was her fantasy to take care of twenty guys at once—or at least one after another—just like it was our fantasy to have her. Who knows?

The only unsettling aspect of it all to me were the phone calls from Annette, who wondered what all the commotion was about. She was used to calling and hearing parties in the background, but this was like no other party we'd hosted.

"Everything is fine, honey," I said the first time she called. "See you when I get home."

Then I dropped my towel and stepped to the plate for another turn at bat.

The next morning, shortly after the girl had departed—we agreed to meet again at some later date, but never did, of course—Annette called again.

"What the hell is going on down there?" she inquired. I could tell she was pissed, and I later found out that word of the gang bang had drifted north during the night—guys calling friends and bragging, I guess. So Annette was quizzing me, really giving me a hard time.

"Nothing is happening," I lied. "I don't know what you're talking about."

At that very moment there was a knock at the door. "Hold on a minute, Annette." I opened the door and saw Weir standing in the hallway, holding a cigarette lighter and a full matte of firecrackers. "Bobby—" I began, but that's as far as I got. He lit the matte and chucked it past me into the room, then pulled the door shut as the fireworks began and held it so tightly that it couldn't be opened.

BAM! BAM! BAM!

As the room filled with the smell of cordite and smoke, and the matte of 'crackers bounced off the carpeting like flaming popcorn, I jumped on the bed and grabbed the phone.

"Annette?" Annette?"

She was gone by this time, and I imagined her thinking, *Gunfire . . . good. I hope the bastard is dead!*

137

The smoke was so thick that I couldn't breathe. My lungs and eyes burned, and I began to panic. So I grabbed a chair and smashed a window. As the cloud dissipated I made my way across the room and opened the door. And there was Weir on the floor in the hallway, laughing his ass off.

Another time, a few years later, we arrived in Pittsburgh on a charter flight (our mode of travel was upgraded significantly in the mid- to late seventies) with a day to kill before setting up for the show the following morning. There were limos there to greet us, and the first couple took off with several of the band members—all except our drummers, Mickey Hart and Billy Kreutzmann. As the limo driver tossed our bags into the trunk, Mickey jumped into the driver's seat and pulled away. That was the beginning of a long and wild night, one that culminated with my calling an escort service and asking them to send over four of their best girls—one for each member of our little party: me, Jackson, Kreutzmann, and Kid.

About an hour later, four cute girls, fresh as the driven snow, showed up at our hotel. Within minutes we learned that this was their very first day on the job, and that they didn't really even know what it meant to be an employee of an "escort service." Not that they were prudish. Far from it. It took almost no time for the party to get into high gear, and it went on all night long. We had an orgy—there's no other way to describe it. Lots of drugs, lots of sex, multiple partners, no act considered out of bounds.

Finally, the next morning, as the girls were getting dressed and preparing to leave, one of them said, "Hey, what about our money."

I waved a finger at her, as if she'd been naughty. "Uh-uh . . . it doesn't work that way."

She seemed surprised. "What do you mean?"

"See, you're supposed to get the money first, then do the job."

They left bewildered, but not angry, in part I think because they'd had a pretty good time, too. In fact, they came to the show the next day, along with the owner of the escort service, who wasn't so much angry as he was disappointed.

"Just trying to break them in properly," I said. "You have to teach these girls the rules. You can't send them out on the street like that, without a crash course in escort ethics. No one's gonna pay them after they get their nut off. You know that. And if they were professionals, they'd know it, too."

He laughed. "Yeah, I suppose."

As it turned out, there were no hard feelings, no lost jobs. In fact, we got together again the next night after the show and did it all over again. This time the girls didn't even ask for money!

To be honest, paying for sex was a rarity, something we did more out of laziness or curiosity than desperation. Women, after all, were everywhere, and they all wanted to bask in the glow of the Grateful Dead. You didn't just meet girls at the show, you met them on airplanes, at rental car counters, in restaurants. If worse came to worst and the flow of groupies dried up, you could always go to the hotel bar and pick up fellow travelers, working women out on the road, away from their husbands and children. They, too, were susceptible to the allure of fame and money. The minute they found out you had anything to do with the Dead, you were beneath their sheets. The funny thing to me was how often and easily it worked. I mean, it *always* fucking worked.

One night in St. Louis, after a show at the Fox Theater, I brought two hairdressers back to the hotel (we stayed at the Stan Musial Inn—I'll spare you the obvious baseball metaphors this time), and we had an amazing time with these chicks. (By "we" I mean just about everybody on the crew—the guys in the band sat this one out, although a few were spectators.) We stayed up all night smoking, drinking, playing cards, and fucking. These girls were into being our little playthings. Why? Who knows? Maybe they just liked sex. Maybe they liked us. Or, more likely, they figured having sex with guys on the crew was the next best thing to fucking Jerry Garcia or Bob Weir.

Anyway, early in the morning, when the party was still going strong, there was a knock at the door. We were on the ground level of the motel, so I threw back the curtains to expose the sliding glass doors leading out to the patio, and there, to my surprise, were four clean-cut young men and women holding pamphlets and smiling. I stepped outside.

"Good morning, sir," one of them said. "We're from the Jehovah's Witnesses. Could we talk with you for a moment?"

I didn't know what to say. Behind me I could hear the sound of laughter, the grunts and groans of exhausted lovemaking. As the musky scent of debauchery drifted out onto the patio, one of them held out a pamphlet and began flipping through the pages, showing me pictures of what appeared to be a Roman orgy. He talked about sin and salvation, and the importance of living the way God intended.

Choking on the irony, I grabbed the pamphlet, physically turned him around, and said, "Please, run for your lives! You are in the wrong place! This is a den of iniquity."

The four of them just smiled some more, nodded, thanked me for my time and urged me to have a nice day. Then they moved on to the next room. Only at times like that did I realize there was another world, that not everyone led such an X-rated existence. It was so normal to us. We lived for the pleasure of the moment. We worked hard, but every day seemed to end with a party, because we felt it was our right to blow off steam. No one could tell us otherwise. Hell, just a little while earlier, on the very same spot where the Jehovah's Witnesses were standing, there had been a six-foot tank of nitrous oxide. We were right out there toking off it in the open. If anyone saw us, we really didn't care.

We were living every adolescent's fantasy, including the one in which you find yourself entertaining and satisfying two women at once. Even to members of the crew, this happened with stunning regularity, although not always by design. Sometimes you'd meet a girl at a show and invite her back to the hotel, only to discover that she was there with a sister or a cousin or a girlfriend. Well, you couldn't just come right out and say, "That's okay, I'll have sex with both of you," even if that was what you were thinking. Instead you had to go through the ritual of drafting a friend to help with your quest. This wasn't usually a problem, but there were times when each of us was left to his own wicked devices, when we succumbed to the urge of luring two girls back to the hotel, knowing full well that there wasn't another man waiting for them. I loved having two women at once—hell, who wouldn't?—and it became something of a forte of mine, although, to be perfectly honest, I must say that it wasn't all that difficult a maneuver to execute. There were hundreds of women at each show who were more than willing to have sex, who in fact wanted noting more than to have sex with someone associated with the Grateful Dead. Sure, their preference might have been Bobby or Jerry or anyone else who played an instrument, but . . . get in line, right?

For those of us on the crew, there was rarely any shortage of flesh, and on the rare occasions when there was, we generously shared the booty, so to speak. We became very good at covering each other and helping each other out. If that sounds improbable or despicable, well, it really wasn't. Not to us, and not at that time. If you picked up a girl and wanted to invite others to the party, all you had to do was leave your door open. Invariably, someone would walk in and take a seat and watch the show. When you were done, you'd give the girl a little kiss and suggest she move over to the next bed, where your friend was waiting. If the girl didn't like that idea, she'd tell you, usually in no uncertain terms. But nine out of ten times, it was no problem at all.

It was the tenth time that got you into trouble.

Example: a show in Oklahoma City, where Rex Jackson met and charmed a beautiful, tall redhead—a truly striking woman—and after which he brought her back to our hotel. I remember that night starting out as relatively quiet. We had rooming lists, and I was paired with

Heard on that night. Neither of us had met a woman at the show, so we just went back to the hotel and hung out and smoked some weed and watched a little televison. Meanwhile, two doors down the hall, Jackson and the redhead were going at it, although I guess Rex lacked stamina or interest that evening, because he finished up in about five minutes—a real quickie—and came wandering down to our room.

"All done, Rex?" Heard chided him.

Jackson nodded, pulled up a chair.

"Poor girl is probably still hungry," I said.

Jackson laughed. "No doubt, man. Why don't you go on down? She's a party girl."

"Yeah?"

"Absolutely," Jackson said.

When I entered the room I saw a pretty young woman sitting up on the bed. She was naked and immediately covered herself with a blanket.

"Where's Don?" she asked, using the first name that none of us ever used—he was always Rex or Jackson, but never "Don."

"Oh, he's around," I said, sitting down next to her. "He asked me to come down here and keep you company."

I sensed right away that she wasn't completely comfortable with the situation, but I figured she was just a little nervous and that she'd soon open up. They always did. So we talked for a few minutes, and as we talked I began stroking her arm, and then her shoulders, and for a moment there I thought everything would work out just fine. But when I subtly slipped my hand down along her neckline and tried to peel back the blanket—WHAM!—she cocked her legs back and kicked me in the stomach as hard as she could. The blow knocked the wind out of me and sent me reeling off the bed and onto the floor.

"Who the hell do you think you are?" she said.

I had no answer, and even if I did I couldn't have articulated it, for I was incapable of speaking—she'd hit me that hard. I was still on one knee, trying to pull myself up, when Jackson walked into the room, doubtless expecting to see the two of us getting it on. What he got was something else entirely. The redhead jumped off the bed, exposing herself completely, and ran straight up to Jackson and slapped him across the face.

"You son of a bitch!" she yelled. "You think I'm your whore or something?"

Jackson said nothing, just held a hand to the side of his face.

"No one treats me like that!" she said, and then she jumped on him, started riding him around the room like a cowboy on a bucking bronco. And all the while she kept biting him, punching him, pulling his hair.

"Jesus Christ!" Jackson yelled. "Calm down."

The redhead wouldn't listen, wouldn't let go. I tried to pry her off, but she responded by biting my arm so hard that she drew blood!

"YAAAH!" My scream startled her, and suddenly she let go and slid off Jackson's back. As he staggered around the room, wounded and dazed, she looked at me and spit out what appeared to be a chunk of my skin.

"You think I'm afraid of you guys?" It was obviously a rhetorical question. "Fuck . . . I grew up with four brothers. I can handle you two pricks."

"No doubt," I said, rubbing my injured arm. "There's obviously been a misunderstanding here. I apologize. I meant no disrespect."

She seemed on the verge of accepting that explanation and ending the battle when Heard walked in, clapped his hands and said, "My turn?"

Oh, shit!

The redhead pounced at Heard like a cougar at a rabbit. She slapped him, kicked him, punched him . . . basically, she humiliated him from one side of the room to the other, until Jackson and I both jumped in and pulled her off. We kept trying to calm her down. We kept apologizing, but she wanted none of it. Every time I loosened my grip, she lashed out again. She was so pissed about Jackson screwing her and then turning her over to the rest of us that nothing short of seeing one of us dead was going to make her happy. How this happened, I don't know. Maybe it was Jackson's idea of a joke. Or, worse, perhaps he thought this was as good a way as any to get rid of her. One drawback of road life was that when you picked somebody up and brought them to the hotel, you were stuck with them . . . and a lot of times you didn't want them there. At least, not once you were through having sex.

In so blatantly disrespecting this woman, however, we'd all made a huge mistake, and now we were paying for it. There were three of us trying to wrestle her to the ground, and still she wouldn't quit. Eventually we got her out into the hall, where we ran into Ramrod, who had heard the commotion and now immediately began scolding us and chastising us. Embarrassed and exhausted, we fell off her one by one, until finally the elevator doors opened and Ramrod guided her inside and stepped in behind her.

She was still cursing, promising to make each one of us pay with our lives, as the doors closed and the elevator carried her safely away.

"Man, what the hell was that?" Heard asked. "That chick is a hellcat, huh?"

The three of us were still standing there nursing our injuries when the elevator returned. We expected to see only Ramrod, but instead were treated to the sight of the redhead on his back, yanking his hair and clawing at his face.

"Christ!" Ramrod howled, blood trickling from his nose. "Get her off me!"

We jumped inside, somehow separated them, and pulled Ramrod out. Then we hit the button and sent the redhead on her way. Then we froze, waiting to see what would happen next. (Years later, when I saw *The Terminator* for the first time, I thought, *Man, Arnold reminds me of that redhead. Just won't quit.*) Indeed, less than two minutes passed before the elevator returned and the doors opened, and there she was again, still inside. Except this time she didn't attack. Instead, she was flat on her back, gasping for breath.

"You bastards," she wheezed. "I'm having an asthma attack, and you brought it on."

Now the worst thoughts started to creep into my mind, thoughts of police and news cameras and unseemly headlines in the next day's paper. I thought of everything that had happened, and while I was pretty sure I'd been guilty of nothing worse than arrogance, I could imagine a district attorney or cop coming up with an entirely different interpretation.

We pulled her out of the elevator and sat with her for a few minutes. We got her some water, helped her get dressed, and then Ramrod and I took her down to the lobby. I tried to calm her down on the way down, not only because I didn't want her to attack me in the lobby and create a big scene, but also because I did feel sorry for her. We put her in a cab, gave the driver twenty bucks, and watched them pull away, hoping like hell that was the last we'd see of her. Then—and this was the kind of karmic episode that happened sometimes on the road—a drunken bum came stumbling past the front entrance of the hotel, stopped right in front of us, and stuck out his hand.

"Got any spare change, fellas?"

Ramrod and I exchanged glances. Then Ramrod dug into his pocket and pulled out a twenty-dollar bill. The bum seemed mystified. He gave the money a little kiss and then balled it up into his fist. "I'm going clean, brother," he said, looking Ramrod right in the eye. "I promise."

Chapter 17

Unlike many rock 'n' roll bands, the Grateful Dead attracted groupies who weren't exclusively young and female. Much has been written over the years about the strange hold the band had (*has*, actually) on so many fans, of the legion of devotees who left home and hearth to travel around the country or the world and pray nightly at the altar of the Grateful Dead. They were hippies, mostly, hanging on to the sixties even well into the seventies and eighties. Most were obscure, of course. But some were not. Over the years there have been scores of celebrities who have became honorary Deadheads, from the obvious (Bob Dylan, John Lennon, Jane Fonda, Bill Walton, Woody Harrelson, Allen Ginsburg) to the interesting (Paul Newman, Phil

Jackson, John F. Kennedy Jr.) to the surprising (Walter Cronkite, Al Gore).

Being a Deadhead, though, was not the same as being part of the family. A greater commitment was required if one sought complete access and acceptance, and no one more fully exemplified this commitment than Loose Bruce Baxter.

Loose Bruce was an interesting man, a jet-setter from Texas whose family was quite well off. Together with a couple guys named Ray and Spider (who seemed to subsist entirely on Dr. Pepper and bacon), Loose Bruce formed the nucleus of something we called the Pleasure Crew. The deal with the Pleasure Crew was this: they loved Jerry and the Grateful Dead, and they liked hanging out with us, but they hadn't the slightest interest in working. Most of them—there were others who came and went—seemed not to have ever done a day's work in their lives. They were people of means, and for whatever reason they decided to make the Dead the focus of their existence. At least for a while. We liked them, naturally, because they bankrolled wild parties, and I will say that they were generally nice folks.

Baxter was a central figure in the party element of the Grateful Dead for many years. He would hang with us and party and travel for months on end. Then, all of a sudden, he'd disappear, and we'd find out later that he gone back to Texas to take care of some family business. Eventually he'd return, ready to do it all over again.

I first met Baxter in the Bay Area, way back in the early days, when I was penniless and living in my car. One night at the end of a party I stood up and said, "Anybody got a buck for a can of oil?" This was actually something I'd done on a number of occasions—I had a shitty car that burned oil like crazy, and I was always bumming cash off friends to keep the engine from dying of thirst—but Loose Bruce had never seen me before, and he found this pronouncement absolutely hilarious.

"A buck for oil, huh?" he said with a laugh. "Not for a hamburger or a beer? Or maybe gas?"

I shrugged. "Not now, man. I need oil."

"I like that," he said, taking out his wallet. "Here you go."

Loose Bruce pressed a five-dollar bill into my palm, and instantly a weird sort of friendship was born. He represented my introduction to the world of the ultrarich, which was like nothing I'd ever seen. Through Bruce I got to know a number of wealthy and wayward Dead-heads, people who had grown up with silver spoons in their mouths but for one reason or another had never really made much of their lives. I guess you'd call them rich kids. And they were all fun-loving, friendly, and more than a bit self-destructive.

There was Peter Sheridan—"Craze" Sheridan, we called him—who had grown up in Washington, D.C., and at one time had worked as a groom, tending horses for Robert Kennedy. Sheridan had a prodigious appetite for LSD. I once saw him so fucked up on acid that he spent an entire show at the Port Chester Capital Theater lying on his back on the floor, laughing like a madman. This guy had gotten around, had tasted a lot of life, and was now pretty much out of his mind, although he was endearing as hell. I spent a fair amount of time with Peter a few years later, when we both got heavily into motorcycles and rubbing elbows with the Hells Angels. Willie Nelson, a longtime friend of the Angels, even dedicated a song to Peter: "Angel Flying Too Close to the Ground," which was fitting even though Peter wasn't a member of the club. A speed freak in every sense of the word, Peter never felt more alive than when he could feel death breathing down his back. He was the kind of guy who would pull up next to you at an intersection and challenge you to a race on his bike. When the light turned green he'd reach over and turn off your ignition. Then he'd hit the accelerator and jump off the line, laughing like a maniac. Peter's life ended in predictably violent fashion shortly after he moved to Hollywood to work as a stunt man. He got hit by a car while riding his bike and was killed instantly. I remember feeling sad upon hearing of his passing, but I also thought it was an appropriate exit for a man whose motto was, "This is America: land of the free, home of the brave. If you're brave enough, everything is free."

Another Pleasure Crew member was a sad and strange woman named Marina. Marina used to come to our shows at the Fillmore East, and then she'd invite everyone back to her house in Manhattan. She lived across the street from Gracie Mansion in a sprawling penthouse apartment staffed by a dozen servants who zipped from room to room in golf carts.

We had a few nitrous parties in the living room of Marina's apartment, and as often as not they deteriorated into complete goofiness. A gas party involving a large number of people was an interesting thing, because people would become highly attached—physically and psychologically—to the hose, that umbilical cord that stretched from the gas tank to the user. That's why the most important person at a nitrous party was the man we jokingly referred to as the "dealer." It was his responsibility to give each person a toke, and to make sure no one inhaled too much—both for safety reasons and because the rest of the group would likely get pissed at anyone who behaved selfishly. At a successful nitrous party the room began to rise, like bubbles to the top of a champagne glass, as people started getting high, acting crazy, speaking from this subconscious place. But as the party progressed, greed was usually a factor, too—you wouldn't want to let go of that hose, because you felt like you were in such a great place. The jaw is a powerful joint, and sometimes people would clamp down on the hose with such force that it was almost impossible to get them to let go. You couldn't pry their mouths open so you'd end up whacking them on the back of the head or neck. Jackson didn't even bother with that— he'd just take his buck knife out and swing down right at the edge of their lips and sever the hose. Understandably, some people didn't like that approach, and so things would get kind of rowdy. That's why we eventually came up with a device known as the octopus: multiple hoses descending from an apparatus attached to a single tank of nitrous oxide. The octopus enabled many people to get high at once, and thus prevented a number of fights. It was a great invention.

On one particularly memorable night, the gas high was intensified through the help of a man I knew only as David. He had a squeeze bottle of LSD, and as you came out of the nitrous fog he would squeeze a dollop of acid on your hand and press it to your lips, and suddenly there would be lights and flashes and you'd be high all over again, although in a manner unlike anything I'd ever experienced. Sheridan was the one we called Craze, but it was David who really needed help. This guy was a madman. The last I heard of him, more than thirty years ago, he'd gotten arrested for trying to dose people with acid on an airplane.

The same night, while wandering around the apartment in a hallucinogenic haze, I walked into Marina's room and saw her sitting all alone on a bed, just staring off into space. I wasn't sure what to say to her. Here she was, in this magnificent but sterile house, surrounded by all these sycophants posing as friends, and she just seemed so lonely. I was several years younger than Marina (she was in her early thirties), and I'd grown up in a world that could not have been more different from the one in which she was raised, but I thought I'd try to cheer her up. So I walked around the room and tried to make conversation. There were framed pictures all over the wall—more like plaques, really—each one depicting a monolithic oil well. It occurred to me then that these were like family to Marina, these lifeless photos of money rising out of the Texas dirt. There were no photos of human beings, no mom or dad, no brothers or sisters. Just oil wells.

"Each one of these represents an oil well owned by your family?" I asked.

It seemed a rhetorical question, but it wasn't. Marina cocked her head and smiled condescendingly. "Darling, each one is an oil *field.*"

I later found out that Marina's grandfather held the patent on the Thompson machine gun, and primarily through his efforts the entire family had become rich as pharaohs. But the money hadn't made her happy. Not long after this she came to California and wound up dying alone in a jail cell.

The partying that went on around the Pleasure Crew was just incredible. I'd go out on the balcony at Marina's apartment and see people throwing cups of yogurt out onto the mayor's house. It was just stupid, childish vandalism, but it also made me think, *Man, these people have a lot of fun,* just like I'd always thought rich people did. And yet, it was obvious that they were totally out of control. We had work to sustain us, to keep us at least somewhat honest. At the end of the day, you see, there was nothing more important than the music. We understood our roles, our function, our purpose. The Pleasure Crew's only purpose was to play. These people didn't have to work. They were accountable to no one.

Loose Bruce was the captain of the Pleasure Crew, and while he could be a shadowy character who was reluctant to reveal much about his personal history, I never doubted the authenticity of his pedigree. He had once dated the daughter of Madame Nhu, the former First Lady of Vietnam, and had the photos to prove it. Similarly, he had a photo of himself at the age of eight, shaking hands with Pope Pius XII. That picture was not merely a chance occurrence during a touristy visit to the Vatican, but rather a memento from a meeting that was scheduled shortly after his family had made a "substantial" contribution to the Catholic Church. Exactly what Bruce meant by the word "substantial," I don't know; he was fairly tight-lipped about such things. But I presume it was slightly more than a fifty-dollar bill in the collection basket.

Bruce brought a wide spectrum of karma to the Grateful Dead scene. He was generous with his money and friendship, and through him we wound up enlisting the services of his sister, Frances Carr, a lovely woman who got hooked up with Sam Cutler and subsequently became our assistant road manager. All in all, there was a lot to like about Loose Bruce.

At the same time, he had an undeniably dark and dangerous and self-destructive side, which took its toll on the band and the crew. For a while in the early seventies Bruce spent a lot of time at Mickey Hart's ranch in Novato. There was a great brotherly feel to the ranch, just as there was at Rucka Rucka. Jackson lived in one of the outbuildings there for a while; so did Billy Kreutzmann. It was a terrific hangout and we had a lot of fun there, and Mickey was great about taking care of the guys on the crew. We always had a place to sleep and a hot meal. But there was a blackness to the place, too, because the partying didn't stop with nitrous or weed or LSD or even cocaine. There was a fair amount of heroin at the ranch, guys snorting and shooting and getting fucked up to a dangerous degree. Not everyone took part, of course. In fact, most of us did not. Personally, because of my experience back East, I hated heroin. Don't get me wrong. I was no angel (I think I've made that abundantly clear). I liked acid, nitrous, pot, and even a line of coke once in a while. Like everyone else on the crew I used speed less as a recreational drug than a tool that allowed me to work the eighteen- and twenty-hour days that were a normal part of our life. I lived the way we all did: on the edge.

But heroin was a whole different deal. I'd taken it once in my life, when I was a teenager in New York, and I didn't like it all. It was too powerful, too nasty. I knew what heroin was capable of doing, had seen it destroy a lot of lives. Two of my closest buddies got hooked. One died of an overdose, the other basically just became a bum. That's what heroin was to me, a bum's drug. It sucked people down the sewer, even the strongest and smartest of people, and the deterioration was just a horrible thing to see. Everyone knew of the dangers, too, which is why it was always surprising to see people get hooked on smack in the first place. You knew it was going to get its hooks into you and hang on until it had ripped every shred of flesh from your bones . . . so why start in the first place? Even the Hells Angels knew how bad heroin could be—that's why the club had a rule forbidding the use of heroin by members. All I can say is, if the Hells Angels think something is too dangerous, then it must be pretty fucking bad.

It took time for heroin to take a serious toll on the band and the crew, and some of the guys pulled themselves back from the brink in admirable fashion. But Loose Bruce was beyond saving, although certainly there were people who tried, most notably and consistently his wife, Tanya, who held him together, body and soul, for as long as she possibly could. In my eyes she was something of a saint, for how else could she have put up with Bruce? This was a guy who kept a five-gallon jug of cough syrup right next to his bed. He would do a few shots before he went to bed each night, regardless of what other shit was coursing through his veins, and he'd take another big swig when he woke up in the morning, so that he never had to face a waking moment sober. He'd hang around most of the day in his pajamas, drifting from one high to the next.

Despite his insatiable thirst for chemicals of all kinds, Loose Bruce insisted on using motorcycles as his primary mode of transportation. The inevitable accidents that followed left him broken and bedridden, addicted to painkillers on top of everything else. When I heard of his passing, I was sorry; it hurt to lose a good friend. But . . . Loose Bruce was lucky to last as long as he did.

I don't mean to imply that there weren't risks involved with the way the rest of us lived, that simply because we avoided heroin we weren't tempting fate on a daily basis. We were. But everyone draws his own line in the sand, and mine was drawn right in front of heroin. The fact is, the people in our circle who seemed to suffer the most damage were those hopelessly drawn to one of three particular drugs: heroin, cocaine, and alcohol.

That's right—good ol' American-as-apple-pie booze. Most of the guys on the crew weren't real big on drinking, for reasons both practical and aesthetic. For one thing, you just couldn't work as hard as we worked if you were drinking. Setup was generally the sober part of the day for us anyway, although on occasion we'd break to have a joint, to take the edge off a bit. But that was about it. There was no throwing back shots of Jack Daniels while setting up scaffolding—the work was too hard, the consequences too severe. We were climbing and working, and we depended on each other not only to make the show a success, but to make the job safe. The truth of the matter was, in our line of work almost any drug was safer than alcohol. Nothing impaired like drinking. And pills seemed to go hand in hand with liquor, resulting in a colossally fucked-up stagehand who was a mortal threat to himself and those with whom he worked. We had a few of those people on the crew over the years, but they were quickly culled from our ranks.

At that time, drinking wasn't big among the band members, either, with one tragic exception: Pigpen McKernan. Everyone close to Pigpen did their best to help him curb his drinking. They'd even dose him on occasion because there was a theory floating around back then that LSD could help cure alcoholism. I developed a friendship with Pigpen in part because he trusted me; he knew I disliked the practice of dosing, that I didn't believe in hitting people with something they didn't expect and probably didn't want. So whenever Pigpen asked for a glass of water or a soda when he was on stage, he knew I'd give it to him straight and clean. It wasn't that I didn't want to help Pigpen, or that I was averse to trying offbeat methods to beat addiction. I just thought the cure had to come from within. Pigpen made a few half-hearted attempts to cut back, but he never seriously embraced recovery. He went to doctors and sought treatment for his physical ailments, but he needed help of a more spiritual and emotional nature. He knew it, too. He knew he had a problem, and yet he rejected the idea of attending Alcoholics Anonymous meetings or anything like that.

Personally, I was somewhat mystified by Pigpen's dependency. I never really understood the appeal of alcohol. As a kid my idea of drinking was to take a bottle of vodka and down it like a soda. I did that a couple times and got so sick that for many years I couldn't even stand the smell of the stuff. I got over that, of course, and like many people in the scene I later developed a taste for alcohol. (I spent many long, long nights with Norman, my favorite bartender, at the Ritz Carlton in New York.)

For a while we didn't realize just how bad Pigpen's problems really were. He'd sit around all night, sipping Southern Comfort, playing the blues, and never seem to lose control. And what a gentle soul he was. He looked like a biker, dressed like a biker, and always wore a cowboy hat, but a sweeter man never walked the planet. Unfortunately, Pigpen had serious health issues, some of which he kept hidden from the band and the crew, at least for a time. I believe that like my father, he suffered from ileitis, a disease that makes the consumption of alcohol at best inadvisable, at worst lethal. They couldn't stop Pigpen, though. Despite the warnings from doctors, and despite his deteriorating condition, he continued to drink. By the end of 1972 he was having more bad days than good. You could see that he was literally poisoning his system, the way his flesh hung from his bones, and his skin took on a ghastly gray pallor. He'd had a girlfriend named Vee, who had taken care of him for a while, but when she developed health problems of her own, Pigpen was left to his own self-destructive tendencies. With no one to watch out for him, no one to at least make sure that he ate reasonably well or visited the emergency room when his colitis flared up, he slipped deeper into the abyss.

The last time I saw Pigpen was in early 1973, when Joe Winslow and I helped him move to a new house in Larkspur. The house sat at the top of a long, steep driveway, and we had a bitch of a time getting Pigpen's 300-pound B-3 Hammond organ from the moving van to the living room. Merl Saunders and Howard Wales also played the B-3, so we had some experience in hauling these things around, But Pigpen's new home presented quite a challenge. No one complained, though, because we knew it would make him happy to have the organ in his house, that it would give him something to do, something to distract him from his own misery. I'm not sure anyone expected more of him at that point. I think we all knew he was in bad shape and unlikely to regain enough strength to return to the band on a regular basis. So we hung out with him that day. We sat around talked and listened to Pigpen play the blues, just as he always had.

Pigpen had also recently acquired a new roommate, a woman from Texas named Angela who came to us, like so many others, through the Pleasure Crew. I thought Angela was a nice woman, so nice in fact that I later developed a romantic relationship with her myself, but for now she was taking care of Pigpen. It probably wasn't merely coincidence that when Angela left for a few days in March of 1973 to tend to family business in Texas, Pigpen passed away—I'm sure her presence had kept him going for longer than he had any right to expect. The coroner's report stated that Pigpen had begun bleeding internally and died of liver failure. Natural causes, they said. But that depends on how you define the word "natural." The truth is, he drank himself to death, and when the end came there was no one by his side. In fact, he lay alone in that house for two days before anyone found him. He was twenty-eight years old.

Pigpen's death left a hole in the band, as well as in our hearts. There was a time, after all, when Pigpen was one of the strongest and most important men in the band. His tenure dated back to 1964, when he teamed up with Jerry Garcia and Bob Weir to form Mother McCree's Uptown Jug Champions. The following year Phil Lesh and Billy Kreutzmann came on board. Changing its name to the Warlocks, the group became Ken Kesey's house band during his infamous Acid Tests, and in late '65 Jerry suggested changing the name again, this time to the Grateful Dead. The first time I hung out with the Pranksters, Kesey pulled out some old eight-millimeter home movies of the acid trips, and I was surprised to see just how central a role Pigpen had played. He was bright-eyed and lucid, and clearly the leader of the band. He seemed so confident, like he was really playing, while the other guys were merely young and learning.

If Pigpen was not quite at his best by the time I came on board, he was still often a sight to behold, standing there at his B-3, singing and playing not from sheet music, but pulling up the blues from somewhere deep in his gut.

"You . . . standing right over there!" he'd shout to someone in the audience as the rest of the band jammed and smiled. "Get your hands out of your pockets, man! Grab that girl next to you, turn her around . . . and put your arms around her! She needs some loving! Come on . . . don't be shy!" The guy would do exactly as he was told and pretty soon they'd be dancing to the music, and Pigpen would throw his head back and laugh. "Good. Now you take that girl home and buy her . . . buy her . . . buy her a new refrigerator, a dishwasher . . . anything she wants! Understand!?"

And of course he did. We all did.

If I have a single, lasting image of Pigpen, it's from 1970. The Dead played a show one night at a club in San Rafael called Euphoria, and as happened on occasion, Janis Joplin was in attendance. At Pigpen's urging she climbed onstage and joined him for a whiskey-soaked duet, the two of them pawing at each other like drunken, infatuated lovers, taking swigs off a bottle of Southern Comfort, and belting out the blues as only they could, while the rest of us looked on in awe.

Chapter 18

H ere's a story that illustrates perfectly the madness of life on the road, and the familial nature of the Grateful Dead.

It was late 1972 and we were out on tour, as usual, crisscrossing the country in an assortment of trucks and vans, hauling our equipment from city to city, and spending a dozen hours at each venue setting up for the show. This was the most frenetic time for the crew of the Dead, when we reached critical mass—that point where it was simply not possible to work any harder, to drive more miles, to fuck more women, or to ingest more chemicals. We were redefining what it meant to burn the candle at both ends.

This was the Heartland portion of the tour, when we got out into the middle of the country, away from the safety and familiarity of the coasts. We did a show in Omaha, Nebraska, then another in Wichita, Kansas. I remember passing through Gardner, Kansas, and then getting to the hotel in Wichita, turning on the black-and-white TV, and being shocked to see the movie *In Cold Blood.*

"Jesus," Jerry said. "This is too weird."

"Why?" I had never seen the movie before and didn't know much about it.

"You'll see."

Indeed I did. The brutal murders depicted in the film had taken place in Gardner, and seeing them acted out on screen gave me a pretty severe case of the creeps. I was happy to be spending only a short time in Wichita. We went to the theater the next morning, spent the entire day setting up, and then did our customary four-hour show. Then we tore everything down, packed up the trucks, and hit the road. There was a big show in Houston the next night, featuring both the Grateful Dead and the Allman Brothers, which meant no rest for the weary.

It was a long straight run from Kansas down to Texas. I rode with Sparky and we agreed that he would drive the first leg while I got some sleep. But there was an incredible thunderstorm raging across the plains that night—lightning cracking, wind howling, rain and hail beating off the windshield with such force that the wipers couldn't possibly keep pace. I tried to get some sleep, but found it nearly impossible, what with nature putting on such a light show and the truck periodically bouncing off onto the shoulder.

The next morning I took over the wheel, despite having been up for more than twenty-four hours. Sparky gave me a Blackbird, also known as a Black Beauty . . . or, as we called it, a Reno Turnaround. So potent was this particular amphetamine that you could take one, drive from Reno to New York, and then turn around and drive right back—without ever taking your foot off the accelerator. That was more legend than fact, of course, but it sure did pack a wallop. I got in the driver's seat and hit the gas, and pretty much kept it floored for the next 500 miles. I mean, I was a crazed mother-fucker of a trucker, my hands glued to the wheel, absorbing every bounce and bump. The speedometer never dipped below seventy-five, which might not sound all that fast, until you consider that this big old bobtail truck was overloaded with tons of equipment. It wasn't the safest of vehicles even in sunshine. In this kind of weather, it was a deathmobile.

But I didn't care. I was twenty-two years old. I was invincible.

"Keep it going," Sparky said at one point. He was too amped to sleep, so he turned on the radio and cranked the volume. Mick Jagger's voice filled the cab, nearly drowning out the storm that continued to rage outside.

"I can't get no . . . satisfaction."

I looked at Sparky. He looked at me. We both shouted at the top of our lungs.

"THOUGH I TRY . . . AND I TRY . . . AND I TRY . . . I CAN'T GET NO!"

To say I wasn't really paying attention to the road would be a dramatic understatement. And I paid for it. All of a sudden I saw flashing lights coming up fast, then whizzing by my window. I saw a big sign: WARNING! CURVE AHEAD! and the number 50, which I presume was the maximum speed recommended for negotiating the curve safely. I hit the brake and pulled back on the steering wheel, as if that would somehow slow the vehicle. But I was already well into the curve and the brakes just locked up in the rain, the wheels sliding as if on ice. I tried to downshift, but that only made things worse. As Sparky and I both screamed, the truck spun off the road and out of control. I remember thinking quite clearly, as the truck tipped over, that I was about to die. I only hoped that it wouldn't hurt too much.

The next thing I knew we were upside down in the cab, two big boys—me at six-foot-four, Sparky at six-two—sandwiched together in the shotgun seat. The rain continued to beat down on the truck, and mud oozed in through the cracked windows. I couldn't say anything at first—I was too shocked to be alive. I just lifted my hand and held it in front of my face. *One-two-three-four-five. All there.* I did the same with the other hand. I wiggled my toes. Remarkably, everything seemed to be in working order. Sparky looked unharmed, too. Shocked, but alive and well.

The truck was buried more than a foot into the ground, and sinking fast, so there was no way to open the doors. The only way out was through the windshield. We both used our boots to kick at the glass. A spider-web crack had already formed on the windshield during the crash so it didn't long to complete the job. As we crawled through the hole and out onto the highway, I could see a woman rushing toward us, tears streaming down her cheeks.

"My God," she cried. "I thought for sure you were dead."

"Don't worry, lady," I said. "We're okay." I looked at the truck, which was crushed so badly that it barely resembled a truck at all. My own words sounded ridiculous. How could we possibly be "okay"?

It wasn't long before Jackson, Ramrod, and Danny Rifkin, our road manager at the time, arrived on the scene in a rental car, and they looked at us as if we were ghosts. They, too, were certain we'd been killed in the crash. No other outcome seemed possible. The truck had been mangled. Not only was the cab crushed, but the back had been shredded, too, leaving all of our wonderful, handcrafted equipment sinking in the Texas mud. And yet, there we were, me and Sparky, standing there without a scratch between us.

Jackson just shook his head and smiled. "Fuck, man. Unbelievable."

Almost equally amazing was the way in which we dealt with this near-death experience. We didn't call for an ambulance, didn't make a trip to the emergency room for a precautionary set of x-rays. We simply went to work. Rifkin stayed with me while Sparky jumped in the rental car with Jackson and Ramrod. They drove to the next town to pick up another truck, while Rifkin and I pulled all of the equipment out of the mud, brushed it off, and stacked up the pieces by the side of the road. Then we loaded the new truck and got back on the highway.

We arrived in Houston around five o'clock that evening and to our amazement discovered that the Allman Brothers had cancelled their portion of the show. Why? Because their bass player had died that day in an automobile accident! Anyway, when we got there and explained what had happened, the guys in the band were completely sympathetic. They asked if we wanted to cancel the show, but of course we rejected that suggestion.

"We're fine," I said. "Let's get to work."

So we set up everything as quickly as we could, and the Dead put on an incredible show, just played their asses off, almost as if they felt they were paying tribute to us. Maybe they were. Later, as I hobbled into my hotel room, exhausted and bruised, I received a visit from Phil Lesh. I'd known Phil to be a very quiet and reserved man. He was one of the more mature members of the group and wasn't inclined to reveal his emotions. On this night, though, I saw a different side of him. As I sat down on my bed and tried to process the events of the day, and suddenly came to the realization that I was remarkably lucky to be alive, the energy rushed out of me like a wave. I was completely and utterly exhausted. I slumped forward on the bed and looked down at my boots, which were caked with slop and dirt.

"Hey, Steve." I looked up and saw Phil standing in the doorway. "Mind if I come in?"

"No, of course not."

Phil walked across the room, leaned over and gave me a hug. "I'm so glad you're alive, man. And I promise you right now—we're going to change things. You guys are no longer going to drive at night. This just isn't worth it."

With that, this soft-spoken man—this bass player who was ten years older than me, and whom I respected and admired—this man whose inherent goodness and warmth were not always visible . . . he got

162

down on his knees and removed my muddy boots. It was such a genuine display of affection, and so entirely unexpected. I didn't know what to say. Really, all I wanted to do was cry.

He took my boots and placed them in the closet. Then he lifted my legs onto the bed and covered me with a blanket.

"Get some sleep," he said. "Everything will be all right."

Chapter 19

W e're wandering around Notre Dame in Paris, me and Ramrod and Phil Lesh. It's an impressive enough place when you're sober, but when you're stoned on acid it's absolutely breathtaking—the stained glass and flying buttresses come alive and transport you to another time. Phil is telling me all about cathedrals and how they were built, and as the sound of his voice echoes off the walls and carries spectacularly, effortlessly, I can't help but think that the Dead could put on a great show here. After a while Phil goes one way and Ramrod and I go another. We ascend time-worn steps to the roof of Notre Dame and look out over the city, and suddenly I find it impossible not to think of Quasimodo, the tragic hero of Victor Hugo's The Hunchback of Notre Dame. I'm electrified by the acid, by the surroundings, by the history and the art of it all. We

*continue walking down a long, dimly lit hall, lined with dark glass. At the end
is a room with a heavy door. I try the handle. It's locked. I feel a chill on my
back and an image comes to mind, the bell ringer swinging madly on his rope.*

Here it is . . . *I think. If ever there was a bell ringer, this is where he lived.*

Phil was a man of his word. After the crash in Texas we moved quickly
into the world of semitrucks and professional drivers, and bid farewell
forever to amphetamine-fueled, all-night treks through the heartland.
More than ever, the crew became part of the Grateful Dead. We
received better pay, better accommodations, better treatment than we
had in the past. And keep in mind that we already wielded more
power and received more perks than any other crew in rock 'n' roll.
The generosity of the band was almost limitless.

If the road became a less perilous place, though, it remained endlessly amusing and challenging—especially when we left the United
States. The Grateful Dead didn't spend a lot of time overseas, in part
because going through customs, especially with our gang, could be
such an enormous hassle. Something always seemed to happen whenever we crossed a border; even when we were completely clean,
things could go wrong, partly because we had in our midst one of the
great practical jokers of all time: Bob Weir. One time in 1974, while
passing through customs in Amsterdam, of all places, I found myself
standing in line with Weir and Kid. The good people of Amsterdam
are reasonably accommodating and open-minded when it comes to
tourists who want to get laid or smoke hash, but there are limits to
their tolerance. By shouting, "He's a smuggler, you know!" as the customs officers looked over Kid's luggage, Bobby pushed the envelope
a bit. Immediately the officers ripped apart Kid's luggage and spread
every article of clothing out on a table for all to see. Then, of course,
they did the same to me and Weir. Kid was pissed, but Bobby was just
being himself. He's still just a smart-ass but a good-natured adolescent at heart.

Not long ago we traveled together to Oregon, to pay our respects at Ken Kesey's funeral. While standing in the security line at the airport, Bobby turned to me and said, loudly enough for everyone to hear, "I don't think that phony passport is gonna work, man." It might not have been the smartest or most thoughtful thing for Bobby to do, but sometimes he can't help himself. He's always loved to poke fun at authority.

Generally speaking, though, messing around with customs was more trouble than it was worth, so we didn't make too many jokes, didn't cop an attitude, and never (well, almost never) tried to smuggle any drugs through customs. That meant we arrived from the United States clean and sober and had to start from scratch. Reloading could be difficult. You had to cultivate new sources each time you crossed a border. Fortunately, with our audience, that was not an impossible task.

But we always encountered problems of one type or another in Europe. Every trip there was an adventure. I remember sitting in a concert hall in Paris one morning in 1972, taking the edge off with a joint. We'd just come from Amsterdam, where we'd procured some marijuana, which was hard to find in Europe. Everyone there smoked hash, or "spleefs," a mix of hash and tobacco. We preferred pure weed but since it was neither wise nor practical to carry it with us from the States, we typically settled for hash. This time, though, we'd lucked out. So we smoked marijuana in Amsterdam and brought a small amount with us to France—crossing borders from one European country into another wasn't nearly as risky a proposition as trying to get through airport customs after flying in from America.

Anyway, I was sitting there smoking a joint, killing time, dropping a switchblade (which I'd bought in Germany) into a wooden floor, over and over, when suddenly a pair of shiny black shoes entered my field of vision. I looked up and froze: the *gendarmes!*

My first thought was, *Holy shit!* After all, I was smoking dope and in possession of a deadly weapon, both of which were felony crimes in the United States at the time, and I was doing it right in front of the cops!

That led to my second thought, which was, *I'm fucked!*

The gendarme, holding a submachine gun casually at his side, took one step closer, cleared his throat, and said, like a schoolteacher scolding a child, "Monsieur, please." He paused and pointed to a NO SMOKING sign. "Your cigarette."

I rolled the joint around in my fingers, nodded humbly, and dropped it to the ground. Then I crushed the joint under my boot heel.

"*Merci,*" he said, smiling approvingly.

"No problem."

That was merely the beginning of a day down the rabbit hole. By the time the show started that evening I was in the midst of a roaring acid trip, courtesy of a badly mixed batch of LSD that was, we later discovered, about ten times stronger than we had intended it to be. And I wasn't alone. The band, the crew . . . just about everyone had sampled this wicked brew, and now we were all wired. Truth be told, the acid made the show all the more enjoyable, but when it came time to break down the stage and load the trucks, things began to go awry. Not so much because we weren't physically capable of doing the job, but because we ran into problems with the French crews and we weren't exactly in the right frame of mind to handle the situation diplomatically. Their hostility had started early in the day, when they realized that Candace Brightman was in charge of our lighting. The French union guys weren't accustomed to working with a woman, let alone taking orders from one, so there was friction right away.

Well, at the end of the night the French crew had some sort of fight with Candace about the lights, and they wound up taking down the truss and dropping it in the middle of the stage. This was not the way we did things. Ever. The lighting truss was supposed to come down last, after we'd cleared all the cables and equipment. The lights were the first thing in and the last thing out. Always. But these guys wanted to give us a hard time, so they dropped the truss and just left it there, effectively fucking up our entire load-out.

The band had departed, leaving me, Jackson, Sparky, Ramrod, Kid, and Winslow to pack up the gear. It was a job we did every night without complaint. But now we had this truss to clean up, as well, and we were all completely wrecked on acid.

"What do we do?" I asked Ramrod, but he had no response. Like me, he could barely form a sentence.

So we sat down there for a while, scratching our heads, yawning, trying to figure out how the hell we were going to pack up all this gear and get to a show the next day in another part of France.

Finally, without saying anything, I stood up and began rolling cable. Miles of it, until I had a dozen or more piles neatly stacked at the back of the stage. Then I took a cabinet—one of the bass cabinets we had built ourselves out of fourteen-ply finished birch plywood—and dragged it down off the scaffolding and out to the truck, grunting and groaning as I tried not to drop it on the wet cobblestone walkway. Then I moved another one. And another. For the better part of the next two hours I worked alone, until more than half the equipment had been carted away. Eventually, as they began to sober up, the other guys joined in. By 3 A.M. we had the truck packed and ready to go. Winslow climbed into the cab, inserted the key into the ignition and . . .

Nothing.

Another hour passed before a mechanic arrived and informed us that some joker had put sugar in the gas tank. It was daylight before we got on the road.

But that's the kind of thing that could happen. As strange and disconnected as road life was in the United States, it was even weirder overseas. It was, by turns, enlightening and confusing, frustrating and fulfilling. And endlessly fascinating.

The '72 European tour was the best and most memorable. We were a young and exuberant all-American gang, intent on bringing the music and message of the Grateful Dead to fans throughout the world, and having one hell of a good time in the process. In some ways I remember that tour as being a zenith of sorts for the band and the crew. We were reasonably healthy and happy, having not yet lost anyone to the misery of addiction. Pigpen was struggling but still alive; cocaine and heroin, and the sickness that went with them, had not yet penetrated our ranks. We weren't jaded, cynical, burned-out rock 'n' rollers; we were wide-eyed tourists, full of life and love and laughter. So positive was the atmosphere surrounding this trip that a decision was made to take an enormous entourage along for the ride. Wives, girlfriends, children, even the recording crew from Alembic— they all tagged along. Annette came with me. Jerry brought Mountain Girl (Mountain Girl was/is Carolyn Adams, the second of his three wives, and the mother of three of his children). There were more than fifty of us in all, divided among two busses, a sprawling American comedy rolling across Europe, looking for fun and fantasy at every stop, and more often than not finding it.

It's funny the way some things stick in your mind. I have this vision, for example, of Sonny Boy Heard creeping from door to door in a German hotel, scooping up dozens of pair of shoes. It was a tradition at many of the finer European hotels for guests to leave their shoes outside their doors at night. Porters would collect the shoes, give them a good shine, and return them the following morning before the guests had awakened. Heard watched this happen a few times and decided it might be funny to switch everyone's shoes. So there he was on this particular night, his already skewed sense of humor further warped by a combination of German beer and marijuana, tiptoeing quickly from room to room, filling his arms with shoes.

"What are you doing, man?" I asked.

Heard just giggled and said, "This is gonna be great."

And it was. The next morning in the lobby of this immaculate, elegant four-star hotel, which catered primarily to clients of ample means, you never saw such a ruckus. There were businessmen holding up women's pumps, screaming at the concierge, demanding to speak with the manager. There were equally outraged women holding up oxfords. It was absolutely hilarious.

A few nights later, in Hamburg, Heard and I went out and discovered a place called the Reperbahn, and let me tell you, in my young American life I'd never seen anything like it. This was, to my eyes, the ultimate red-light district, a place so open and inviting in its carnality that it made Times Square look like Disneyworld. (I know, Times Square in the twenty-first century, with its family-friendly atmosphere, has pretty much *become* Disneyworld. Back then, though, it was still a deliciously seamy place. And yet it was G-rated fare in comparison to the Reperbahn.) We walked down a block, turned a corner, then made our way around a large partition clearly designed to separate the Reperbahn from the rest of the city. On the other side of the partition was every sexual dream you could imagine, a full city block of what could euphemistically be called "adult entertainment."

There were hosts and hostesses at every door, of course, luring patrons to come inside and sample the goods. Despite Heard's recommendation—"take your time, Steve"—I didn't get past the first shop. I marched right up and began chatting with the madame. She explained that for the whopping sum of ten American dollars I could fulfill any fantasy, from the tame to the lurid. There were women in leather, women in lace. There were fat women and lithe women. There women who looked like men, and women who surely were men.

"Take your pick," she said in a thick German accent.

Like a kid in a candy store I fumbled for my wallet. That Annette was back at the hotel, nursing a case of the flu, didn't slow me down for a moment. I don't say that with pride, but merely as an honest reflection. I was too young and selfish to be involved in a serious relationship. I really didn't think Annette would care all that much that I was hanging out at the Reperbahn, and if she did . . . well, too bad. Any lingering doubts about whether I was doing something wrong subsided when I walked into the brothel and chose a demure young woman who was hanging out by the bar. As she took my hand and led me into a back room, I could hear music coming from a radio. Familiar music. The music of the Grateful Dead.

Everyone had their own way of handling the road—of enjoying the perks and enduring the hard times. When we stopped in Ypres, France, during a long bus ride through Europe, my bones just chilled, for I knew that I was on the site of the bloodiest battle of World War I. I'd read *All Quiet on the Western Front,* which described that battle in detail, and so I was overcome with respect and awe, not unlike the feeling you get when you visit Gettysburg in the United States. There is a palpable sense of sadness at the loss of life and the horror of war.

That was my take on it, anyway. Heard just sort of looked up from beneath his cowboy hat and snorted. "Ypres," he said dismissively. "I think my grandfather bombed the shit out of this place."

But there were other moments that brought us together, that made us feel as though we really were on some sort of mission, like the time we were riding through the Swiss countryside, on our way to a hotel in Lucerne. We passed over a bridge spanning a lake, illuminated by an incredible double rainbow, and when I turned around to watch the rainbow fade in the distance, I noticed that the bridge seemed to be made out of iron lattice work. But as I continued to stare, another picture came into focus: it wasn't latticework. It was a series of skeletons—steel skeletons!

"What the hell is that about?" I said to no one in particular. The answer was provided by a man named Alan Trist, a friend of Jerry's who was a native of Great Britain and had spend most of his life in California. He proved to be a wonderful, knowledgeable guide.

Alan smiled. "That," he said, pausing for effect, "is the bridge of the Grateful Dead."

That's where I first heard of the legend—of the importance of helping people in your travels—right there in the shadow of the bridge itself, on a beautiful day in Switzerland.

Like so many days on the road, however, it ended oddly. Our road manager, Sam Cutler, had booked us into a storybook hotel right on Lake Lucerne. When we arrived, two footmen with wigs came running out and unfurled a red carpet. Then they stood sentry as the doors of the bus opened. As soon as they got one look at us—a horde of ugly Americans—they quickly rolled up the carpet and retreated into the hotel, presumably to warn the rest of the staff.

Two years later we returned to Europe, and the atmosphere could not have been more different. Tired and grumpy and still grieving over the loss of Pigpen, we left our friends and families behind this time. Cocaine use was on the rise, and with it came anxiety, irresponsibility, hostility.

Strictly from a technical standpoint, it was a more challenging tour, for this time we brought the Wall of Sound, something we hadn't done in '72. Trying to haul this massive PA around Europe was like trying to make a bull elephant go somewhere he didn't want to go. We were getting burned out from too much work, travel, and drugs, and we were trying to set up a sound system in places where the crews simply weren't prepared to deal with it. Moreover, the crews in Europe were generally slower and less finicky about their work than we were. They didn't understand our attitude, the way we were always rushing them and yelling at them.

A lot of us were going through personal changes, too. My relationship with Annette was almost dead, and yet I was spending hundreds of dollars on phone bills trying to keep it alive. I don't know why. It was like I was banging my head against a wall.

Sometimes we took out our frustrations on each other; more typically, though, we vented at the locals. On one memorable trip to a club called the Eros in Munich, Germany, my own simmering anger bubbled over. The Eros, as you might have guessed, was a bordello. I went there with Sparky after a long day of smoking dope and drinking heavy German beer, and I wasn't in a mood to be pushed around. While we were examining the merchandise, an older woman interrupted us. "This isn't a bus station, boys," she said. "Make a choice or move along." So I picked out a pleasant-looking woman and went into a back room. There, to my amazement, she tried to rip me off. She took my money and then refused to have sex with me. I don't know why. Maybe because I was drunk and she was scared. Whatever the reason, I had a refund coming, but none was forthcoming. So I exploded. I destroyed the room, just tore it apart, and began screaming that I wanted my money back. The hooker ran out of the room and yelled for help from one of the bouncers, a small, wiry fellow named Hans.

"Come on, Hans!" I shouted as I chased her down the hall. "I'm ready!"

Hans, who was a good six inches shorter than me, and probably seventy-five pounds lighter, wanted no part of a confrontation. When he saw me, he turned and ran. Meanwhile, I kept tearing the place apart, rampaging like a wild man. Sparky eventually heard me and came running. At first he tried to calm me down, but when I told him what had happened he joined in the mayhem. We knocked over tables, punched holes in the walls, threw steins of beer all over the place. As we marched down a flight of stairs toward the exit, a busload of Japanese tourists—all male, all wearing business suits—walked in the front door. They looked up at Sparky and me, and froze in their tracks.

"What's the matter?!" I bellowed. "Haven't you ever seen anyone get pissed off before?"

We ran right through them, knocking them down like candlepins, and stumbled out into the street. Then we jumped into a cab and headed back to our hotel. As we pulled away I saw the riot squad arriving at the bordello. Cops spilled out of their cars and began rounding up the Japanese tourists, handcuffing them and hauling them away.

By the end of our European tour in '74 we were a band on the verge of collapse. (Indeed, the Grateful Dead would go on hiatus shortly after we returned home.) We were all homesick and miserable, largely I think because of the debilitating and isolating nature of cocaine, which had eclipsed acid and even marijuana as the drug of choice among many of the guys in the band and crew. Not everyone, mind you. Bob Weir stayed pretty clean during that time, and Mickey Hart was in self-imposed exile from the Dead. But Jerry was heavily into coke and on his way to developing a smack habit, too. Billy Kreutzmann loved coke, so much that it became a quest for him. He'd jack people up for a snort right away, as soon as he met them. As for the crew, well, we were all into it, although some of us more than others. It got to the point where everyone was acting so weird, so paranoid, that Jackson made a public suggestion: "Let's all stop. Right now. No more coke. It's ruining the band, and it's going to kill us."

He was right, of course. So we all got together one night and threw our coke spoons and our coke bottles and any other paraphernalia into a garbage can. That was it, we promised each other. No more cocaine. Ironically, Jackson was the first to break the vow. He went on a terrific coke jag and was absolutely wracked with guilt about it afterward. The rest of us just saw his failure as an excuse to get back into it ourselves, and pretty soon we were snorting our way across Europe again.

Everyone suffered to a degree during this time, but no one more so than Rock Scully. Rock was our road manager and his drug use had become a serious impediment to our ability to function as a cohesive unit. It became something of a joke with Rock over the years, because here he was, a manager, and yet he was hopelessly disorganized and disheveled. Admittedly, he was a funny, sweet man, willing and eager to help you with almost anything. As John Kahn once said, "Whatever ails you, Rock's got the cure. Gravel in your urine? Don't worry. Rock's got a pill for you." He usually did, too, but his fascination with pharmacology eventually led to significant problems, and it was in Europe, in '74, that they first came to light.

It happened at the end of the tour, at a time when we were all in black moods. We just wanted to get home, and on the day of our departure we were sitting on the bus, waiting for Rock to arrive with our plane tickets so that we could drive to the airport in Paris and catch our flight. A half hour went by, but there was no sign of Rock. So a couple of us went up to his hotel room, where we found Rock in something of a stupor. His clothes were all laid out—he hadn't even packed!—and he was mumbling something about not being able to find the tickets, so we turned the room upside down, and eventually Rock said, "Got 'em!" and we left.

What a solemn bunch we were on the ride through Paris. Two years earlier we'd had such a wonderful trip, and now here we were, in the same spot, and the unhappiness was pervasive. And it was about to get worse. Rock suddenly jumped out of his seat and ordered the bus driver to pull over. Before any of us had a chance to react, he opened the door and disappeared into a crowd.

Jackson, who had seen a fair amount of strange behavior in his day, shook his head. "What the fuck was that?"

"I have no idea."

We sat there for a while, too stunned and tired to do much of anything. But when it became apparent that Rock wasn't coming back anytime soon, and that we needed his help to get out of the country, Jackson and I decided to go look for him. We found Rock at a café a couple blocks away, standing in a phone booth, whimpering something about "lost tickets."

It seemed impossible. The road manager doesn't lose tickets. The road manager's primary responsibility is making sure that the tickets *don't* get lost. But Rock was clearly a man in distress at this point, and there was no point beating him about it. Instead, we dragged him out of the café and back to the bus. Then we drove to the airport and talked our way onto the plane. We were fortunate to encounter a compassionate ticket clerk at the TWA counter, and he made a few phone calls that cleared everything up. We were given new tickets and boarding passes and soon were on our way back home.

But Rock wasn't with us. He stayed behind in Europe for a few months, supposedly to travel and spend time with some woman he'd met. I don't mean to come down too hard on Rock, though. Believe me, I'm not laying blame at his doorstep. He was only caught up in the same madness that eventually gripped all of us.

Chapter 20

L ife is all about finding people and connecting with them, maybe loving them . . . and eventually losing them. When they're gone you mourn, of course, but after a while, when the ache subsides, you take the good parts—the laughter, the warmth, the generosity—and add them to yourself, and in that way they live on inside you, in your heart. You become a reflection of the people you knew best, and with whom you've shared your life.

Two years after Pigpen's death, I lost one of my best friends. Like Pig, Badger was bigger than life, and therefor perhaps destined to check out early. Badger was a Hells Angel, which meant he loved riding bikes, because that was true of all the Angels. But I'd never met anyone more at home on the back of a Harley than Badger. He was a pure rider, sure-handed and utterly fearless, to the point where he became convinced that he could not be killed. I remember him limping into my living room one night in the pouring rain, after losing control of his bike on a slick stretch of highway near my house in Stinson. I had to cut off his boot with a knife because he'd broken his ankle and the joint was now swollen to the size of a cantaloupe. He was soaking wet, covered with mud and grease, and clearly in pain, yet he had this goofy grin on his face, like he'd gotten away with something. Which he had, I guess.

Badger died on my twenty-fifth birthday, May 17, 1975, while riding with a pack of the Richmond Hells Angels on their annual trip to Bass Lake. Angelo gave me the details, said that Badger had taken a lot of LSD before the ride. Acid was big among the Angels then (Big Vinnie once told me it helped him fight better, which I never really quite understood), and no one had a heartier appetite than Badger. That day he must have taken a particularly potent dose, for while climbing a hill on a winding stretch of Route 4 near Calaveras, Badger drifted over the center line and was hit head-on by another motorcycle. Three people died in that accident—Badger and the driver and passenger on the other bike. But Badger, tough bastard that he was, didn't die right away. As they put him on a stretcher and loaded him into an ambulance, his body broken and bleeding, his face covered with Indian war paint, Badger was asked his name by one of the paramedics.

According to Angelo, this was his reply:

"Richmond Hells Angels! That's my fucking name!"

Those were Badger's last words.

A few days later, at the funeral, I couldn't stop crying, couldn't stop the tears from flowing even in the presence of all those hard-ass Hells Angels. Badger was just a big, happy guy, a friend to almost everyone he met. He was smart, too. He may have looked like a wild man, and he may have flirted with death and danger in an unhealthy way, but he was the kind of man you could talk to about almost anything. His loss was monumental, and I miss him to this day. I still have the wallet he was carrying when he died—Angelo gave it to me—and I still take it out sometimes and look through it, just to feel close to Badger, to take strength from his spirit.

Badger was a profound and wonderful character in so many ways. The freakiest thing, though, was how well he knew people, how he could see into the deepest recesses of their souls. He knew me, that's for sure. He knew me better than I knew myself. Years earlier we used to sit around and smoke dope and he'd tell me exactly what I was going to do with my life, and how I was going to become an important part of the Grateful Dead scene. I had no clue, no plan for making something of my life.

It was because of Badger that I began riding motorcycles. He'd always encouraged me to get one, said I had the attitude and outlook of a biker. In fact, the last time I saw him, just a day before he died, Badger had said, "Come one, Steve, you gotta get a motorcycle. This is ridiculous. And if you don't buy one, I'm gonna steal one for you."

After Badger died I figured the least I could do was grant him one last wish. So, through Jeff, another Hells Angel, I was introduced to a club member named Little Rick, who was legendary for being an *Angels Angel,* if you know what I mean. He was a hardcore biker, fearless to the point of craziness. If you know San Francisco at all, you know it's a city of hills, and a skilled biker can do amazing things on those hills; you can practically fly from one hill to the next. Little Rick was one of the best. He'd jump over police cars at intersections, just sail right over the top of them and then hit the gas when he landed.

As far as I know, Little Rick never got caught jumping cop cars, but he'd been in jail on several occasions by the time I got to know him. He'd been stabbed seven or eight times and had the scars to prove it. If you caught him in a particularly good mood he'd have you pull up a chair and he'd start rolling up his sleeve and laughing, revealing all the details of the fight that left him with a withered arm. It had started when Rick pissed off some guy in a bar one night. The guy left for a while and returned with a hunting rifle and took a shot at Rick, blowing his arm to bits. Surgeons had miraculously saved the limb, but even now, years later, there wasn't much left, just a mangled ribbon of flesh and misshapen bones connecting his hand to his elbow. That Rick was able to ride like Evel Knievel with basically one arm was just one of the many things that made him something of a mythic figure. As the name implied, Little Rick was not a big man, but he was full of piss and vinegar, always blowing up and challenging people—he reminded me of Yosemite Sam.

I didn't know Rick all that well, and I'm not sure whatever became of him. I know he parted ways with the Angels, and I think the cops were looking for him, too. No great surprise, considering he was, in every sense of the word, an outlaw. For whatever reason, though, he sort of liked me, and even offered to build me a bike. I began making periodic trips to his house in Sonoma, where I'd give him some cash to cover the cost of building this bike (although I couldn't compensate him for his time and expertise, which were substantial). In the end it was worth it, because I wound up with one mother-fucker of a bike, a beautiful rigid frame with big ape-hanger bars . . . a full chopper. But the process was at times exhausting and even frightening.

First of all, Little Rick lived out in the country, in a small house on five acres of land, really isolated, so right off the bat it was kind of creepy to visit. As soon as you pulled up you could hear the stereo blasting full force, usually Bob Seger, although he liked all kinds of rockin' music. After a few minutes Rick would come out, with his faithful dog Champ by his side. Champ . . . man, that dog was about as ornery as a snake, and a hell of a lot more dangerous. Champ was a pit bull, weighed maybe seventy-five pounds, always drooling and snarling and looking like he wanted to take a chunk out of your leg just for the pure fun of it. Although he wasn't on a leash, he never left Little Rick's side. They were inseparable, like Bill Sykes and his mutt in *Oliver Twist*. You couldn't get near Little Rick when Champ was around—not unless Rick gave the okay. It was a game with Rick. He loved to use Champ to scare the shit out of people . . . and believe me, this was a scary pup. Rick used to say he was raised on gunpowder, and I didn't doubt it.

As much as he looked like a wild animal, though, Champ was completely subservient and obedient to Little Rick. If Rick gave an order, Champ executed it, no matter how ridiculous it might have seemed. Several times I saw Rick tease the dog with a beer can, get him all riled up. Then he'd take the can, pass it in front of the dog's nose, yell "Get it, Champ!" and then throw the can onto the roof of the house. At first Champ would naturally go nuts, like any dog dying of frustration and embarrassment. But Champ wasn't just any dog. After sprinting back and forth for a few minutes, with his eyes focused on the roof, Champ would suddenly jump up on a big fifty-gallon oil drum near the side of the house, and then, I'm not kidding you, he'd stand on that drum and he'd jump up as high as he could, and with his teeth he'd latch onto the drainpipe of the house. He'd hang there for a few moments, catching his breath, I guess, or maybe contemplating the insanity of his actions, before clawing his way onto the roof of the house! And then he'd strut up to the beer can, his nuts hanging low and proud, and pick it up in his teeth. Finally he'd leap off the roof and land upright on all fours—like a fucking cat!—and return the can to Rick, who'd give him a little kiss and a scratch behind the ears.

Rick and Champ were alarmingly, unnaturally close. He used to brag about all the women he'd fucked, but it wasn't so much the conquest that made Rick proudest, it was the fact that he shared his good fortune with Champ.

"Any lady wants to blow me?" Rick used to say. "She's gonna have to blow Champ first."

Honest to Christ, that's what he said, and if at first I thought it was just a sick joke, I later came to believe it was true. I didn't actually see anyone service the dog, but I saw Rick in action a couple times, with Champ nearby, and . . . well, let's just say I don't think Rick was lying. When it came to Champ, Little Rick's affection knew no bounds, and any guests were wise to remember that. One time, for example, we came in the house and the stereo was roaring, as usual, and Champ was sacked out on a chair, flat on his back, with his legs sticking straight up in the air. Like an ant on the front of a can of bug spray.

"What the hell is wrong with Champ?" I asked, innocently enough, or so I thought. "It looks like he has rigor mortis."

Rick frowned, clapped his hands, yelled, "Up! Nine! Ten!" and I'm telling you that dog flipped over and leaped from the chair to where I was sitting in one motion, and was ready to rip me apart. Fortunately, Rick was sitting on the couch right next to me; he reached out and grabbed the collar inches from my face. If he'd been one second slower that dog would have taken my lips off.

"Now, what did you say about my dog?" Rick asked.

I took a deep breath, tried not to move. "I said, 'Champ is the most beautiful dog I've ever seen in my life. He's gorgeous.' "

Little Rick kept Champ there for a minute or so, snarling and salivating, before giving the order to back off.

"Don't fuck with my dog," he said. "Remember that."

Rick was also a serious drinker who made this thing called Sonoma Punch. He'd get a galvanized steel basin and fill it with Kool-Aid, orange juice, and vodka. Then he'd add a couple bottles of Everclear—100 percent alcohol—just for good measure. This stuff was so strong it would make your eyeballs burn when you drank it, and it would seriously fuck you up. But I got the impression that Rick had been weaned on the stuff. I met his mother and father once, when they came out for a visit from Oklahoma. His mom was drinking heavily the whole day; at one point when she got up to go in the house, she kicked over her purse . . . and out fell a handgun. No shit! Little Rick's mom was packing a .38-caliber revolver.

No question about it, Little Rick was Oklahoma crazy, but he built me a beautiful bike, and I cherished it. I got into bikes in a big way for a while, me and a bunch of guys on the crew. Jackson had one first. Then I got one. Then Heard and Ramrod and Kid. And finally even

Harry Popick, our monitor man, Dan Healy, and Robbie Taylor, our production manager. There would be days when there were ten bikes parked outside the Front Street studio. The New York Hells Angels gave one to Mickey Hart—he was the only guy in the band who really got into riding, but others openly lusted after bikes. (I was given a magnificent '57 panhead chopper by Angelo on behalf of the Richmond Hells Angels, which I cherish to this day.) For a while in the mid- to late seventies we rode all the time. We almost quit driving our cars because it was so much more fun to ride a bike. There was such a feeling of exhilaration, of freedom. I used to ride my bike right up to the stage and begin playing it with the band. See, when I was doing the drums for Mickey we built a back riser, and it became the setting for a big rhythm section, and the band wanted us to play too. So I'd jump up and started playing steel drums, maracas, whatever. We called ourselves the Rhythm Devils. Some of the guys didn't really like it all that much, but I really got into it. When the band would play "Not Fade Away," I'd fire up my bike and lay down the beat on the pipes:

"*VROOM-VROOM-VROOM . . . VROOM-VROOM.*"

The thing about riding a motorcycle is that it changes you. It toughens you up, makes you stronger. We were fearless and reckless and oblivious to our own mortality, despite having lost Pigpen and Badger. We did stupid things on our bikes. We went to bars and drank all night, picked up chicks, and rode drunk till dawn. There's nothing quite as stupid and suicidal and irresponsible as driving drunk, because you lose all perspective. I remember driving home one night with both of my hands holding the throttle wide open, going at least 100 mph. Just crazy. But it was fun. I can't deny that. The camaraderie of riding . . . staying out all night with the Hells Angels . . . drinking . . . smoking . . . seeing the sun come up when you're crossing the Golden Gate Bridge—it brought us closer together. It tightened a crew that was already the best in the business.

Chapter 21

After the European tour of 1974, the Grateful Dead went on hiatus for a while. Although the Jerry Garcia Band continued to play and perform, and other members of the Dead became involved in their own various projects, the Grateful Dead was silenced. At least temporarily. By the time we all got back together in '75, a number of things had changed. Pigpen was gone, of course, and Mickey Hart had returned to the fold after an absence of four years. The psychedelic wave of the 1960s had crested and in its place was a newfound fascination with harder and more debilitating drugs, most notably cocaine and heroin, both of which, in one way or another, wreaked havoc on the Grateful Dead and many in its circle.

One of the hardest hit was my dear friend Rex Jackson, who in early 1976 decided for some reason to walk through the revolving door that led to the Grateful Dead management offices. It was a bold move on Rex's part, one he made not only because he wanted a bigger challenge out of life, but because he honestly felt he could do the job as well if not better than it had ever been done. We'd seen so many people come and go over the years: Mickey's father, Ron Rakow, Danny Rifkin, Rock Scully, Sam Cutler, John McIntire. Everyone who tried their hand at management seemed to collapse under the weight of responsibility and expectation. It became something of a joke to those of us on the crew: *Want to keep your sanity? Stay the fuck out of management.*

Rex was one of the most vocal proponents of this philosophy, too. Like the rest of us, he believed that if you kept your hands on the gear, you'd be locked into something strong and permanent, something meaningful. Everything else—the finances, the scheduling, the personnel changes—was shapeless and crazy and uncontrollable. The music was the only constant, and without the equipment there was no music. The gear was always there, physically; whatever other problems a crew member had, he could always fall back on what he did best, because without him the show could not go on. Management? That was madness on a daily basis, like waking up every morning and trying to walk through quicksand. We saw it on the faces of everyone who tried to get their arms around the job. It was a no-win proposition. So when Rex announced one day that he wanted to become road manager of the Grateful Dead, I was both shocked and concerned, for it seemed to be a bad move on so many levels. Rex knew the equipment. He was a great crew member and an even better friend, and I was worried that I'd lose both.

In most bands this wouldn't have been an issue, for there was little chance of a roadie moving up to management; but the Grateful Dead was unlike any other band. Jackson was a comrade, a friend, a trusted ally, and so his request, his ambition, was met not with laughter or derision, but a pat on the back. And soon enough Rex Jackson became road manager of the Grateful Dead.

It's easy and perhaps true to say that the job was beyond him, but it might have been beyond anyone at that time. Suddenly the carnival that was life on the road became volatile and dangerous in ways we'd never anticipated. I'm not saying we were sweet and innocent prior to this, but there was a difference, and the difference was cocaine. Coke hit the scene hot and heavy just about the time Rex took over. There had always been drugs around the Grateful Dead, but we favored the less lethal, more communal highs of pot, acid, and nitrous oxide. Speed, as I said, was less a recreational drug than a tool of the trade, and coke was more of a party favor, used only sporadically and carefully. By the mid-seventies, though, coke was pervasive. It seemed everyone you met carried an assortment of spoons and the name of his dealer on the speed dial. It became easier to procure a few lines of coke than an ounce of weed. It was just crazy.

New York was the capital of the cocaine world, and we spent a lot of time in New York. Somehow we got adopted by a group from Bay Ridge, Brooklyn (home to Tony Manero in *Saturday Night Fever*), and they'd come to all of our shows whenever we were in New York, always armed to the teeth with weed and coke and other shit. They were all quasi-drug dealers of one type or another, and they used drugs to curry favor with the band and the crew and thus gain access and hanging-out privileges. That's the way it worked: girls used sex to gain entree to the inner circle; guys used drugs. And cocaine opened doors like no other drug before. I was fortunate in that I never really became cocaine crazy, like so many other people. I did my share, don't get me wrong. But I didn't enjoy it the way so many people did, maybe because I knew it was a short jump from one serious drug to the other, from cocaine to heroin. Or maybe it was because I saw how it seemed to have a death grip on so many of my friends. It became clear that they couldn't function without it, that nothing was more important to them than that next line of blow. Some of the guys on the crew claimed they did it because the drug gave them a feeling of strength and boundless energy; they couldn't understand why I wouldn't want that.

"How can you do all that weed and still work?" they'd ask. "Aren't you tired?"

The truth was, no, I wasn't tired. I always had more energy than the other guys on the crew, and sometimes it seemed the only way to harness that energy, to take the edge off, was to smoke a joint. A few times I did coke after a show, prior to loading the truck, and indeed it did provide an electric rush that made me feel like Superman. It also made me edgy and nervous and even a little bit nauseous. I'd be tossing equipment around, grinding my teeth, sweating. The euphoria lasted only a few minutes and was quickly replaced by paranoia and irritability. To be perfectly blunt, cocaine didn't work for me until a few years later, when I started drinking a little, and discovered that one balanced the other and left you with a more manageable, albeit potentially lethal high.

Jackson, though, got hooked. Big time. The enormity of his problem became clear to me in the summer of '76, after a show in New York. It had been a wild night, a wild show, really out of control. Johnny Hagen was with us then, too. Johnny was a Pendleton boy who came to work for the Dead along with Ramrod. He'd gotten connected through his brother, Mike, who hung out with Kesey and the Merry Pranksters. Ramrod and Hagen were old buddies who'd spent some time in a Mexican jail. (As I said, there was a lot of history with these guys.) Johnny had come and gone by the time I arrived on the scene, but now he was back again, as crazy as ever. He came from a long line of wheat people, and once on a road trip we stopped at his family's farm in Pendleton and hung out with his folks. During one road trip a year or so earlier, when I was rooming with Johnny, I took a call from his girlfriend, Rhonda, who was howling into the phone, just screaming, "I need to talk to Johnny!" Rhonda was pregnant at the time, and it turned out she'd gone into labor that night and was having the baby, Johnny's baby, all by herself—no nurse, no doctor, no midwife—in a farmhouse out in Sonoma County.

It was sad in a way, of course, but I also thought it was natural and beautiful and impressive, that this woman was having a baby right at the moment, while talking to me on the phone.

"She's like a true Indian," I told Johnny.

He smiled. "You know, that's what I should call the kid: Indian."

But he didn't. Instead, he named his son "Whip," which is what I used to call Johnny when we were working on the road. It was something I got from my buddy Ray. "Come on, Whip, get moving!" Ray would say when the workload got heavy and he wanted us to pick up the pace. So Johnny Hagen's boy became Whip Hagen. A little unorthodox, I know, but then, Johnny was a quirky man. This was a guy who stopped doing his laundry on the road because he claimed the machines were always ripping him off. Instead he'd buy two or three pairs of blue jeans (which was all he ever wore) every week.

He was a good, fun-loving guy, Hagen, but strange. No doubt about it. And he was totally enamored with all these Brooklyn people, to whom he'd dispense backstage passes like so much candy. Our world became filled with these shady characters—dope dealers, tough guys, bikers—especially when we were in New York, and while it could be fun and interesting to have them around, it created a bit of friction, too. Bob Weir, for instance, was really getting uptight about our ever-expanding circle of "friends," many of whom wound up backstage or, even worse, crawling all over the stage, trying to become part of the show. Hagen was a big part of this, primarily because he got caught up in cocaine. We all loved Johnny deeply, but he was in trouble.

On this night, though, Jackson had decided to try to clean up the stage. Weir had been griping incessantly (and understandably so) about the number of freeloaders who somehow wound up in places that were intended to be the band's sanctuary, so Jackson took it upon himself to clean things up. Early in the show he started grabbing people by the shirt, handing them tickets, and coaxing them out of the stage area and into the audience. Frankly, I was stunned to see him do this. It was dangerous enough to push around a bunch of low-rent drug dealers from Brooklyn, but to disrespect the Hells Angels, no matter how slightly . . . well, that was lunacy. They didn't like it, either, but Jackson was afraid of almost nothing, and he wasn't going to stop just because they were wearing their patches.

His courage was great, but his chemical dependence was even greater. He called me up to his hotel room a few hours later and showed me a one-gallon Ziploc bag filled with cocaine. When it came to drugs, there wasn't much that surprised me, but this did. I'd never seen so much cocaine in one place before. It was ridiculous for anyone other than a dealer to carry that much coke. And Jackson was no dealer.

"What are you doing, Rex?" I asked.

He lowered his head, squeezed the bag lovingly, pathetically. "If you don't take this, Steve, I'm going to kill myself with it." He looked up at me. "Please. Help me."

It was a strange moment, a strange transaction, because while Jackson didn't want to keep the coke, neither did he want to throw it away. I mean, he could have just flushed it down the toilet. But he didn't. Instead, he asked me to hold it for him. "There's no one else I can give it to," he said.

I thought about it for a few seconds, and though it was one of the hardest things I've ever done, I turned him down.

"Sorry, Rex. I don't want anything to do with carrying that much coke."

That was the only time I ever refused Jackson anything, and I did feel bad about it afterward. I left the room not knowing whether I'd ever see him again, and in fact he did disappear for a couple days shortly thereafter. Somehow Rex found this girl in New York and hooked up with her. She was an exotic kind of zaftig girl named Rene, a real New York girl all the way, and suddenly Jackson was in love with her. When the tour ended he brought her back to the West Coast and their relationship began the painful, inevitable process of erosion.

Jackson was not the "settling down" type. Actually, he was the type who often couldn't stand the sight of a woman after he'd had sex with her. So he and Rene never had a chance. The fact that he had just endured a nasty breakup only a few months earlier, combined with his escalating coke habit, pretty much doomed their romance.

By Labor Day Jackson was tired of Rene, overwhelmed by management responsibilities, and exhausted and sick from a month-long coke jag. He used to tease me about my lack of interest in coke—"You can't handle it, huh?"—and maybe he was right. But as far as I could tell, almost no one seemed to handle coke very well, least of all Jackson. He still carried that Ziploc bag around with him, its contents diminishing daily, and his mood was increasingly dark. He was really disturbed about a lot of things, including my having caught him at my house after a tryst with Angela, at a time when she and I were romantically involved. That had bothered me, but it had bothered Rex even more.

That Labor Day weekend we drove up to San Anselmo to hang out with our friend Billy Crowe. Crowe was originally from New York but had moved to California after meeting us on the road. He was a good guy, liked his weed, but wasn't into coke at all. The three of us spent a few hours together, smoking pot and talking the way friends do. It was a quiet, low-key time, but I could tell there was something on Jackson's mind, something he was reluctant to share. Pot usually brought out a lightness in Rex, but now he seemed to be in a funk. He talked about his son, Cole, who had been born to his girlfriend Betty (who had also been our recording engineer) a year earlier, and how much he loved the boy. But there was a sadness to him, a bleakness that I couldn't understand. He kept talking about the emptiness of his life, which later blew my mind because it seemed as though he knew he was on some sort of a rendevous with death. He fretted about the future, about what would happen with Cole and Betty, and how he was going to end his tangled relationship with Rene. Late that afternoon Jackson dropped me off at my house. I don't remember our parting words. I do know that I never saw him again.

Jackson, you have to understand, was a fantastic driver. He could drive a truck, a car, motorcycle . . . anything on wheels. He'd been a hot-rodder back in Pendleton and I'd heard countless stories from the other guys about how Jackson was always toying with the cops, outrunning them in his souped-up '57 Chevy, just for sport. Sometimes I'd call him "Thunder Road" (after the Robert Mitchum movie, not the Bruce Springsteen song). Jackson was like Badger in a way: he felt he had an angel sitting on his shoulder. He'd say, "Man, I've had so many near-death experiences in cars, there's no way I'm ever gonna die behind the wheel." He believed that, and he said it so many times that I believed it, too. I'd been with him when he drove his way out of seemingly impossible situations; I'd been on the back of his motorcycle when we both almost died. There was no question about his driving ability. When it came to riding shotgun, I trusted him like I trusted no one else. But that night while he was coming home on Highway 101, something went inexplicably, terribly wrong.

A jogger out on his morning run spotted Jackson's car in a ravine off Highway 101, near the Mill Valley exit. The police report said the driver had failed to negotiate a steep turn and simply lost control of the car, which left the road and flipped over several times before settling on its roof in a ravine. The driver was killed instantly.

Word of Jackson's death spread quickly. The car was discovered around 8 A.M., and by eleven o'clock everyone had gathered at my house in Mill Valley. And not just the guys on the crew—every member of the band was there, too. We were all stunned, as if we'd been hit between the eyes. Of all of us, Jackson had been the most indestructible, and now he was gone. It seemed impossible. After a few hours we all went to Ramrod's house, where we decided to hold an impromptu rock 'n' roll wake, one that Jackson surely would have appreciated. We sat around all day and night, drinking tequila and eulogizing Jackson, telling stores that left us breathless with laughter.

Maybe the best Jackson story, though, was revealed several months later. Jeff, the Richmond Hells Angels who had been hanging out with us for a while, had a girlfriend named Charlie, who worked on the ferry boats between Larkspur and San Francisco. Like a lot of us in the greater Grateful Dead family, Charlie wore a Grateful Dead necklace, one of the originals, and one day while working she was approached by a passenger on the ferry, who recognized the necklace.

"Do you know anyone in the Grateful Dead?" he asked.

"As a matter of fact, yes," Charlie replied.

They talked for a while, and eventually the man asked Charlie if she knew anything about that guy on the crew, the one who had died in a car accident. Again, Charlie said yes, she did. His name was Jackson. The man nodded, looked around to make sure no one was listening, and then said, "It wasn't just an accident."

The story he told was this: The cops had pulled him over two weeks after Jackson's death because he was a driving a powder-blue Citron, which happened to be the same type of car Jackson had been driving. They had chased Jackson's car at a high speed for a while before losing track of it, the cops explained, and now, after all this time, they couldn't believe their luck at having stumbled upon the same vehicle. But they were mistaken, of course, and after jacking the guy up and interrogating him for the better part of an hour, they realized it and sent him on his way. Why hadn't these cops heard about Jackson's death? I don't know. Maybe they represented a different municipality than the one that investigated the accident. Maybe, after Jackson went off the road and sailed into that ravine, the cops went flying right by, never even knowing that their prey was already dead. Maybe, for some reason, no one ever bothered to put the pieces of the puzzle together.

Or, maybe, the guy on the ferry boat was an inveterate liar.

Personally, I like the idea of Jackson going out that way, with the cops in hot pursuit, just like in the old days, when he was tearing up county roads around Pendleton. He would have liked that. I prefer not to think of the most likely alternative scenario: that it had been a long day, that he was depressed and sick and not at all like the Donald Rex Jackson I'd known and loved. I prefer not to think that in some way he had sold his soul to cocaine, and that the drug had killed him, either directly or indirectly. Cocaine could do that. It was a drug that took a lot out of you and gave nothing back. It speeded things up to a breakneck pace and left you exhausted, empty, alone.

I really don't know whether Rex wanted to die that night, or whether he was merely trying to cheat death. Maybe it doesn't matter. All I know is this: the last time I saw Rex, it seemed like death was sitting on his shoulder, stalking him.

And he knew it.

Chapter 22

1978-

The first time Lowell George walks into the Grateful Dead's Front Street studio in San Rafael, he doesn't exactly look the part of a musical genius. He's wearing tattered overalls and carrying with him nothing but a guitar and a good-time Southern attitude. He's here to produce the Dead's latest album, Shakedown Street. The title mirrors our nickname for the studio. We call it Shakedown Street because it is located in kind of a seedy neighborhood, directly across the street from a rundown motel filled with cheap-ass hookers.

Appearances to the contrary notwithstanding, Lowell is a smart boy and a hell of a musician. He's the lead guitarist/singer/songwriter for Little Feat, a quirky Southern blues band whose work is admired by all of us, especially Jerry. It's a tricky thing when you bring in another musician to produce your album, especially one who is accustomed to running the show, the way Lowell is. There's a period of acclimation in the studio, when goals are established and roles become understood. If egos run rampant, the process can become unbearable and the whole project can fall apart.

This won't be a problem on Shakedown Street, as we discover that very first day. We're hanging out in the studio, waiting for Lowell, when Rock Scully walks in with a big envelope. Smiling, he rips off the top of the envelope and dumps the contents onto a table. The cocaine falls like virgin snow. Instantly we're all out of our seats, pushing each other to get a spot at the table. Straws come out, dollar bills are rolled, and heads collide over this remarkable little mound of coke. We're laughing at the absurdity of it, jostling for position, and suddenly the table begins to quiver. To our horror, the mound collapses and slides toward the edge of the table—an avalanche of cocaine rushing to the floor. Everyone freezes for a moment as the powder settles onto the carpet and a small cloud rises from the floor. How much money was just wasted? How many hours in the orgasmic world of the cocaine high?

A rhetorical question, as it turns out, for nothing will be wasted. The next thing you know we're all on our hands and knees, dragging our faces across the floor, inhaling cocaine and dirt and bug parts and God knows what else. We're in the midst of this ridiculous cocaine orgy when the door opens and Lowell George walks in.

"Hey, guys!" he says.

We stop and look up. I wonder what must be going through his mind. I wonder how ridiculous we must look. And I wonder how quickly he'll turn and walk out of here rather than work with this crazy bunch of cokeheads. But then Ramrod is on his feet. He pulls out a buck knife, shoves everyone aside, and cuts out a big chunk of carpet. He picks it up and slaps it on the table, then clears his throat proudly. Lowell takes a look at this funky brown coke-stained slab of rug, pauses for a moment, then drops his guitar case and jumps right in.

At that moment it seems pretty obvious that Lowell George is our kind of people. Too bad this will be one of his last projects. Within a year Lowell will be *gone. The official cause of death will be heart failure. As for the underlying cause, well . . . your guess is as good as mine.*

In hindsight, I realize there was no greater enemy to our lives, and to the health of the band, than those powders, cocaine and heroin—especially heroin—and all of the things accompanying their use: the needle play, the violent crowd they attracted, the immediate and profound effect they had on the mind and body. They destroyed not only your social instincts, but your creativity, your spirit, your will.

Cocaine, particularly when freebased, was bad enough. But nothing was quite like heroin. And mixing the two together—a lethal combination known as a speedball—was as good as playing Russian roulette. I knew all of this. I'd seen enough heroin use in my youth and had never forgotten the ugly images. So, in the winter of '75, when I saw Jerry Garcia snort a line of heroin for the very first time, I couldn't help but think, *Uh-oh . . . this is not good.*

For a while he kept it hidden, snorting smack in his room, or smoking "rat," as we called it, Persian-based morphine sulphate. Kid and I tried rat with Jerry once, as part of a pathetic bonding exercise, and to show him that it really wasn't all that big a deal. Maybe if it didn't appear to be such a forbidden fruit, we reasoned, he wouldn't want it so badly.

Wrong! Rat whacked me like no drug I'd ever experienced. Kid and I were on the floor, totally wrecked, and Jerry was just standing there, laughing and shaking his head, like a junkie pro, saying, "Man, you guys don't know what you're doing." I never tried rat again. It was a horrible drug, one that consumed you and controlled you. I couldn't understand why anyone would want to live like that, hopelessly hooked on that shit. But for Jerry and some of the guys he was running with (John Kahn and Keith Godchaux, among others), rat was like the elixir of life: the more they had, the more they wanted.

Jerry was our idol, our spiritual and musical leader, and when he started messing around with heroin and freebasing cocaine, others naturally followed suit. It wasn't long before they reached the point where their addiction started to interfere with the music. I'd notice that some of the guys weren't rehearsing as much, and that Jerry, who had always been the first person to arrive and the last to leave— who could never get enough of his guitar—was now hiding out in the bathroom, freebasing, snorting heroin, whatever. We'd be out there in the studio, twiddling our thumbs, waiting for him, waiting for this man who was the greatest musician of his time to get his fix and clean up and walk out of the bathroom and pretend he was clear-headed enough to continue working. It became a silly game in which doing drugs was no longer an enjoyable, communal experience, a twisted but fun reward for a hard day's work, but rather an excuse not to work. That's what being a junkie is all about: excuses. *Why didn't you do this? Why didn't you do that. Why couldn't you come here?*

"Sorry, it was the shit, man. Fucked me up. Won't happen again."

Yeah, right.

Those two drugs—heroin and cocaine—changed Jerry, weakened him. The deterioration became evident in the late seventies, both in his appearance and his work, and it saddened me greatly, but there was only so much you could do for him. Jerry was an intensely private, strong-willed person who did not want anyone to interfere with his life. He detested anyone who tried to turn over his rock and shine a flashlight on his life. This put me in a difficult position, because although Jerry was my friend, he was also my boss. More than most of the guys on the crew, I owed my livelihood and career to Jerry.

First of all, of course, there was my role in the Garcia Band. I was Jerry's right-hand man in that venture, the person who not only handled his guitars and amp, but also hung out with him on the road. I wouldn't go so far as to say I was irreplaceable—I'm not that deluded—but I do know that he liked me and appreciated my work, and that I made his job easier, which is one reason why I was able to take over as manager of the Garcia Band in the mid-1980s.

But that's only part of the story. The other part has to do with my role with the Grateful Dead, and the deterioration of my relationship with Mickey Hart, an undeniably brilliant musician whose desire for perfection, combined with his temperamental nature, made him an extremely difficult and demanding boss. I'd been doing Billy Kreutzmann's drums for several years, and he had been a good friend and an easy guy to work with. But when Mickey returned to the band in '74, I began handling his equipment, and we had problems almost from the outset. I'd never worked with anyone like Mickey before. Everyone else in the band had a fairly laid back attitude and treated the crew with respect and dignity. Mickey was a taskmaster. He'd want me to sit there and stare at him, watch his every move so that I'd know exactly what he wanted and what he expected. That was his prerogative, of course. He was in charge. But after a while I got the impression that he was at times putting me through the paces for no good reason, that there was some sort of personal agenda.

We stayed together for nearly four years, even as our fighting escalated to the point where I thought we might actually come to blows. Fortunately, everybody on the crew and in the band knew what Mickey was like. They loved his talent and creativity, but he could be a difficult personality. So they sympathized with me and encouraged me to hang in there. And I did, until finally, in 1978, we both decided a change was not only wise, but absolutely necessary.

I told Ramrod of our impending split one day at the Front Street Studio. "Mickey wants me out of here," I said. "I think I might have to leave the crew. Unless . . ."

"Unless what?"

I hesitated, for I found it hard to ask for favors, especially one as large as this.

"Any chance you'd be willing switch to with me?"

This was not a minor thing. Ramrod was king of the crew, the longest-tenured man on the job, and one who had already put in his time working with Mickey many years earlier and who now had the enviable task of working with Jerry. In theory the switch would work, for Ramrod knew how to handle Mickey's drums, and I'd become thoroughly adept at setting up Jerry's guitars. Still, it was a lot for me to ask of him. And yet he didn't hesitate.

"Okay," Ramrod said. "Let's do it."

"Really? You're sure?"

"Absolutely. We've got a good thing going here. Let's not bust it up."

Ramrod's response was nothing short of mind-blowing. I knew he was a good man and a good friend, but this gesture required immense sacrifice. It was not the rock 'n' roll crews; hell, it wasn't the kind of thing you saw in any work environment. People just didn't care about each other that much. But we did.

The transition didn't happen overnight; there was a little more to it than just a handshake between me and Ramrod. I had to talk to Jerry about it, and Ramrod had to talk with Mickey. They were both cool with the plan. But I also had to get Bob Weir's approval, because he'd been the rock of the Grateful Dead, the steadiest, most level-headed component of a machine that was now always teetering on the brink of collapse. Bobby was no longer responsible only for his own job; he was a guitar player and songwriter and singer. In each of those roles he was backup to Jerry, and Jerry was faltering. Jerry needed a lot of attention and support, and Bobby usually provided it. The last thing he needed was the headache of dealing with personality conflicts between band members and crew, especially when they resulted in a shift in duties, such as this. Bobby just wanted to make sure that I was up to the task of handling Jerry's equipment within the framework of the Grateful Dead, admittedly a more demanding job than taking care of his guitars when he played with the Garcia Band. Everything about the Dead was bigger, more cumbersome, more pressurized.

Good man that he is, though, Bobby signed off on the deal, and Jerry agreed to take full responsibility for me and my performance. So Ramrod and I switched jobs, and Mickey and I made our peace, and life went on pretty much as usual. I liked doing Jerry's guitars, the feeling of being connected to such a brilliant musician. The job wasn't that much different than it was when I worked for the Garcia Band, but the stakes were definitely higher. I liked that. What I hadn't anticipated was the development of a secondary role. As Jerry's addiction worsened I became not just his guitar roadie, and not just his friend, but something much more complicated. It was my job to be there for him whenever he needed help, in whatever form that might entail. Sometimes that meant lending an ear, sometimes it meant becoming involved on a far more personal level.

I don't mean to imply that Jerry stopped working. He remained, for a while at least, one of the most driven and creative of artists. But whereas he once worked incessantly, because it wasn't really work at all to him, now he worked when and where the mood struck him. Everything had to be done on his terms, according to his schedule and needs, and always the first thing on his "to-do" list was: *get fucked up*. It was all about the drugs, about freebasing or smoking rat or snorting heroin. I tried to stay out of the whole thing, to concentrate on my role as a member of the crew. If I did my job professionally and efficiently, I figured everything else would work out. But that was a naive and simplistic outlook. As Jerry fell deeper into the blackness of addiction, he turned to me more frequently for help.

We'd be out on tour with the Garcia Band, for instance, and he'd ask me if I would hold his Persian. "I've got too much right now," he'd say. As with Jackson, I found it difficult to say no to him. I'd think to myself, *Well, maybe Jerry's trying to wean himself, do a little chip-chop thing, and eventually he'll kick this shit for good.* What a silly, stupid thing that was, because every two minutes Jerry would want more of his stash. I was angry that he'd ask me to be in that position.

The thing about addiction is that it isn't always a free-fall. It's much more complex than that, more like a roller-coaster ride, with periods of hope and productivity, alternating with periods of despair and self-destruction. And so it was with Jerry. Life went on, and more often than not it was a good life. We partied and played and created music that made a lot of people happy. Increasingly, though, recklessness got in the way.

On the night of February 7, 1979, we were preparing for a Grateful Dead concert at Southern Illinois University in Carbondale, Illinois. (Our hotel was located in nearby Normal, Illinois, which, given our completely bizarre, even amoral, existence on the road, lent an ironic twist to things.) I spent most of that day (after setup) backstage with Jerry and Kid Candelario. The three of us hung out together a lot, even on Dead tours, because we'd gotten to know each other so well through our time with the Garcia Band. The mood on this night was light, playful. Despite his ongoing problems with cocaine and heroin, Jerry seemed to be in a pretty good place at the moment. We ate dinner together in the dressing room, smoked a few joints, then I brought Jerry his guitar and he began warming up. We were just sitting around, laughing, telling jokes, getting ready for the show, when Rock Scully popped in. Rock, who was still road manager, must have sensed the happy vibe in the room—a party waiting to happen—because next thing I knew he held out his hand and said, "Look what I've got, boys."

In his palm were four little blue pills, instantly recognizable as Valium. I don't blame Rock for what happened next, any more than I blame myself or Kid. Pills were part of our lives, day in and day out. I think Rock was just in a good mood and wanted to let us know that he'd be bringing something to the party later on. I'm sure he intended to split the candy. What he could not have known—what none of us could have predicted—was that Jerry, perhaps almost as a joke, or perhaps not, would suddenly leap out of his chair, sweep Rock's hand clean, and gulp all four pills in a single swallow.

For a moment we all froze, as Jerry stood there smiling a tight-lipped smile. A part of me hoped he had faked it, but when he started to laugh, and it was clear that his mouth was empty, I realized we were in trouble. I looked at the dressing room clock. We were due to hit the stage in less than thirty minutes.

"What did you do, man?" I asked incredulously. I'd never seen Jerry do anything like this before, not before a show.

Jerry said nothing, just shrugged and went back to playing his guitar.

By the time Kid and I led Jerry out of the dressing room and onto the stage, his legs were wobbly, his eyes heavy. No one in the band had any idea what had happened, at least not until the lights went down and they launched into the first song of the first set, "Don't Ease Me In." Instead of a neat, tight intro, what the 10,000 Deadheads at SIU heard was a single, ear-splitting jack-hammer of a chord as Jerry's hand fell heavily across the strings of his guitar.

SPRRRROINGG!

Everyone in the band stopped playing and turned to look at Jerry. It was almost comical, in a strange sort of way, but it was sad, too, to see one of the world's greatest guitar players too fucked up to play. But the band soldiered on, veering almost immediately from the planned set list to a series of tunes on which Bobby would sing and play lead guitar, even as Jerry sort of wobbled in place, half conscious.

It was an abbreviated set, after which we took Jerry backstage and did our best to revive him. The scene in the dressing room was not unlike that of a boxing match, in which a trainer tries to revive a punch-drunk fighter. We talked to Jerry, tried to encourage him, walked him around. We pumped coffee into him, of course, and when that didn't work we turned to our own private stashes. To counter the effects of the Valium, Jerry ingested all manner of substances: Black Beauties and Bennies were dispensed by the truck drivers; cocaine appeared out of nowhere; anything and everything to wake him up and help him get back on the stage and play.

All of this sounds crazy, I know, and undoubtedly it was. But it also worked. Jerry went out and played the second set—admittedly, fidgeting and twitching like a laboratory rabbit—and the fans went home happy. Or, at least, not disappointed. Jerry never offered an explanation for what happened, and I never asked for one. I'm sure he felt bad about it, because it was totally uncharacteristic of him to risk the music. That was a line he simply did not cross. Not deliberately, anyway. In some way, though, I guess it was a sign of things to come, further indication that he was losing control.

Later that year, when Jerry first admitted that he wasn't merely a user, but a full-fledged heroin addict, I considered it a potential sign of recovery. The first step, as it were. Jerry was living in an apartment below Rock Scully's house at the time, and boy was that a mistake, since Rock's place was about as safe and sedate as Caligula's. I'd gotten a call from Richard Lauren, who was then manager of the Garcia Band, asking me to pick him up and drive to Jerry's place. He didn't say why, but I liked Richard and trusted his judgment. We used to hang out together at his office and smoke a lot of weed, and eventually, when coke and heroin replaced pot as the drug of choice among some people in our circle—most notably Jerry—Richard decided we had to do something. So we picked up Jerry in a white Garcia Band van and drove him to the private residence of a physician named Allen Spanek.

The idea was to help Jerry kick heroin through the use of a new and unorthodox treatment called a Narcan Flush. I knew nothing about it, wasn't even sure that it was safe or made sense, but Dr. Spanek gave a convincing presentation. As we sat in his big beautiful house, the centerpiece of which was a giant fish tank filed with piranha, Dr. Spanek explained what was about to happen. Richard and I were subdued. Jerry was shaking like a leaf, partly out of fear and anxiety, I'm sure, but also because he hadn't had a hit of smack in a while and he was already going through withdrawal. Narcan, the doctor explained, was a chemical that quickly flushed the body's receptor sites. So basically it was like a concentrated "kick." When a junkie kicks heroin he typically goes cold turkey or goes to a rehab center, and within a few hours he starts craving the drug. If he doesn't get it, the misery escalates over the course of a several days, hammering him with what can charitably and euphemistically be called "flulike symptoms." Narcan accomplished this same agonizing process in a few short hours.

I should say here that I am not, by any means, "antidrug," at least not in the traditional sense of the term. I've never been through rehab, never endured the introspective torture and spiritual mumbo-jumbo of a twelve-step program. Although I've left most so-called hard drugs behind, I still light up a joint every so often ("often" being the operative term). I believe that drugs are a part of man, and that when used properly there is nothing wrong with them. There is a reason the body produces endorphins, the effect of which is not unlike the effect of heroin. The pain-killing properties of opiates are well documented, and I think the world is a better place for their existence. But that doesn't mean they're meant to be used recreationally, or that they can be used safely and casually, the way cannabis can. Jerry was proof of that. He needed help, and Dr. Spanek's office was a place to start. I had no idea whether the procedure would work or not, but it seemed to be worth a try.

Jerry took the first of four shots of Narcan, and almost instantly the kick started coming on. He started sweating, crying, throwing up. Dr. Spanek tried to relieve some of the symptoms through the use of electro-acupuncture, but that didn't appear to help much. Jerry was in severe pain throughout the night. I tried to comfort him as much as I could, simply by talking to him, holding him, reassuring him in any way possible. Boundaries that had been between us for years crumbled. I hadn't seen anyone kick junk since I was a teen at Rikers Island, and as I watched Jerry suffer the aches and pains, the nausea, the chills, that whole horrible experience came rushing back to me. In that moment I hated heroin more than ever, because it was destroying someone I cared so much about, someone who had such a good heart and so much to offer the world.

I'll say this, though: Jerry was pretty tough about it. At one point as he sat shaking on the floor, drenched with sweat, he said to me, "Steve, I've got King Kong on my back, huh?"

"Looks that way, man."

And then he laughed, retched a little more, and took another shot of Narcan. It was an amazingly intense experience, and I was impressed by his willingness to endure it. He didn't fall apart completely, I'll give him that. At around one o'clock in the morning, when the nausea and chills subsided, I asked Jerry if he wanted to crash there for the night.

"No," he said. "Let's go home."

Richard lived near Dr. Spanek in Mill Valley, so I dropped him off first, then drove Jerry to San Rafael. We'd been sitting three abreast in the front seat—me driving, Richard riding shotgun, and Jerry in between—but even after Richard got out, Jerry stayed in the middle, leaning against me, half asleep. Although he was eight years older than me and brilliant in ways I could only imagine; even though he was the boss and I was the employee, I felt in that instant as though our relationship had been turned inside out. Suddenly I was the parent and he was the child. He needed me. It was as simple as that.

So we pulled up in front of his place and sat there for a moment, not saying anything at all. It was a crucial moment in our friendship, and in Jerry's road to recovery, if such a road even existed.

"Let me come in with you," I finally said. "I can help you get set up, and then I'll sleep on the floor."

Jerry was thoroughly wrung out from the Narcan flush and obviously needed some assistance, but that wasn't really why I made the offer. I thought Jerry might have drugs in the house. At that moment he was clean, probably for the first time in three or four years. He'd gone through hell to get there, and now he had at least a chance to stay clean, to kick the junk forever, or at least for a while (which was probably a more reasonable goal). I thought if I could help him get through the night without using, if I could convince him to toss out whatever shit he had in the house, maybe it would stick.

"No, I'll be all right," he said, opening the door. "But thanks anyway. For everything."

He shuffled away from the van like an old man and disappeared into his house. I drove away filled with a sense of regret, rather than accomplishment. I don't know how quickly Jerry turned to heroin, but I'm sure it wasn't long. Maybe even that night. Really, though, the Narcan flush had no chance to work. To me it was nothing more than a junkie's cure, a way to clean out your system for the express purpose of getting high all over again from scratch. Not that doctors looked at it that way. I'm sure they thought it was a truly helpful and compassionate way to beat addiction. But it really wasn't. It was a finger in the dike. Nothing more.

Chapter 23

Even in the weirdest and most turbulent of times, those of us who traveled and lived as part of the Grateful Dead family enjoyed moments of joy and laughter and nearly transcendent beauty. The road was by turns sad and sweet, maddening and mystical.

In the fall of 1978 we played a series of shows in Egypt. It was an unforgettable, almost mythical trip, including as it did performances in the shadows of the great pyramids and the Sphinx, and innumerable opportunities to expand our cultural horizons. Like our first tour of Europe, this trip was a family affair. Spouses, children, friends, associates (including Kesey and the Pranksters, who chartered their own jet to be with us, and basketball star and longtime

Deadhead Bill Walton)—all were part of the massive Grateful Dead entourage that descended on the desert. There were more than sixty of us in all, and despite some of the problems we were experiencing at the time—the personnel and personal issues that occasionally flared and made life challenging for everyone—it was a great experience.

Thanks in no small part to Jimmy Carter and his efforts to bring peace to the region through the Camp David Accords, this wasn't a bad time to be an American in Egypt. It was, for the most part, a warm and friendly place, and we found ourselves not only tolerated, but embraced by the locals. Each of us was, in a sense, adopted by one or more Egyptians. They would act as hosts, guides, friends. Sometimes they would have these funny little arguments among themselves, heated debates about who had been assigned to help whom. And we came to understand that they were as curious about us as we were about them. One evening Bill Walton and I were out riding camels, along with an Egyptian man named Abdul, who befriended me and assisted me throughout our stay.

"Mr. Steve," Abdul said at one point. "I want to come see you in America."

"No problem, Abdul," I said. "Come to my village. It's a place called San Rafael." I paused and pointed at one of the pyramids. "I have two of those back home. I'll show you."

Abdul just nodded. I came to realize that he took everything I said pretty much at face value, for America to him was an incomprehensible place; what little information he had was gleaned from snippets of popular culture.

"Mr. Steve?" he asked me one day.

"Yes, Abdul."

"How do you make a living in America?"

"Well, we do this. We make music for the people."

He shook his head. "No, no. I mean, how do you do that?"

"Do what?"

He stopped. Clearly he was frustrated at my confusion.

"How do you travel around your country? Aren't you afraid?"

"Afraid of what, Abdul?"

He spread his arms, as if to understate the obvious. "The Indians, Mr. Steve. What about the Indians?"

As it turned out, much of Abdul's knowledge of America had been obtained from watching a handful of old Western movies. To him, it was incomprehensible that anyone could move freely about the United States without being savagely attacked.

"That's not really a problem for us," I told Abdul.

"No?"

"No. You see,"—I looked around conspiratorially, pretended I was letting him on a big secret—"the government pays us to kill the Indians."

Happy to have been supplied with an answer that made sense, Abdul smiled and nodded. "Ahhh," he said. "I see."

Every day in Egypt brought some new and unforgettable experience: a thick, black cloud of sand fleas that descended on us like a plague of locusts during a casual ride through the desert; a solitary stroll behind one of the pyramids in the middle of one of the Grateful Dead's concerts so that I could scatter the ashes of a friend's mother, in accordance with her wishes.

To be perfectly honest, the only time I felt unwelcome in Egypt was during an unpleasant encounter with an American. This happened one afternoon while Johnny Hagen and I were hanging out on stage at the Theater of the Sphinx, right next to the pyramids, taking a break during preparation for that night's show. We watched with amusement as a bus filled with tourists pulled up and disgorged its contents. They spilled out onto the desert floor, waving cameras and pointing and acting appropriately awed—not only by the sight of the pyramids and the Sphinx, but by the incongruity of a rock band setting up in the midst of some much ancient history.

One person, however, found the scene not just amusing, but completely inappropriate. He stepped off the bus, took one look at me and Johnny—with our tie-dyed T-shirts and long hair, surrounded by the tools of of the rock 'n' roll trade—and immediately marched right up to us. He identified himself as an American military officer, a retired general, no less, and demanded to know what we were doing.

"Why are you here?" he asked, his face glowing crimson in the desert sun.

"We're with the Grateful Dead," I responded. "We have a show tonight."

This was not the answer he wanted. I believe he was looking for something more abstract, philosophical, something that would legitimize our presence. What he wanted was for us to understand that our very presence in this place was offensive to him and an affront to all he represented. He had come all this way, to visit a land supposedly untouched by American trash culture, and what does he find?

Rock 'n' roll garbage.

"Who gave you permission to do this?" the general demanded.

Trying to maintain my composure, I explained that our trip, and our performances, had been approved by the U.S. State Department and the Egyptian State Department.

"Names!" he said. "I want a name."

Now I was getting pissed, so I gave him a name, completely fabricated, along with a fictional title. "Check it out," I said. "It's all cool."

The general shook his head in disgust. "You people are a blight on the antiquities of the world."

With that, Hagen laughed and flipped off the general, raising his middle finger so casually and cavalierly that the general went into a temporary state of shock. He wasn't accustomed to dealing with people like Hagen, people who had little or no use for mindless authoritarianism. Finally, the general raised his hand, pointed at us, and shouted, "I want you out of here! Right now!"

Hagen flipped him off again. We were both laughing as the general turned and stormed away, vowing, like MacArthur, to return with a vengeance.

But we never saw him again. We went on with our tour as planned. We bonded with the people of Egypt, and we learned about a whole different culture. We were treated with dignity and respect, and we offered the same in return. And we came to find that despite our differences, there was much we had in common with our Egyptian brothers. For example, around this time the King Tut exhibit was touring the United States. But numerous artifacts from the tomb had been left behind in the Cairo Museum. I was wandering through the museum one day, peering in at all the mundane, everyday things that were reflective of the king's life, when I noticed, deep in the corner, a small basket . . . filled with cannabis seeds!

Hmmmmm . . . wonder why they didn't take that *on the tour.*

Although it was somewhat amusing to imagine the debate over which artifacts would be included in the traveling King Tut exhibit—*"Death masks, yes! Cannabis, no!"*—I felt nothing so much as satisfaction. I felt a oneness with the world, knowing that this ancient civilization had grown pot. It sustained them. It was part of their everyday lives, just as it was part of mine.

And, startlingly, it remained that way even now. In fact, the thing that really blew our minds was that it seemed as though everyone in Egypt had hashish—the young and the old—and they were always trying to give you a piece. Everywhere we went, people were always trying to press bits of hash into our palms, either as a token of their appreciation for something we had done, or simply as a gesture of goodwill and friendship. Man, we loved that.

Of course, coming home to the United States from an environment in which hashish and cannabis are not just tolerated but openly embraced can cause something of a shock to the system. We had nearly seventy-five tons of equipment on the Egyptian tour; as usual, transporting it overseas was a major hassle. The gear arrived at New

York's JFK Airport roughly two weeks after the band and crew. Kid and I drove out in a rental car. Our job was to sign for the equipment, clear it through customs, and pack it up in a truck. Then it would be shipped back to the West Coast. Well, on the way out to the airport, of course, Kid and I shared a joint. (We had a small duffel bag filled with various items, including a small amount of marijuana.) When we arrived at the airport, the joint was snuffed and the weed packed away. But Kid had the bag slung over his shoulder as we strolled through the airport.

We found our gear piled high in a vast room, almost as large as an airplane hanger. Kid and I sat down and waited for the customs officers to arrive so that we could sign for the equipment and get home. A few minutes later a car pulled up, and out stepped two men . . . and a large German Shepherd. We knew right away it was a drug-sniffing dog, and that within seconds he'd be all over the equipment. But we weren't really concerned because it was an unwritten rule among the crew that drugs were never to be transported with the equipment. And we adhered to that rule. But there was one other little problem: the duffel bag. If this dog was any good, he'd eventually make his way to Kid and the bag, and the customs officers would discover the marijuana. It was a small amount, to be sure, but considering the situation—we were sitting in an airport, trying to claim hundreds of thousands of dollars worth of equipment that had been overseas for the past couple months—even this small transgression would result in a major hassle. So Kid stood up and discreetly walked outside and put the duffel bag in the truck. Moments later the dog was turned loose. He leaped up onto the pile of equipment like a mountain goat and began rooting all around, sniffing like crazy. He found nothing, of course, because there was nothing to find.

As Kid and were signing the customs papers, though, the dog suddenly ran across the room and jumped up onto the table where Kid had placed the duffel bag just a short time earlier. The dog went wild, sniffing and whimpering and pawing at something that wasn't there.

"What's wrong with him?" one of the customs officers wondered.

The dog's master walked over, ran his hand across the surface of the table, peered beneath and behind it, then gave the shepherd a friendly scratch behind the ear.

"That's okay, boy," he said. "Nothing here."

Chapter 24

These are people who died,
died. These are people who
died, died. They were all my
friends . . . and they died.

—JIM CARROLL

We lost Heard in 1980, although in truth we'd lost him much earlier than that.

His full name was Clifford Dale Heard, although I never heard anyone call him "Cliff" or "Clifford" and certainly not "Dale." He was "Sonny" or "Sonny Boy" or "C. D." or "C. D. Rambler." Big Mac was his CB handle, and the nickname he preferred, but not many people called him that.

Heard was a ne'er-do-well and a troublemaker, no question about it, but I believe he came by his feistiness honestly. He used to tell me stories about his childhood back in Pendleton (stories corroborated by Ramrod and Jackson, incidentally), and how as a scrawny youngster he routinely got his ass kicked by nearly everyone in town. Then one summer he went off to work at a logging camp and came back a far brawnier lad and got his retribution.

Heard was not the type of guy to worry about burning bridges. He acted and reacted straight from the gut, consequences be damned, and as a result he could be difficult to work with. Heard had problems with most of the people on the crew at one time or another, and with some of the band members, too, but it was an escalating feud with Jackson that led to his being fired from the crew of the Grateful Dead in 1973. Heard was deeply angered by his dismissal, but he continued to hang around the scene for several years afterward. Candace Bright-man took him under her wing and gave him a job on the lighting crew, which sustained him for a few years, until he burned out completely and went back home to Pendleton.

I still don't know why he chose to go back there. It was too small a town for him, with far too much history. I guess he figured had no place else to go. Anyway, Heard wound up marrying a girl and together they had a couple kids and tried to settle down. They used to visit me when the band played up in Portland, and I was always struck by what a wild and untamed region it seemed to be. Pendleton was located in the northeast corner of Oregon, near the Columbia River. It was a rugged, beautiful setting, just the kind of place you'd expect to produce a guy like Sonny Boy Heard. It was also a place fairly teem-ing with outlaw activity.

Heard was not the quiet, introspective sort. He could be a kind and pleasant man when the mood struck him, but he could also be a bully and a braggart—qualities bound to get you in trouble when you're in a small town. Somehow people got it in their heads that Heard had a stash of money at his house, presumably because he was shooting his mouth off and probably flashing a wad of bills now and then. Inevitably, a couple dirtbags came to visit Heard one night at his trailer outside town and tried to rip him off at gunpoint. Even more inevitably, Heard put up a fight and got himself shot. As I understand it, he chased them out of his home while gushing blood from a hole in his chest and died hugging a fencepost on his property. Far from rocket scientists, the assholes who shot Heard were caught almost immediately and sent to prison. Of course, no one much cared about them or the guy they killed.

But I cared, and so did most of the guys on the crew and in the band. Just as we had after Jackson died, we all flew up to Pendelton to attend Heard's funeral and to pay our respects to his family. I'd spent most of the day after Jackson's funeral with his father, and at one point he asked me about Heard, who by that time had been fired from the Dead.

"Whatever happened to that Heard boy?" Mr. Jackson had wondered. "He'd come over in the morning to get Don and give him a ride to high school, and he'd go into his room and steal all his clothes." Mr. Jackson paused, laughed. "Funny kid."

Yes, he was. And when he was at his peak, in the late sixties, early seventies, he was the best of us, a strong, big-hearted man who could work his ass off. Heard was the kind of guy who would walk into a hotel lobby—and I'm talking about some of the finest hotels in the world—and throw his leather satchel thirty feet across the floor, where it would stop only after crashing into the registration desk. Then he'd walk up to the receptionist, slam his fist on the counter and shout, "Heard's the name, rock 'n' roll's the game. Gimme my fuckin' room!" Everyone would be shocked. Except us, of course. We'd just laugh and shake our heads. That was Heard at his best, and it's the way I'll always remember him.

That same year saw the death of Keith Godchaux, another indirect casualty of drugs. Keith had been dismissed from the Grateful Dead in 1979, ostensibly for "creative differences." But it was more complicated than that.

To put it bluntly, Keith and Jerry were both junkies, and they were junkies together, along with John Kahn. One of the most sinister things about addiction is the way it changes people, makes them nervous and paranoid and focused primarily on the pursuit of the next high. In time they learn to put their trust primarily in other junkies, and so cliques are formed. Over the years I watched many of my friends succumb to this illness, and saw firsthand the terrible toll it took on their personalities as well as their bodies, especially when we were off in the Garcia Band and there were fewer buffers between the crew and the band. I'm not saying we didn't get along, or that we fought incessantly over drug use. It wasn't like that, mainly because none of us was Simon pure. I liked my weed, acid, nitrous, and an occasional toot of coke. Though I knew in my heart that heroin was a different animal, one with extraordinary parasitic ability, I wasn't aggressive in rooting out the users or confronting them on their behavior. Right or wrong, I didn't feel it was my place to judge them. Looking back on it, I wish I had been stronger.

But we remained friends even through the worst of times. You can't hang out together on the road for ten years, or twenty years, making every joke possible, examining every nook and cranny of the human experience, getting to know the most intimate details of each person's life, without forming a bond of steel. We had always talked with each other openly and freely. We were friends. We were family. And that didn't change. The heroin and the coke never stood in the way of our friendships; but they made things more complicated. You'd be hanging out together, having fun, and suddenly, one by one, the junkies would drift off, and you knew precisely what was happening. They'd pretend that it wasn't any big deal, but the very fact that they had disappeared reflected a level of self-consciousness and embarrassment that spoke volumes. We smoked pot right out in the open. We had nitrous parties. We whipped up fucking vats of acid punch. Heroin was done in the dark, in the shadows, in places that weren't meant to be seen.

Jerry, Keith, and John were all in the same sad shape, and as a result they became thick as thieves, united in their never-ending quest to score. These guys shared dealers, they shared drugs, they shared paraphernalia. They shared secrets and lies. Jerry remained one of the most gifted and charismatic artists in rock 'n' roll. He was the Grateful Dead, and it was possible, even necessary, to forgive him almost anything, and to indulge all manner of bad behavior. Keith didn't have that luxury, which is why he was nudged off the stage.

After leaving the Grateful Dead, Keith and Donna formed the Heart of Gold Band, but that group never released an album and performed only one live concert before Keith was killed in an automobile accident in Marin County on July 23, 1980. He was thirty-three years old.

The band lost another friend in the spring of 1982, when John Belushi passed away. We'd gotten to know John through a strange set of circumstances, beginning with a Grateful Dead show at Winterland in 1976, which also happened to be the landmark first season of NBC's *Saturday Night Live*. In the middle of the show two guys in their late twenties came bounding up the steps leading to the stage. They looked respectable and harmless enough, but I had no idea who they were or what business they had in our sanctuary. So I did what I typically did in those situations: I blocked their path.

"Can I help you gentlemen?"

"Yeah, we're friends of Candace Brightman."

I said nothing.

"The lighting girl?"

"Yeah . . . so what?"

They looked at each other, as if confused by the fact that I wasn't impressed by their name-dropping.

"She said we could come up here and hang out."

I put one hand on each of their shoulders and started to turn them around. "Tell you what. Why don't you get the fuck out of here? And tell Candace to keep her friends out there with her. Okay?"

They shrugged and walked away, presumably to watch the show with the rest of the audience. I really didn't give it another thought until I talked with Candace a few days later and she explained who they were: Al Franken and Tom Davis, a couple of Deadheads who were also writers for *Saturday Night Live.* And they were indeed good friends with Candace. But I didn't apologize for tossing them off the stage. We were overrun with fans and friends who wanted to hang out backstage or onstage or right next to the stage, and we had to be fairly aggressive in keeping the place clean and clear (and we never really could accomplish that).

Well, about a month later, while out on tour with the Garcia Band, we came back to the hotel after a Saturday night show, just to grab a shower. Then we'd get in the trucks and drive to the next city for the next show. I was getting undressed as *Saturday Night Live* came on the air. Art Garfunkel was the host. I sort of half-watched the opening monologue and then ducked into the shower just as they started a skit. By the time I came out there was a commercial break. I got dressed, turned off the TV, and left the hotel.

The next day I got more than a dozen phones calls from friends and relatives.

"Hey, Steve, did you see *Saturday Night Live?*"

"No, why?"

Apparently, while I was in the shower, I had missed the debut of the infamous "Steve Parish Sketch," in which John Belushi played an overzealous and basically clueless backstage sentry at a rock concert. Some of details were changed—it was a KISS concert, rather than a Grateful Dead concert—but the point was clear. Belushi's character played hard-ass with a couple record company executives, refusing to grant them backstage access, even as dozens of shady characters—

including some carting tanks of nitrous oxide—sneaked in. In the end one of the record company suits asked Belushi for his name.

"Steve Parish," he said, thrusting his chest forward.

The record company executive frowned and said, "Parish, you'll never work in this business again."

So Franken and Davis got their revenge, and I got a chance to be immortalized in a sketch featuring the great John Belushi. Shortly thereafter, John started hanging out with us. He was a great guy, so funny and sensitive and energetic. And what timing he had. In 1977, when the Grateful Dead were in New York trying to finish up the *Terrapin Station* album, things were pretty bad between me and Mickey. We were approaching the end of our working relationship, and we were fighting like crazy. He was accusing me of trying to undermine his efforts, and, worse, of being unattentive, which was ridiculous. Whatever flaws I may have had, a reluctance to work was not one of them. Anyway, I was just exasperated by Mickey and his outrageous demands. We hadn't been able to complete overdubs in the studio in California, so I had to bring all of Mickey's stuff to New York, where we were doing a week-long run at Madison Square Garden. Every night we'd finish the show, and then Mickey, Jerry, Ramrod, and I would trek off to a studio in Manhattan to work on the album. We wouldn't get to sleep until six or seven in the morning, which left all of us exhausted and irritable.

I don't mean to rag on Mickey too badly. The truth is, he's an amazing musician who comes up with ingenious ways to capture sounds that previously existed only in his mind. We'd hang brake drums from the ceiling and beat on them with hammers. We'd utilize car doors, firecrackers—anything and everything at our disposal. Mickey's creativity and attention to detail later helped him land the job as a composer for the soundtrack of *Apocalypse Now*, which was another interesting, tension-filled project, because the director, Francis Ford Coppola, was every bit as much of a neurotic perfectionist as was Mickey.

So I appreciated and admired Mickey's ability, but I just couldn't stand working with him any longer. And he didn't want me working for him. The hostility boiled over in the studio late one night (or early in the morning—it was 4 A.M.!) when Mickey asked me to set up an "instrument" he needed for a particular sound effect. Basically, it was just a collection of seashells dangling from a series of wires. When tickled just right, they would produce the breezy, delicate sound that Mickey wanted. Unfortunately, just as we were about to begin recording, the shells tipped over and smashed on the floor. Mickey froze for a moment and then glared at me. I could tell he was about to blow up, and if he had, I was prepared to get right back in his face. All of a sudden, in walked John Belushi. I don't know whether John sensed trouble, or if he simply did this sort of thing all the time, but his entrance defused the situation beautifully. He blew in through the door and immediately went into his most famous move, that whirling, off-balance cartwheel that so often highlighted his performances with the Blues Brothers. It was amazing to see him do that in person, not only because he was pretty nimble for a rotund lad, but also because . . . well, because nobody did that kind of thing. But John did, and at that moment we were all thankful for his spontaneity and joyous sense of humor. It was a great rock 'n' roll moment. Everyone laughed, including me and Mickey. We sat around shot the breeze with John for a while, then I fixed the seashells, and we all went back to work.

The last time I saw John was about ten days before he died. It was during a show at UCLA's Pauly Pavilion and John was hanging around backstage. He was in great comedic form, wearing his porkpie hat and glasses, his black Blues Brothers suit—even when he wasn't performing he sometime adopted the persona of Jake Blues, which was kind of weird, but also pretty cool. At one point that night he came up to me and said, slyly, "Steve, what do you want?" Then he opened his jacket to reveal an elastic strip sewn into the breast. Running the length of the strip were more than a dozen plastic or glass vials filled with powders and pills of every color and size. "I got it all, man. Just tell me what you need."

As we all later discovered, John was on the bender to end all benders around that time. On March 5, 1982, he was discovered in a Hollywood bungalow, the victim of a lethal speedball injection. He was only thirty-one years old.

And then there was Nicky Hopkins, the great British keyboard player. From the mid 1960s to the early 1980s, Nicky was among the busiest of session players, lending his creative genius to an astonishing list of A-list performers, including the Beatles, the Who, the Kinks, Eric Clapton, the Rolling Stones, Jeff Beck, Jefferson Airplane, and Rod Stewart. I got to know Nicky when he joined the Garcia Band for a while in the mid- to late seventies. Nicky was a brilliant piano player and a wonderful, funny guy, but life had dealt him more than his fair share of personal problems.

The road was too much for Nicky, who was a prodigious drinker (his beverage of choice was a tall glass of tequila tempered only by a few drops of orange juice) with an assortment of physical ailments. And though he preferred session work, the road was at times his escape hatch. Nicky had a crazy home life that included a temperamental wife who was a former groupie from England. She and Nicky were always fighting over one thing or another, and when it got to be too much for him he'd head out on the road. But Nicky required a lot of baby-sitting. More than once I can recall sitting at the airport, preparing to board a flight, and discovering that Nicky was missing. I'd find him a little while later, lying on top of a counter, stone drunk, crying his eyes out.

"Christ, Steve . . . I lost me mates," he'd wail. "I lost me mates!"

Nicky preferred the shadows to the spotlight, but sometimes when the booze took over, he'd nudge his way toward the center of the stage. I remember one particular Garcia Band gig at the Oasis in Sacramento, on a hot, sticky night, when Nicky grabbed the microphone and shouted, "You don't mind if I take me shirt off, do you?"

Caught off guard, Jerry just stopped playing and stared at Nicky, no doubt wondering what would happen next.

"See . . . I've got this great big scar here," Nicky went on, pulling shirt up over his head to reveal a long, purple ribbon of gnarled flesh stretching across his belly—an Englishman's scar, we called it, emblematic as it was of what we saw as the Brits' tendency to have stomach problems. So here was Nicky, rail thin and bare-chested, drinking his awful firewater, standing over his keyboard. But instead of playing, or even explaining the scar that supposedly precipitated this interlude in the first place, he launched into a story about his favorite pet, a cat named Pig whose periodic strolls across the top of Nicky's keyboard inspired some of his greatest work. And then the story was over and the concert went on.

That's what it was like with Nicky. For a while, anyway. He lasted only a short time with the Garcia Band, and though he recorded with the likes of Steve Miller, Graham Parker, and Paul McCartney in the 1980s, his health continued to decline. Nicky passed away in 1994, at the age of fifty, from what was described as complications related to previous intestinal surgeries. He was a gentle soul, and I'll always miss him.

Chapter 25

1981-

We were in the middle of a load-out at one of Bill Graham's Bay Area clubs, a place called the old Waldorf, the first time I saw her. She was tall and lean, with reddish-blond hair and friendly eyes, and I couldn't stop looking at her. Eventually our eyes locked and she smiled, and I took that opportunity to strike up a conversation, even as I continued to reel in a couple miles of cable. Her name was Lorraine Doremus and she was originally from New York. Like a lot of people who had moved to California, Lorraine was in the process of finding herself. She'd graduated from high school, served time in the

U.S. Army, and then worked for a while as a topless dancer, none of which made her very happy. So she'd drifted out to the West Coast and was now staying with some friends in San Mateo while planning the next phase of her life.

There was an exchange of phone numbers, a couple interactions that could generously be called "dates," and then for some reason she fell in love with me, and I fell in love with her, despite the fact that I was about the worst candidate imaginable for domestication. Although I hadn't succumbed to the lure of heroin and cocaine the way so many others in our circle had, I was nevertheless leading a dangerous and wild life. I was on the road all the time, working for both the Garcia Band and the Grateful Dead, and when I wasn't on the road I lived on the back of a motorcycle. I was so wild that around this time I got really drunk one night, crashed my bike, and wound up breaking my shoulder in four places. (The injury was severe enough that I had to bring my dear friend and motorcycle mechanic, Billy Grillo, on the road to help out with the Grateful Dead. Billy and Corky—George Varra—became part of my hand-picked Garcia crew.) To put it mildly, I was not the "settling down" type.

But that was okay with Lorraine. Within a couple weeks of our first meeting she had moved in with me, apparently content to share her life with a man who wanted no part of a traditional family, and who had no idea what the word "commitment" meant, proclamations of love notwithstanding. This happened to a lot of guys on the crew and in the band. We all had women who hung out with us; those who eventually moved into our homes were often referred to as "housekeepers." It wasn't a term of derision, really, but it certainly wasn't born of respect. Rather, it was a way to categorize the relationship in clinical terms. I didn't want a wife or a mother or, God forbid, a soulmate. I wanted someone to have sex with . . . someone who would clean the house and cook my meals and be happy that I was paying the bills, so happy that they wouldn't care what I did while I was on the road. They would ask nothing of me and expect even less. But a funny thing sometimes happened with these types of arrangements: you'd be hanging out together, essentially playing house, and things would change. It was inevitable. You'd be sleeping together, having fun, sharing major parts of your life, and suddenly you'd develop feelings you hadn't anticipated. Feelings that had some legitimate depth.

That's what happened with me and Lorraine. Sort of. I can say with complete honesty that I loved her, but I didn't respect her enough to abandon my selfish ways. I continued to have one life at home and another life on the road. I wasn't going to deny myself anything. In one sense, though, I'd made some progress: I didn't lie. I told Lorraine what I was like and how I lived my life and that I had no intention of changing. I'm sure she didn't like that, but she put up with it pretty well. So well, in fact, that for a while she was willing to share our home and our bed with other women.

One of them was Suzette, another gorgeous exotic dancer I met in Denver, right around the same time I met Lorraine. Dancers were usually a lot of fun, and I'd gotten to know many of them throughout the country. They liked to come to the shows, they liked to party, and they had low expectations. By this time I'd spent enough time walking on the wild side to know exactly what it was like to be with two women at one time, and how to make that fantasy happen, if only for a few hours, maybe a few days. For some reason, though, I got it into my head that I could have two women for an extended period of time, that both Lorraine and Suzette would be happy living with me, sharing me. You know, like *Three's Company*, only better, because we'd actually be having sex.

It was a crazy idea, really. I'd seen other guys—like Dan Healy—try it out, and it was difficult and required an enormous amount of patience (a quality I lacked). Most of us preferred the "girl in every port" approach. They were much easier to please and manipulate, for you saw them only a few times each year. But two old ladies under a single roof? That was rare.

Somehow I thought I could be the exception to the rule, the one man who could smoothly incorporate multiple women into his home life without anyone getting jealous or angry or petty. So I started bringing Suzette out to California, where she'd stay with me and Lorraine for a few days at a time. Before long the three of us were living together, and we developed an amazingly open and generous three-way relationship. Then I met Joanne, a beautiful girl from San Diego, and after she moved north it became a four-way relationship, and I was—how can I put this?—well, I was in heaven.

Then the strangest and most unexpected thing began to happen: Instead of becoming more sensitive to their needs, and more caring and nurturing to these three wonderful women, I became an asshole. Instead of the women experiencing jealousy or envy or regret, or any other feelings that would cause our complicated relationship to crumble, I was the one who became weird about the whole thing. I'd favor one woman over the other. I'd treat them differently for no reason at all. Or maybe there was a reason. Maybe, subconsciously, I wanted it to fall apart. Maybe that's why I started leaning on Lorraine, treating her more like a domestic partner and less like a plaything, while not extending the same courtesy to the others. Whatever the reason, we soon drifted apart. Joanne was the first to go, although there was no bitter breakup, no face-slapping, no venom of any kind. In fact, I will always consider her a good friend and a remarkable woman. And then Suzette started to drift off, again, with no hard feelings, but rather with the idea that it was simply time to move on. That left Lorraine, who walked out of the bedroom one day with a smile on her face and told me she was pregnant, and that I was the father, and the air rushed out of me in a single breath and the world turned upside down.

I'd been told news of this sort only once before, several years earlier. But the circumstances and outcome were much different. I came home one rainy afternoon and found my girlfriend sitting in the living room, looking sad and depressed. I asked what was bothering her and she told me she'd just returned from the doctor's office, where she'd had an abortion. My initial reaction, I'm embarrassed to say, was not sympathy, but anger. I hadn't even known that she was pregnant.

"You're kidding!" I said. "Why didn't you consult me? Don't I have any say in this?"

She shook her head, wiped away a tear. "Are you kidding? I'm going to have a child with you? The way you live? It's out of the question."

She was absolutely right, of course. Still, at the time, it hurt to know that I might have been a father, and to have been denied any input into the decision-making process. So when Lorraine woke up that morning in December of 1982 and said, "I've been late, I just took a test, and I'm pregnant," all I could do was smile. I was filled with awe. A baby! And she wanted to have it—with me! And I wanted to have it. God only knows why, but I did.

For a brief, mind-boggling time, I honestly felt that I was up to the task of being a husband and a father. I wasn't, though. Pretty soon I was back out on the road, living the way I had always lived. Along the way Lorraine hinted a few times at the possibility of our getting married, but I wouldn't even consider it. I covered all her medical expenses, made sure the bills were paid at home, and that she could afford to buy whatever she needed in the way of clothing and food. When I was home we slept together and held hands and acted like a young couple in love, a couple about to become a family.

Jennifer was born on September 3, 1983. I'd like to say that I was there at Lorraine's side, coaching her through labor, wiping her brow as she did all the work. But that would be another lie. I was on a stage in Park City, Utah, working a Grateful Dead concert. At the very moment Jennifer was born, I was crawling across the stage floor to fix something on Bob Weir's gear. When I got it fixed and returned backstage, Danny Rifkin told me Lorraine was on the phone, and that I had a baby girl. It saddened me not to be there, and I did feel some guilt and shame about that, although not so much that it prevented me from partying wildly at the hotel later that night, celebrating the birth of my baby daughter by having mad sex with a bunch of strippers a thousand miles from home. That's the kind of man I was, that's the kind of life I led.

Ready or not, responsibility was thrown at me in clumps. First a child, then a new job. In 1984, for reasons that I couldn't really articulate clearly at the time, I followed Jackson and others down the dark path of management. It happened more out of necessity than anything else. It wasn't like I was hungry for power or control. The fact is, Rock Scully, who was managing the Garcia Band and was publicist for the Grateful Dead, had become so dysfunctional that everyone was beginning to suffer. Everywhere we went, people were talking about him: "Where's Rock? What's wrong with him? Is he going to be okay?" Covering up for him and compensating for his problems became an overwhelming chore.

Rock wrote a book a while back in which he accused me of sandbagging him at a meeting, but that wasn't my view of it. We'd all been talking about Rock and his inability to function for some time. As a rule, though, confrontation was not a strong suit of the members of the Grateful Dead. Problems were allowed to fester for almost unlimited amounts of time, until someone either quit or died and the problem went away. This time, though, I stood up at a meeting and confronted Rock. I told him, in no uncertain terms, "Rock, this can't go on any longer." Everyone else agreed, and Rock was dismissed. I felt bad about his departure and my role in it, but I also felt it was necessary if the two bands were to avoid chaos and self-destruction.

It was a natural move for me to step into the dual role of road manager and band manager for the Garcia Band, not only because I'd been working so closely with Jerry for nearly fifteen years, but also because I'd kept a close eye on the managers who had gone before me. I'd followed their accomplishments and their mistakes, and I was reasonably sure that I could avoid many of the pitfalls that had ruined their careers. It helped that I had a wonderful and capable assistant in Sue Stephens, who had been taking care of the Garcia Band's paperwork for years. It also helped that Jerry was a generous and trusting employer, especially when it came to money. By industry standards, everyone associated with the Garcia Band was compensated extremely well. We'd finish a tour and Jerry would say, "How much money did we make?" I'd tell him and he'd just smile and nod. "Good. Now make sure you pay everyone well. You've all earned it." Jerry never dictated salaries, never sat around and counted the money. He left that to me, partly because he knew we'd be fair, but also because he just hated dealing with those kinds of things. Business, as most people know, was not one of Jerry's strong suits. He was first, foremost, and always, an artist. I felt a tremendous responsibility to prove myself worthy of his trust, to the point where I gave everyone in the band as much money as I possibly could, certainly more than I ever paid myself. The crew was paid handsomely, too—I still worked as a member of the crew of the Grateful Dead and I understood and sympathized with them, so I made sure they felt their efforts were appreciated. And Jerry wanted it that way. Whatever problems he may have had, whatever demons tormented him, Jerry always loved and respected anyone who was dedicated to him and his music.

Included in that group, of course, was Bill Graham, a true giant in the industry. I had learned a great deal about the music business from Bill, so when I took over as manager of the Garcia Band, one of my goals was to enrich our relationship with him. At the time, Bill was handling promotion for our West Coast shows, while John Scher, another dear friend, handled promotion on the East Coast. I spent a lot of time hanging out with Bill after shows in the Bay Area, talking and drinking and smoking, and sometimes we'd discuss the possibility of him becoming more involved, of promoting some of our shows back East, just as he'd done in the early days. But this was a tricky concept, since we also had a strong relationship with John Scher.

"If we're going to work together on the East Coast," I said to Bill, "it can't be in one of John's theaters. It's going to have to be something really unique."

Bill agreed, and together we came up with the idea of bringing the Garcia Band to Broadway. Not just for a night or two, but for an extended run. And that's how the Jerry Garcia Band became the first rock 'n' roll act to play Broadway. We played twelve shows in fourteen days at the Lunt-Fontanne Theatre in late 1987. It was an exhausting but successful engagement that opened the door for us to work with Bill anywhere in the country.

By working with both John Scher and Bill Graham, two of the best in the business, I got a crash course in management and promotion. I watched the way they worked, and I compared their styles. I absorbed as much as I could. Admittedly, by doing this I not only helped myself, but jeopardized my personal and professional relationship with John. But he proved to be an even better friend than I had suspected. I know John was hurt by our decision to work with Bill on the East Coast, but he did not hold a grudge, and he continued to promote some of our shows.

While coping with my new professional responsibilities, I tried to be a decent father, though I really didn't know what that entailed. I hadn't planned on starting a family, but I had one nonetheless, and I was surprised by the feelings it engendered. We bought a little house together in Sonoma County, and several months later, in the spring of 1984, Lorraine became pregnant again. I was shocked at how quickly it had happened, until I talked with Kesey one night and he just laughed and put the proper cosmic spin on the situation.

"Man, didn't you ever have puppies when you were a boy?"

"Nah, I was a city kid."

"Well, all females get pregnant real quick when they're nesting. Remember that next time, huh?"

It was Lorraine's idea to get married. She'd brought it up a few times in the past, but never in a hostile or threatening way. I had always said no, never thought it was all that important. Now, though, everything was changing. I had one child and a second on the way. Lorraine asked me again one day to marry her. She didn't beg, didn't yell or cry, just expressed her desire earnestly and simply, as was her custom.

"All right," I said. "Why not?"

In some abstract way I liked the idea of getting married, settling down, raising a family. My desire to take care of these two little babies was completely sincere, although in reality I wasn't even remotely prepared for the task. Nevertheless, our union was formally and legally recognized during a small civil ceremony in Marin County. There was no honeymoon, no "wedding." Just me and Lorraine and a friend of ours named Janet Knudsen, a secretary for the band who had agreed to act as a witness. We exchanged vows, rings, kisses . . . and then we went home.

The months rolled by. As usual I spent a lot of my time on the road. Professionally, I'd never been busier. I liked the challenge of managing the Garcia Band, and I still enjoyed working as part of the Dead crew. Regardless of which band I was with, I never let go of the equipment, because that's where my heart was. Through the equipment I was connected to the music, which was bigger and more important than any job.

As for my home life, well, everything had changed . . . and nothing had changed. Lorraine and I got along just fine, and Jennifer was a beautiful little girl, toddling all over the house, crashing into things and smiling from the moment she woke until the time she fell asleep in her mother's arms. Or, sometimes, in my arms. I'd cradle her and sing to her, and like any new father I was awed by the very fact of her existence. When I was around, that is. Most of the time I was neither a husband nor a father; I was just a man who happened to have a wife and a child and another child on the way. On the road I behaved pretty much as I'd always behaved. A part of me wanted to change, but it was a small part. I wasn't ready.

Lorraine didn't push me, either. She was reasonably content to stay home and raise our family without much help from me. I bought her a Buick station wagon and sent her to driving school so that she could be self-sufficient when I was away, but she was a slow learner. Even after she got her license and learned how to traverse the tricky back roads of Marin County—the winding, mountainous county two-lanes that are far less traveled but no less dangerous than the interstates—she was never more than a competent driver. But she was careful. She always told me that.

On December 27, 1984, the night before the Grateful Dead was scheduled to begin their three-day run-up to their annual New Year's Eve show at Civic Center in San Francisco, the strangest and most mystifying thing happened. (I don't particularly care if anyone believes it or not.) While Jennifer slept peacefully in the next room, Lorraine and I were lying in bed together, watching an old movie on television. Lorraine had never seen *It's a Wonderful Life,* and of course she thought it was a beautiful story with a wonderful, life-affirming message. Sure it's sappy, but when you're eight and a half months pregnant and it's the Christmas season, cynicism doesn't come easily. When the movie ended, I turned out the light and held Lorraine close. I put a hand on her belly and felt the baby stir. She was in the final weeks of her pregnancy then, and while she was tired and uncomfortable, she was in generally good spirits. She was thrilled at the prospect of having another child, and so was I. In fact, I was trying to be a better person, a better father and husband. I didn't want to deny my family. I wanted to be there for them.

The next morning, around seven o'clock, Lorraine woke up screaming. She'd been having a nightmare.

"Something is pulling me off this earth!" she gasped. I rolled over and put my arms around, tried to comfort her. She pushed me back, looked me straight in the eyes, and said it again. "Steve . . . something is pulling me."

"It's okay," I said, kissing her forehead. "Everything will be all right."

Late that morning I drove into town to start setting up for the show. We'd been to a holiday party at a friend's house in Woodacre the previous evening, and Lorraine had mistakenly left her purse behind. She said she was going to drive there to retrieve the purse in the afternoon, and then call me to discuss the possibility of joining me at the show.

I checked in a few hours later, just as Lorraine was getting ready to leave. She was running late and hadn't yet picked up her purse. I told her I'd see her when I got home. I told her to drive carefully.

When I walked through the front door shortly after midnight, I was immediately struck by the stillness of our house. It was never that quiet, not even when Lorraine and Jennifer were sleeping. I checked the bedrooms. Both empty. I paced the floor for a few minutes, wondering where they might be. I tried not jump to conclusions, tried not to panic. Then I sat down in a chair and waited. This will probably sound strange, but I didn't call the police, or anyone else for that matter. Something did not feel right. I thought about the dream, and about Lorraine and Jennifer out there on the road somewhere. It didn't make sense that she would just disappear like this, that she wouldn't call.

I didn't sleep at all, just sat there in the living room, staring out the window, waiting for them to come home. Finally, around eight o'clock, there was a knock at the door, and I opened it to find a dour-looking gentleman with hat in hand standing on my front steps.

"Mr. Parish?"

"Yes."

"I'm very sorry," he said. "I have some bad news."

My knees buckled. I had trouble breathing. "They're dead, aren't they?"

He lowered his head. "Please . . . may I come in?"

"Not the baby, too. God . . . not the baby."

He held me up and walked me into the house. Then we sat down together in the living room as he delivered the kind of news that no one should have to deliver. He was the county coroner, so I'm sure he'd done this sort of thing before, but that made it no less painful. He told me there had been a car accident the previous night, that Lorraine was apparently driving back home from Woodacre when she failed to negotiate a sharp turn and crashed into a tree. She had died at the scene, along with our unborn child. Jennifer had survived the initial crash but was critically injured. Paramedics had taken her to a nearby hospital and worked furiously to save her life, but it was too late. She died shortly after arriving.

The next thing I knew I was out in the street, crying, running. A neighbor came out and stopped me. She grabbed me by the arms and pulled me close. "I'm so sorry," she said. "I thought you knew. The police were here last night and I told them you were working in the city. Why didn't they come and tell you?"

I had no answer. I had no answer for anything. All I knew was that my world had collapsed, that my entire family had been wiped off the planet with a single breath. Just like that. They were all gone.

I went back into the house and called Lorraine's parents. We had met once before, when Lorraine and I took Jennifer back East for a visit, but I didn't know them well. I'd spent most of my time on that trip working with the band, which was playing in New York. It was always work for me. Work, work, work. Work came first. Play came second. Family third. Always. I don't really remember exactly what I told them. I remember kind of spitting out the grim facts and then handing the phone off to the coroner to let him finish the job as Lorraine's mom and dad cried on the other end. Then I got a phone call from Peter Barsotti, one of Bill Graham's lieutenants, who had a question about the show, and I told him what had happened. He made a few phone calls and quickly the word spread. People started coming over. By early afternoon my house was full. Everyone from the crew had stopped by to offer their condolences, to do whatever they could, which, of course, was nothing. Everyone from the band came, too—

everyone except Jerry, who was too disturbed and shaken by the incident to come by in person. He could be that way: socially awkward to the point of embarrassment.

I forget who first made the suggestion, but it was quickly determined that the Grateful Dead should cancel its shows for the next few days. But I said, no, that would serve no purpose. Again, I know it sounds crazy, but I felt the only way I could survive that experience was to get back to work, to be with the band and the crew, making music, doing the things I loved. It was distraction therapy, I know, but I had no alternative. I'd lost two children and a wife. I wasn't thinking clearly. I knew only that I couldn't just sit there and cry. Nothing made sense. Nothing except the music.

So we did the show that night, and the night after that, and the night after that. And it was remarkable experience, the way the guys in the band and the guys on the crew all rallied around me and hugged me and propped me up and told me how much they loved me. I should also say that Billy Crowe, along with Mickey Hart, insisted on going to the coroner's office to identify the body so that I wouldn't have to do it. They didn't think I could handle that sort of trauma, and maybe they were right. I don't know. Several people from the band stayed with me for the next several weeks, taking turns feeding me, talking with me, making sure I was all right. Phil Lesh and his wife, Jill, were immensely giving and thoughtful. They were just starting their lives together, and their love was so strong and pure and clear that it had a palpable effect on me. It made me smile, made me think of the possibilities that life can bring. Bobby Weir stayed with me for days on end, listening to music, talking, just hanging out, the way friends do.

And then there was Jerry . . .

That first night, when I got to the show, Jerry approached me backstage and gave me a hug. He seemed so sad, so moved by my loss. And then, in a twisted but genuinely loving gesture, he did something that astounded me.

"Hey, man," he said, his eyes brimming with tears. "You want some heroin? It'll kill the pain."

I thanked him but declined the offer. "If I did anything right now—one snort, one drink—I'd never stop."

He nodded and told me again how sorry he was. In that instant I felt more pity for Jerry than I did for myself, because he really was trying to help. He just didn't know any other way.

Chapter 26

Death was no stranger to me. I'd lost a number of friends and felt the pain of their absence on an almost daily basis. Jackson, Heard, Pigpen, Badger, Keith—the world, or at least my little corner of it, was a sadder, quieter place without them in it. But this was entirely different. The death of a child, especially, points out the inherent unpredictability, unfairness, and fragility of life. Nothing is certain, nothing is secure.

I became well acquainted with grief after the accident. First I tried to deal with it by sweeping Lorraine and the children out of my life, by putting all of their pictures in boxes and turning the nursery into a guest bedroom. *Out of sight, out of mind,* I told myself. But of course I was wrong. Grief, I learned, is something that can't be ignored. It must be dealt with and released. If you let it stay inside, it boils up and completely dominates your life. It can and will make you sick, so you have to get it out of you. I accomplished this process—or perhaps I just avoided it—in a way that seemed perfectly natural to me, a way that suited my lifestyle, a way that you might consider silly or selfish or shallow. But it worked. I used sex to get over my loss.

There were so many women in the Bay Area whom I considered to be my friends, and they came to me and held me and cried with me and slept with me. Friends offered me their wives and girlfriends (I know how that sounds, but it really wasn't a grotesque gesture; it was a gesture borne of kindness and tenderness). It was, for me, a sexual healing. I was still numb with grief, and this was a way to feel something, to feel good for a short time, and to connect with another human being in the most intimate way possible. It was a respite from the solitude and the suffering, strange as that may sound.

On the day Lorraine and Jennifer died, Billy Crowe held me close and whispered, "Life will draw you back into it, man. Just have faith." I had my doubts for a while, but after taking a couple months off from work I started to get restless, and I knew it was time to get back on the road. Pretty soon I was doing double-duty all over again, managing the Garcia Band and working with the Grateful Dead crew, and feeling useful and alive, if not completely whole.

It's interesting how our lives become intertwined in so many unusual ways. Years earlier, back in the early 1970s, we used to stay at the Watergate Hotel whenever we were in Washington, D.C. (That's right, the very same Watergate where Richard Nixon had his problems.) On one stop with the Garcia Band I met a young lady named Barbara who ran the hotel limousine service. She was a tall, athletically built girl with a big taste for partying and we hit it off right away. She became my Washington girlfriend, someone I saw whenever I was in town with either the Dead or the Garcia Band. Barbara had grown up in San Diego and was, despite her relocation to the East Coast, a real fun-loving California girl. I enjoyed spending time with her and we kept in touch over the years, even after we stopped sleeping together. She was a good friend and under different circumstances we might have ended up together, but she was smart enough to know that I was a bad investment back then, that I was just too wild and crazy.

Anyway, Barbara eventually moved back to San Diego. A few months after Lorraine died, the Grateful Dead was scheduled to play a show in Irvine, California, which is roughly halfway between Los Angeles and San Diego. When we got into town I called Barbara, ostensibly just to chat, although I'm sure that in the back of my mind I was hoping she'd show up and contribute to my healing process. She was a loving and compassionate person—I had no doubt she'd rush to my side.

And I was right. Sort of.

"I'm coming to the show," she said. I smiled at the receiver. It had been a few years since Barbara and I had been together, and I was looking forward to seeing her. "And I'm bringing my friend Marilyn with me."

"Marilyn?"

"Yeah . . . you'll like her. See you in a while."

This wasn't exactly what I had planned, but I quickly warmed to the idea. Maybe this evening would turn out even better than I had anticipated.

Marilyn was a longtime friend of Barbara who could not in any way be described as a Deadhead. Nor was she into the party scene that was so much a part of the Grateful Dead experience. What she was, in a word, was . . . stunning. I'd left passes for them at the back door and told security to page me when they showed up, which turned out to be halfway through the show, during a break between sets. I had my own little spot on the stage, from which I directed traffic and barked out orders. As they walked into view I waved at Barbara, and she waved back. Then my eyes moved to Marilyn . . . and the lightning bolt struck.

240

I can honestly say that what I experienced was love at first sight. Marilyn was tall, poised, well proportioned, with shimmering blonde hair and the face of an angel. Like Barbara she appeared to be a true California girl, so I was surprised to learn that she'd actually grown up in Great Falls, Montana. I couldn't imagine a place like that holding her, keeping her in check, and indeed it couldn't. Marilyn had left home shortly after graduating from high school and settled in Los Angeles, where she received her college degree and worked in the fashion industry. Our conversation was light and comfortable, and I did my best to be cool, despite the fact that I was enormously attracted to her. She told me that she'd also worked as a flight attendant and hadn't cared for it, and that she'd been married briefly and hadn't care for that, either. She was divorced now, but had no children. She was looking for a change in her life, she said, and I sensed by the way she said it that she wasn't the type to run off to a hotel room with a man she'd just met. Maybe she had been at one time—I didn't know for sure—but not anymore. She was a grownup, and a formidable one at that.

I acted like a goofy schoolboy around her, a reaction she'd surely provoked in the past, but she didn't seem to mind. She was three years younger than me but clearly wise to the ways of the world. As the break came to an end we exchanged phone numbers. Then, as they walked away, I picked up a bullhorn and proclaimed my undying love for Marilyn:

"I AM GOING TO MARRY THIS WOMAN!"

Marilyn just laughed. "Let's see if you even call me," she said. Then she waved goodbye.

I did call her. The very next day, in fact. And the day after that. For the next two weeks we talked just about every day on the phone and got to know each other a little bit. Then Marilyn flew up to the Bay Area to take in another show, and we wound up spending a very passionate couple of days together. We hit it off really well, physically, emotionally, mentally. In addition to being beautiful, I thought Marilyn was a genuinely warm and sensitive person. She liked me, too, she said, although she did acknowledge a certain apprehension about the world in which I lived. She thought my job was strange (which it was), and she was concerned about all the scary and dangerous people who seemed to exist at the corners of the Grateful Dead scene—mainly the bikers, both causal and hardcore. My whole lifestyle was just too weird for her.

"You seem like a good guy," she said before returning to Los Angeles. "But I don't know where I'd fit into any of this. It's just a little too bizarre."

Not that Marilyn was an innocent. She'd been through a few things, enough to know what she wanted and did not want out of life. What she hadn't experienced, and had no desire to experience, was the life of a Deadhead. To me the rock 'n' roll life, with its abundance of drugs, groupies, and Hells Angels, was perfectly normal. To Marilyn it was like something out of a bad dream. She wasn't a hippie at all. She was a smart, lucid woman who didn't want to waste her time with someone who simply wouldn't be there for her when she needed him; someone whose lifestyle was so narcissistic that he couldn't possibly make a good partner.

But I wouldn't let her go that easily. Knowing how much we liked each other, we continued to talk on the phone, trying to figure out if there was a way to make the relationship work. We were four hundred miles apart and leading lives that could not have been more different. Still, I couldn't stop thinking about her, obsessing about her, really; she affected me in a way that no one else ever had, and I refused to let her go.

"I'm coming to L.A.," I told her one night. "With Jerry's band. Let's get together."

And so we did. Over the course of a few days we fell in love, and before leaving to return to the Bay Area I asked Marilyn to spend the rest of her life with me.

"I know it's too soon," I said. "I know it's crazy. But I think we can make it work. Please . . . come up and live with me."

She hesitated at first, which was obviously the right and sensible reaction. I was damaged goods: a rock 'n' roll widower who rode motorcycles, lived out of a suitcase, and smoked too much pot. And yet, there was something that led her to take a chance. Maybe it was because her job was falling apart and she wanted out of Los Angeles. Maybe it had something to do with her age—she had just turned thirty and had made it clear to me that she hoped to have children someday (I could almost hear the biological clock ticking). Or maybe she simply fell for me as hard as I fell for her.

"It's destiny," I pleaded. "I can feel it."

Just about everyone thought we were crazy, but in early May Marilyn accepted my proposal and we set a date to get married. Less than one month later we drove to Lake Tahoe with Barbara, who would serve as maid of honor and witness. Along the way I stopped at the funeral of a friend, a Hells Angel named Fu Man Chu who had been killed in a head-on collision near Fresno. Afterward Marilyn and I had a long talk, during which she made it clear that while she understood my sadness over losing Fu, she thought it was time for me to make some changes in my life.

"You have to begin extricating yourself from this world," she said. "All this dangerous stuff . . . it's not good for you, and it's not good for us."

She was right, of course, and it wasn't like I hadn't given the matter some thought, in part because the FBI had just completed its notorious Rough Rider investigation, a nationwide sting in which scores of Hells Angels were arrested on drug-related charges. Several of the higher-ranking members of the cub wound up doing serious time, and hundreds of "associates" were implicated in one way or another. Needless to say, I was an associate, and so were several other people in the band and crew. All of our names were dragged through the mud. I was accused by a federal informant of being some sort of a conduit between the band and the motorcycle club, which was just complete and total bullshit. I couldn't really hold any of the guys in the club responsible for what happened, because they hadn't said a word about the Dead, hadn't made up any lies to save their own necks. They'd simply been victimized by a snitch. Still, it was disconcerting, to say the least, to be accused of things I hadn't done. So by the time Marilyn politely suggested that I start taming my lifestyle, I'd already begun moving in that direction. Not since my brief but unforgettable trip to Rikers Island had I exchanged any drugs for money, and it was frankly shocking to find myself being implicated in a significant drug trafficking sting. So I was ready for a change.

Marilyn asked me to tone down my relationship with the Hells Angels and to curtail my motorcycle lifestyle. Which I did. (At the same time, California passed a helmet law, which curbed my enthusiasm anyway.) I still had lots of friends in the club, people who meant a great deal to me, and we continued to spend time together.

"The Angels will never hurt us," I often said. "Believe me. They love you guys like family."

And they did. I don't doubt that for a second. But some things were obviously beyond their control, beyond my control. My personal involvement in the Rough Rider investigation stemmed from a concert at the Saratoga Performing Arts Center in Saratoga Springs, New York. There were dozens of Hells Angels at the show—they were in the midst of some kind of run—and they introduced me to a biker from another club. He turned out to be an informant. We chatted for all of about two minutes, but that one conversation somehow produced volumes of information, almost all of it bogus. The U.S. government wound up with an indictment against the Hells Angels, and my name was everywhere. I hadn't done anything illegal. Nevertheless, I was repeatedly listed as an associate. I was righteously pissed at myself for being so naive. I thought I could hang out with the club and be friends with some of them, and that would be the end of it. But I was wrong. I realized that if the club was hassled by the federal government, some of it was going to bleed over onto me. And if I was hurt, so, too, were the people I loved.

Marilyn got pregnant right away—in fact, as near as we could figure, our first child was conceived on our wedding night. I looked at the pregnancy as a gift from God, a sign that I had found the right woman and was prepared for a second chance in life. Not everyone agreed, of course. When I told my mother, she said, "What?! Already?" A lot of my friends were really concerned, too. They were certain I'd simply latched on to the first woman foolish enough to take me in. I can't blame them for feeling that way, but in my heart, I knew . . . I just knew.

At least I thought I did.

After a couple months reality began to set in, and Marilyn realized that her initial suspicions had been correct: I was an enormously fucked-up individual. I had problems and issues. I'd acquired a family under unusual circumstances, had never properly cared for that family, and then lost them in the worst way possible. Protestations to the contrary notwithstanding, I'd never allowed myself to fully grieve in the wake of their deaths, and now I was paying for it. I was overwhelmed with guilt and sadness and hostility. Through it all, Marilyn was marvelous. She held me and talked to me and helped me understand what I was feeling. In the end, though, she cut me no slack. She was pregnant and she wanted—no, she needed—a husband who would love her and take care of her. She needed a partner, not a second child. I was on the road a lot during her pregnancy, and while she was tolerant of my absences, she made no secret of that fact that she expected loyalty and maturity in a husband. Without going into details, let's just say that first year was hard. My sexual compulsion didn't disappear right away. I turned off the animal spigot gradually and completely. Marilyn didn't believe in polygamy and open marriages. She was a striking woman and could have had any number of men, but that wasn't the idea. That wasn't what she wanted. Thanks to Marilyn I came to understand that monogamy and fidelity mean something to a long-term relationship. Actually, they mean almost everything. If you don't love somebody you can't be faithful, and I loved her with every inch of my being.

Lauren Parish was born on February 22, 1986. A gorgeous baby girl, I held her in my arms the moment she slid into the world, wet and wailing, and told her I'd never let anything happen to her. I still sometimes call her my savior. Then Tony came along on October 3, 1989. I was there for his birth too. Wouldn't have missed it for the world. Marilyn and I have been married for seventeen years now, and sometimes I can't believe how lucky I am. To have two wonderful, healthy children, a compassionate wife whose beauty still takes my breath away . . .

There are times when I feel a bit like Mac Sledge, the broken-down, alcoholic former country music star portrayed by Robert Duval in *Tender Mercies,* who finds salvation and redemption in the arms of a saintly woman who runs a roadside motel in the middle of Nowhere, Texas. In the movie's final scene, Sledge tends to a small garden and weeps quietly after learning that the daughter he abandoned has been killed in a car accident. His final words are: *"I don't trust happiness. Never have . . . never will."*

Neither do I, but I'm trying.

Chapter 27

*T*alk about weird synchronicity. I'm hanging out at the Grateful Dead's Front Street studio, and there in front of me, only a few feet away, is one of the greatest poets of our time, Bob Dylan. He walked in a few hours earlier to help out with a studio session, and unlike so many stars of his stature, he came with no entourage at all. No agent, no manager, no assistant. In fact, he didn't even bring a guitar or harmonica. Just walked through the front door, grunted a little hello, and said he was ready to work.

For me, this is more than a minor thrill. When I was fifteen, sixteen years old, I worshiped Dylan. I had all his records, listened to them constantly, spent endless hours listening to that mangled voice of his, trying to figure out what the hell he was saying. Needless to say, my folks didn't think too much of Dylan.

"Kid can't sing worth a damn!" my father would bark. I remember once sitting on the couch in our living room, arguing with my parents—not arguing, really, but discussing, in passionate terms—what it was we liked and did not like about Dylan and his music. To them, Dylan's success and popularity were a mystery. He wasn't like Sinatra, didn't have that silken voice, so what the hell was the big deal? I tried to explain the appeal, that Dylan was the voice of a generation, but they just didn't get it.

A decade later my mother bought some new furniture and shipped the old couch to my house in California. As the years went by and I acquired some furnishings of my own, that couch made it down to the Front Street studio. So imagine how strange it seems to me now, to be staring at Bob Dylan as he lies curled in a fetal position, napping in the shank of the day, on that very same couch. I'd defended him from that spot, had argued on behalf of his brilliance with every tool at my disposal. And now here he is, with me watching over him. As I said . . . pretty weird.

Dylan toured with the Grateful Dead in 1986. He had no trouble fitting in, despite the fact that he wasn't an easy guy to get to know. He was, in fact, exactly as advertised: reticent, shy, prone to speaking in grunts and hiccups. He was pleasant enough, though. It wasn't like he was rude or self-important. I think he was just a very quiet, private man. Like Jerry Garcia, Dylan was first and foremost an artist—you sensed whenever you were with him that he was somewhat distracted, like his mind was elsewhere. As far as I could tell, Dylan was content to write songs, play his guitar, and smoke a little pot. He liked Jerry a lot and was a big fan of the music of the Grateful Dead, so I can only imagine what he thought as he traveled around the country with us, watching Jerry deteriorate before his eyes.

Things were pretty bad by this time. As heroin and (to a lesser degree) cocaine took their toll on the band in general and Jerry in particular, attempts at intervention were made by various people. John McIntire was the first to attempt a realistic approach to the problem, one that involved not trash cans and symbolic dope fires and half-assed promises to clean up, but rather serious counseling and therapy. I cooperated as much as possible, but it was kind of pathetic, really, because the group as a whole wasn't prepared to deal with any of this. We'd meet with counselors and therapists, but no one would really talk. There was one particular night when we made something of a breakthrough, when one after another people from the band and the crew stood up and discussed their weaknesses and their concerns. It was, in large part, a team effort to get Jerry to face the fact that his was the greatest problem of all, not only because his addiction centered around heroin, which threatened his very existence, but also because he was the heart and soul of the band. Without him, there was no Grateful Dead. Not really, anyway. And there certainly wasn't a Jerry Garcia Band.

But for all its good intentions, even this soul-baring session devolved into silliness when I seized upon a quiet moment to declare my own personal concerns.

"You know," I said, in all honesty, "I think maybe I'm smoking too much pot."

There was a long pause as everyone sat and stared at me. And then suddenly the room erupted with laughter.

"Come on, man," Jerry said. "We're trying to be serious here."

I sat down and retreated into the background. What else could I say? I hadn't intended any sort of joke. I was completely serious. I was trying to be supportive and forthcoming and candid. But such was the atmosphere surrounding the Grateful Dead at this point that anything less than a life-threatening heroin or coke habit was considered trivial.

There were other, more aggressive attempts to shake some sense into Jerry, to make him realize that we loved him and wanted nothing but the best for him, even if that meant hurting him. The most memorable of these occurred in 1986, when the entire band and crew went to Jerry's house one night. Ramrod and I were right at the front of the line, and I can still hear the bitterness in Jerry's voice as he answered the door and looked down the sidewalk at the crowd of people, his supposed friends and coworkers, and said, while shaking his head, "Look at them all . . . coming to get me." I hated the way he said it, like we were betraying him somehow, but we believed in what we were doing, so we all piled into the house as Jerry stood outside and held the door. When the last person crossed the threshold, Jerry slammed the door behind us and walked down the street.

He didn't get off that easily, though. We went after him and confronted him again and convinced him that we had something worthwhile to say. But Jerry took off in his car, and although we tried to tail him, he sped away like he was fleeing the scene of a crime and lost us within a matter if minutes. It was shortly thereafter that he got popped for possession in Golden Gate Park, but that didn't deter him, either. Jerry was by now a slave to his own addiction.

Predictably, word got out that he was using, and I quickly found myself in the unenviable position of trying to keep him healthy and sober enough to conduct business. It got worse as the years went on, not merely because of my position as the manager of the Garcia Band, but also because of my deepening personal relationship with Jerry. He had very few close friends, especially after heroin got its hooks into him, and I became one of the few nonusers he felt he could trust. Unfortunately, that made me look like something of an enabler. In later years, just about everybody who wanted to see Jerry had to go through me, and I'm sure many of them thought I was protecting him or pillowing him. But it was much more complicated than that. This was the way the guy lived. He made a decision to be a heroin addict. I ached when I saw what heroin did to Jerry. We all did. And we tried so hard . . . we tried every way imaginable to help him. But you can't help someone who doesn't really want to be helped, especially someone like Jerry, who had spent much of his life erecting barriers around himself. Jerry had this weird notion that you simply didn't interfere with someone else's personal life—I say "weird" because we were like a big extended family, and there was no way to ignore the pain of a brother or sister. But that's the way Jerry wanted it . . . so that's the way it was.

Complicating matters further was the fact that despite his deepening addiction, Jerry frequently got the job done, both in the studio and on stage. See, what heroin brings with it, more than anything else, are lies. Life becomes little more than an endless game of deception. The addict is consumed with chasing the next high, and yet he insists to those around him—those who love him and work with him and need him—that he has no problem. Jerry usually dismissed with a laugh or a wave of the hand any suggestion that he might have a serious problem, and for a long time we wanted to believe him. Here was this strong, brilliant man, playing every night, still working as hard as he could, making wonderful music that brought joy to millions of fans. But I was with him every day, and after a while I started to pick up on the subtle signs of decomposition. He wasn't coming in early anymore, and when he did come in, he'd flop down in a chair and ask me to bring him his guitar.

By the summer of 1986, the vintage version of Jerry Garcia was all but gone, replaced by a bloated, graying man who had neither the energy nor the inclination to devote himself fully to the art that had defined his life. He staggered through the tour with Dylan, teetering on the brink of collapse. Each performance seemed as though it might be his last, but somehow he'd take a day or two to recuperate and hit the stage again. Jerry was in terrible shape by this point, his body ravaged by years of drug abuse and poor dietary habits and a complete lack of exercise. He'd been neglecting his health for years, and now it was all catching up to him. I remember talking to him one night around this time and being struck by how he had aged, how the boyish face had grown sad and pale. The same sort of thing had happened to Keith Moon, the late, great drummer for The Who. If you look at albums and concert footage from the band's early days, you'll see a kid (Moon was only fifteen when he joined The Who) full of youthful exuberance, always smiling, laughing, playing from somewhere deep in his soul. Later, as alcoholism ravaged his system and spirit, Moon's entire appearance changed. By the time he was thirty he looked like a fifty-year-old man. And a broken-down fifty-year-old at that. (Here's another example: a few years later, while Jerry and I were killing time one day at JFK Airport in New York, before flying back to San Francisco, we found ourselves sitting next to Jack LaLanne. Jack was a Bay Area legend, of course. One of the healthiest men on the planet, and a pioneer in the field of diet and fitness, Jack was a tremendous athlete whose exploits included pulling a string of rowboats across San Francisco Bay with his hands tied behind his back. He was amazing! Even more amazing was the sight of Jack, so fit and trim and muscular, shaking hands and chatting with Jerry. I couldn't help but think, *Here's a seventy-year-old man who looks like he's forty, and a forty-year-old man who looks like he's seventy.*)

The same sort of thing was happening to Jerry, the unraveling of the mind and body. And there was no stopping it. I think on that tour we all sort of knew he was headed for a crash of some sort; it was just a matter of when and how. The answer came during a concert at JFK Stadium in Washington, D.C. If you've ever been to Washington, you know what a swamp it can be in the summertime. This particular day was oppressively hot and humid. I glanced at a thermometer before the band went out on stage. It was 104 degrees! Everyone—the band and the crew—drank gallons of water that day during setup and sound check. Except Jerry. I barely saw him prior to the show. No one did. Anyway, by the time Jerry walked up on stage, it was apparent to all of us that he was in rough shape. Sweating like crazy, panting like a horse in the moments after a race, he looked like a man on the verge of a heart attack. But it wasn't his heart that was the problem. For several days Jerry had been complaining of a busy bladder. He was constantly in the bathroom, pissing all the time, regardless of how much liquid he consumed. Because of my family history and my teenage fascination with anatomy and biology, I knew a little about diabetes, and I suspected maybe this was Jerry's affliction. Maybe his kidneys were shutting down, not an uncommon occurrence among junkies. As it turned out, I was right.

In the middle of the show, as the Dead played in front of tens of thousands of screaming fans, Jerry turned to me and yelled, "Get me something to piss in!"

I was shocked, frankly, not only because it seemed an unreasonable and alarming request, but because I had no idea how he intended to complete the act with even a modicum of privacy. This was a packed stadium, and, as always, every eye was focused on Jerry. He was, after all, the star of the show, so it was a practical impossibility to empty your bladder on stage without causing something of a scene. Nevertheless, I did as ordered. I retrieved a garbage can from the side of the stage and dragged it out behind the amp. Jerry sort of strolled over behind his amp during one of the band's many extended jams, sidled up to it as closely as possible, and tried to urinate. After about thirty seconds of strained effort, he gave up.

"Can't do it," he said. It was clear that he was in serious distress. So he put down his guitar and walked off the stage in search of a bathroom. Meanwhile, the band played on. A few minutes later Jerry returned, his discomfort temporarily relieved, but his overall condition worsening by the minute.

That was the last show of the tour. We all went home that night, and a few days later Jerry was discovered unconscious by a woman named Nora, with whom he'd been sharing time of late. She was part housekeeper, part girlfriend, and she also sold his art for him, although Jerry never publicly acknowledged any sort of a romantic link between the two of them. But it was fortunate that she was around, for if she hadn't stopped by Jerry's house that day, God only knows what might have happened.

The doctors said his blood had coagulated and he'd gone into shock. Who knows what prompted it? Heroin was surely a contributing factor, if not the direct cause, but the end result was a diabetic coma. It was a scary time for all of us, of course, because there was a distinct possibility that Jerry might not recover. But there was hope, too, for while he was in that coma, he was kicking junk; his body was leeching itself of the toxins that had brought him to this awful place. I spent hours at Jerry's bedside while he was hospitalized, even while he was comatose. Later, when he woke up, he talked about the visions he'd experienced, strange and vivid fever dreams, mostly centering on his own demise. As the days and weeks wore on, and his health naturally improved, Jerry opened up in ways he hadn't before—not recently, anyway. He talked about his hopes and his fears, and the thing that frightened him most was not the prospect of dying young, or dying at all. What scared the shit out of Jerry, what really depressed him, was the possibility that he might never recapture the genius of his youth; that he'd never play the guitar like he had in the sixties, or create the kind of music that once seemed to pour out of him like lava from a volcano. He questioned whether a life without art was a life worth living.

I considered all of this to be progress. It seemed apparent then that Jerry wanted to get better, that he still had dreams and aspirations. Slowly, through the help of friends and musicians (particularly Merle Saunders) and family, he began to recover—physically, emotionally, spiritually, creatively. Everyone in the band and crew helped. We took turns watching over him, hanging out with him, cooking his meals, helping with laundry and housekeeping, and generally just making sure he knew he wasn't alone.

After about a month or so Jerry picked up a guitar and started to play again. He'd sit in a chair at home and noodle all afternoon, just to get his rhythm back. It wasn't long before his confidence returned and he told me he wanted to get back on stage. We started small, with a Garcia Band show at the Kaiser Auditorium in Oakland. I remember the way Jerry looked that night, not exactly the picture of health, but happy and fairly robust nonetheless. For the first time in years he was clean. Completely clean? I don't know. That might be a stretch. I wasn't with Jerry every waking moment, and he was notorious for sneaking off and getting high the second you turned your back. But this wasn't long after his forced rehabilitation, and the effect was startling. There was a sharpness to his playing that hadn't been there for a while. More important, there was a glint of happiness in his eye, as if he realized for the very first time just how important performing was to him, and how much he had missed it. When he came off the stage and gave me a hug, I was filled with pride. And with hope.

Around this same time Mountain Girl and two of Jerry's daughters began to take an active role in his recovery. They tried to get him a place that would give him roots and stability and some semblance of a "normal" American life. Truthfully, though, that was the last thing Jerry wanted. At heart he remained a vagabond, a beatnik. But his family meant well and I admired their interest so I tried to help them out. I took them on a vacation in '86. We rented a houseboat and we swam and and hung out and had a good relaxing time. While there we came up with the idea of a bigger vacation, something longer and more involved.

"Hawaii," I told him. "That's where we should go."

The Dead had played in Hawaii before, but Jerry had never spent an extended amount of time there. It seemed like the perfect place for a troubled soul to find some peace, and to reconnect with family and friends. Far from the macho road trips of our younger days, this was a fairly wholesome family affair. I took Marilyn and Lauren, who was barely a year old. Jerry traveled with Mountain Girl and his daughters. Robert Hunter and his wife Maureen also joined us. We got a big house on the beach on Kauai, all of us under one roof. Bob Weir stayed in a separate place just down the road, as did Billy Kreutzmann. We spent more than a month in Hawaii, just eating and hanging out, enjoying the ocean and the weather and the good company of friends. Near the end of our stay we decided to do some diving. I'd taken an introductory course prior to this trip so I knew a little about it, and I'd told Jerry repeatedly about how beautiful the underworld could be.

He was intrigued enough to give it a try. So Bobby, Jerry, and I went for a dive off the southern tip of Kauai. To be honest, it wasn't that great a dive. The current was too strong for optimal viewing, but Jerry didn't seem to mind at all. In fact, he was in heaven. Jerry had never been much of an athlete, and it had been years since he'd gotten any sort of exercise at all, but suddenly he was excited about the prospect of getting in shape. "This is a sport I can do," he told me. "I want to learn more."

It wasn't so much that he enjoyed the exertion. He just liked spending time underwater, exploring an alien world, and to do that effectively, he knew he'd have to get in better shape. So when we got back home, Jerry, Bobby, Bill Kreutzmann, and I signed up for a scuba course and got certified as divers. We completed the deep-water phase of the training the following year in Hawaii. There we had a dear friend named Vicky Jensen, a lifelong Grateful Dead family member who had moved to the big island of Hawaii in the early '80s. Vicky was an avid diver who introduced us to Jeff and Terry at Jack's Dive Locker in Kona. With the help of these people, diving became a passion for Jerry, perhaps the first healthy obsession (other than music) in his life. So strong was his interest that he vowed to take a month's vacation each year in Hawaii. We went there in 1987, just as we had in '86, a big group of us sharing several houses on the beach. This time, though, we went diving every day. Jerry was completely hooked, to the extent that he let down his guard even when in the company of complete strangers. People would come up to him on the beach, or on private diving excursions, and naturally they'd be shocked to see Jerry Garcia in a wet suit with a tank on his back (talk about a lack of context!). They'd want to chat with him, but not in the usual way that fans want to chat. They weren't interested in autographs or handshakes. They wanted to talk about diving, and Jerry was more than happy to oblige. For the first time in years he seemed to be relaxed, content. There was a ripple effect, too, because I found it easier in this setting to retreat from the mentality of a manager, whose primary function is to protect his client. As a roadie I'd spent a lot of time throwing unruly fans off stages; now I was manager of the Garcia Band and thus responsible for a large portion of Jerry's working life. My usual response when he was approached by fans was to intervene on his behalf, to keep the meeting short and sweet, and to make sure no harm came to him. In this setting, though, intervention wasn't necessary. Hawaii was so restorative and beautiful that it was impossible to be grumpy or combative there, even when your personal life was in turmoil.

Certainly this was the case with Jerry, who decided during that second trip to Hawaii that after so many years, his roller-coaster relationship with Mountain Girl had run its course. He didn't want to be with her anymore, but Jerry was terribly weak when it came to confrontation, so he typically ended one affair by simply diving headlong into another. And so it was that he became involved with Menasha Matheson, a Deadhead who had been following the band and who loved Jerry with all her heart and soul. Menasha was a sweet, ethereal little thing, but she was so young and so pure, and she spent countless hours trying to analyze her relationship with Jerry—trying in vain to figure out her place in his world, and in our world, the world of the Grateful Dead.

Menasha meant well, but there were times when she tried my patience. She didn't understand the machinations of the road, the armor we donned while traveling, the pace of our lives. She was young and naive, and sometimes she'd do silly, irresponsible things, like taking off in a limo without asking, and thus stranding members of the band. Her transgressions were never malicious or anything—she just didn't *get it*, and, I'm sorry to say, sometimes this provoked hostility. I know there were times when I did not treat her as well as I might have, and I feel bad about that now, because she really was a good person. But my first responsibility was to Jerry . . . to the band. That's why thick skin was a prerequisite for anyone who ever tried to have a relationship with Jerry. They had to understand that he would be shared with another handmaiden, and her name was the Grateful Dead. To a degree, it was that way for all of us.

At times the band was merely an obligation, a job like any other that required commitment and travel and professional expertise, often at the expense of "quality time" with our families. Other times, though, the job served as a coverup, a boys' club, a place to hide. Once you jumped into the world of the Grateful Dead and earned the trust of your brothers, the doors locked behind you. I can remember Jerry coming to the studio one day in the 1970s with a girlfriend in hot pursuit. They'd had some kind of blowup, then she followed him to the studio and banged on the doors and screamed until her voice went raw. We instantly rallied around him; we closed ranks for our boy.

Menasha wasn't easily dissuaded, however, so their relationship lasted for a few years. They had a child together, and slowly but surely Jerry fell back into the routine of self-destructive behavior. I suppose this was his way of coping with all the stress.

Jerry's relationship with Menasha effectively ended with the arrival of an old high school sweetheart named Barbara Meier. She came to a show one night in late 1992, they talked for a while, and pretty soon they became a couple. It wasn't that simple, of course, or that romantic. The truth is, we all liked Barbara and were more than happy to see her replace Menasha on Jerry's arm. So we nudged them along, meddled in their personal business, helped him slide out of one affair and into another. It was that deliberate. I remember everyone from the band attending a Christmas party at my house, during which we spent a lot of time devising ways for Jerry to go to Hawaii with Barbara. Everyone agreed it was all for the best. Jerry was miserable with Menasha, and Barbara seemed like the answer to our prayers. Robert Hunter, one of Jerry's oldest friends, had known Barbara for years, and he, too, gave the plan a stamp of approval. None of this was particularly nice on our part. Menasha was hurt. But there seemed no recourse. So when Jerry flew off to Hawaii with Barbara, we all breathed a sigh of relief.

A month later they were back, and to my eyes it was painfully obvious that Jerry had slipped into the abyss once again. I don't know what happened, whether their trip was less than Jerry hoped it would be, or whether he'd simply said, "Fuck it! I miss heroin." Whatever the reason, he was, once again, an active junkie. Most people didn't pick up on it right away, but I could tell. And so could Barbara. She went on the road with us in 1993, and one night I got a disturbing call from Jerry.

"Come on down here," he said. "I need some help."

"What's wrong?"

"Barbara and I had a big fight. She's leaving me."

Their fight, of course, had been about Jerry's drug use. Barbara had gotten only a glimpse of it, and she'd immediately confronted him. Unlike so many of Jerry's girlfriends, Barbara wasn't content to share her life with Jerry's demons. She had told him, in effect, "I am not going to put up with it. You want to kill yourself, go right ahead, But you do it alone."

I admired her spunk, her courage. It was, after all, more than I could muster. Barbara had some experience with junkies. She'd endured the lies and the cheating and the downward spiral of deception and self-destruction. She wasn't about to do it again.

Chapter 28

I don't mean to imply that the late 1980s and early '90s brought a seachange to the Grateful Dead, ushering in a new era of clean, healthy living. That wasn't really the case. Believe me, we were never a smoke-free band or anything like that. We all overindulged on occasion, but not to the extent that we had in the early days. You grow up, right? You lose the energy and the desire to get completely fucked up all the time. You take greater joy in your family and friends, and just hanging out, talking, spending time with those you love. Some of us never left the wild life behind, though. Jerry was one example. Brent Mydland was another.

They were different in so many ways—Brent had grown up in a religious family (his father was a chaplain in the U.S. Army) and knew only a little of the hardcore rock 'n' roll life before joining the Grateful Dead in 1979—but in other ways he and Jerry were similar. Both were sensitive and caring individuals whose tenderness infused their music on every level. And both were compulsive, hard-working types who turned to hardcore drugs as a way of coping with stress and insecurity.

When Brent was brought in to replace Keith Godchaux on keyboards, he seemed fresh and talented. In practically no time at all he established himself as not only a formidable stage performer, but an accomplished composer as well. Two of his songs, "Far From Me" and "Easy to Love," were recorded for the Dead's 1980 release, *Go to Heaven*. Nine years later, when the Dead released their final studio album, *Built to Last*, Brent was a dominant creative force: he wrote four of the songs on that album. Sadly, in the interim, his life had unraveled in many ways.

Brent arrived at a time when we were all running at a frenzied pace. The band was enormously popular, so the money and drugs and groupies flowed like water. Brent, a peaceful, soft-spoken kid, for some reason felt a need to play catch-up. He started drinking heavily and quickly graduated to everything else, including heroin and cocaine. The scene and the lifestyle ate him up. He just wasn't wired for it. He'd listen to all the war stories and I think in some ways he felt left out. To compensate for his shyness and sensitivity, Brent drank too much, which I guess made him feel more comfortable. The sad part was, he never looked very happy to me when he drank. In fact, he could be a sullen, angry drunk. He'd stagger around hotels, banging on doors, demanding to know where the party was. It wasn't long before he bumped up against heroin somehow, in one of the dark corners of our world (you didn't have to look too hard to find it), and, tragically, he was the perfect candidate for addiction.

After that, Brent's decline was precipitous. To my eyes, one of the worst things you could do was get real drunk and then start doing heroin. The combination was at best stultifying, at worst, lethal. But that's what Brent did—many, many times. Unlike Jerry his taste for heroin knew no bounds. As I said, Jerry didn't like needles and typically ingested heroin by smoking it—a dangerous practice, to be sure, but not nearly as dangerous as taking it intravenously. Once you decided to shoot heroin, you were on a different and far lonelier plane, and that's where Brent lived, right up until the day he died of an overdose in July of 1990. His death was enormously disheartening to all of us, because Brent was a guy who seemed to have everything: a beautiful wife, a nice house, two kids, an income that had soared in recent years. He had friends. He had talent. He had so much to live for. To hear that Brent had been found dead on the floor of his neat suburban home in Lafayette, California, all alone, was shocking and sad. I remember not being able to focus very well at the funeral. It was a strange day, almost surreal. Brent had been with us for ten years, and now he was gone. It had been a while since we'd buried anyone, and I'm not sure we were equipped to deal with it. I recall feeling vaguely uncomfortable and dispirited, and even a little angry. Maybe we just weren't absorbing it at the time, because his death didn't seem real . . . didn't seem possible.

Life went on, of course, as it always does. The first person to step into the fray and fill the gap created by Brent's death was Bruce Hornsby, an adventurous and versatile musician whose top-forty hits represented only a fraction of what he was capable of doing. Here's a guy who graduated from the Berklee School of Music, spent years struggling to make a name for himself, and then finally hit the big time with his 1986 album, *The Way It Is,* which spawned several hit singles and made its author a very rich and famous man. So what did Bruce do? He stretched and experimented and over the course of the next four years moved light-years away from the pop formula that had made him so successful. There was nothing he couldn't play: jazz, soul, folk, R&B, and all found their ways into his studio and stage work. It wasn't that Bruce rejected stardom in that arrogant way that some artists do; he simply played what he wanted to play, with little concern for how it would be met by critics and the record-buying public. His goal was to become a better musician. How could you not admire him for that?

Attitude alone made Bruce an ideal fit for the Grateful Dead. The fact that he was also a longtime fan of the band was merely a bonus. He got up to speed in no time and clearly enjoyed the free-flowing, semi-improvisational nature of a Grateful Dead concert. He was a good guy and a talented musician, and everyone liked having him around. By his own choice, though, he never really became part of the family. Once he stepped in for Brent and hung out with us for a while, and got to see what our scene was all about, Bruce retreated just a bit. He was squeaky clean, a total nondrug user whose idea of a good time on the road was to head out to the local YMCA or playground and find a kick-ass game of pickup basketball. He was always there for a smile, a laugh, a good vibe, and his musicianship was indisputably a boost to the band. He knew the music like the back of his hand. In college he'd done Grateful Dead cover tunes, and more recently he and his band had opened for the Dead. Sometimes, after his set, Bruce would sit in with Jerry and the band. So he really was the perfect choice to replace Brent.

Almost.

The problem was, Bruce hadn't anticipated an environment that seemed to revolve so heavily around drugs and partying. As I said, many of us had slowed down or otherwise cleaned up a bit, but Jerry was still the center of attention, and he was in sorry shape. Like a lot of musicians, Bruce idolized Jerry, and I think he found it extremely difficult and painful to see what had become of this once great and vibrant artist. To play alongside Jerry each night in those days was often an exercise in frustration and sadness. Most of us had grown accustomed to it; we were resigned to the fact that he wasn't going to help himself, and so we did what we could to prop him up and keep him going, all the while clinging to the hope that maybe he'd experience some sort of epiphany. That approach wouldn't work for Bruce. It was just too hard. And, anyway, Bruce had his own solo career to consider. It was never his goal to be the full-time keyboard player for the Grateful Dead. So he left, and his place was taken by former Tubes keyboard player Vince Welnick, a solid musician and a less conflicted man who simply jumped on board and enjoyed the ride for the better part of the next five years.

There were good times in that period, too, despite Jerry's deteriorating health and ongoing struggle with heroin. I don't mean to give the impression that being part of the Grateful Dead or the Jerry Garcia Band became a miserable, depressing experience, because that wasn't the case at all. We still had fun, made good music, and enjoyed each other's company. To the very end Jerry remained a fascinating, generous man—a good friend—and some of my most vivid memories involved times when we were alone together, which happened with some regularity after I became manager of the Garcia Band.

There was the time in New York, for example, when Jerry and I stayed behind after the end of a Grateful Dead tour. I'd arranged for members of the Garcia Band to fly into New York to meet us, so that we could immediately begin a second tour. The plan called for the guys in the band to arrive at JFK Airport, where they'd board a helicopter and fly to the heliport on Fifty-ninth Street in Manhattan, next to the Hudson River. Jerry and I were to meet them there with a van.

So we drove out to the heliport on a cold, rainy night. I was going to go by myself, but Jerry didn't feel like hanging out alone at the hotel, so he tagged along. He did that with me sometimes when we were on the road, especially in New York, which was one of his favorite cities. We'd go on these excursions to Harlem, Little Italy, Chinatown, and just wander around and soak up the culture. Anyway, we drove out to the heliport, and of course the chopper was delayed because of bad weather. It was not a busy night at the heliport—in fact there was only one other customer in the terminal when I walked in (Jerry waited in the van). He was seated on a bench, all alone, with a garment bag at his feet. He had a round, weathered face, and gray hair showing beneath his hat. As he read his newspaper, I stared at him for a moment, thinking he looked vaguely familiar. But it wasn't until he looked up and our eyes met that I realized who he was.

My God . . . Frank Sinatra!

I didn't hesitate for a second. My parents—especially my mother—adored Sinatra, and I wasn't about to pass up the opportunity to chat with him one-on-one. He was on his way down to Atlantic City, but the weather had scuttled his plans, at least temporarily, so he didn't mind talking for a while. I told him who I was and why I was there, and I told him it would mean the world to my mom if he would give her an autograph, and, despite the fact that he was notoriously uncooperative when it came to signing autographs, he graciously obliged. Then we started talking about the Grateful Dead, and to my surprise it turned out that Sinatra knew all about the band. I wouldn't go so far as to call him a Deadhead, but he certainly was aware of Jerry's talent and his contributions to popular music.

"You know," I said. "He's here."

"Who?"

"Jerry Garcia. He's outside in the limo."

Sinatra smiled. "Really? I'd like to meet him."

So I went out and got Jerry and brought him into the terminal. Jerry was nervous about these types of things—hanging with other celebrities—and he wasn't exactly a Rat Pack fan or anything. But he had great admiration for Sinatra. Jerry was a fan of all types of music, and he understood better than most people what it was that made Sinatra unique. "That voice," he'd say, shaking his head. "Just amazing." Sinatra had a gift, just like Jerry. Each had used music to leave his mark on the world; each had brought joy to millions of fans. Yes, they were of different generations, and they were different types of artists. But they *were* artists. And that was a bond that transcended almost anything. So there they were, shaking hands, exchanging pleasantries in an empty heliport terminal on the banks of the Hudson River. As I watched them, Sinatra clean-shaven, wearing a neatly pressed suit, Jerry bearded and unkempt as always, in a black T-shirt, I couldn't help but think, *Now there's a meeting for the ages.*

And there was another trip to New York, this one in 1988, when the great jazz saxophonist Ornette Coleman asked Jerry to play on his *Virgin Beauty* album. Jerry was like a wide-eyed child on that trip, sitting at the knee of this wonderful, eloquent gentleman of jazz. Ornette would give Jerry history lessons and music lessons, and Jerry would soak it all up. And then they'd sit together and play, and it was obvious that the respect was mutual, that Ornette was awed by Jerry's ability to listen to a piece only once and then play it flawlessly. As for me, I felt privileged simply to be in their presence, to see art in its purest form.

In the world of rock 'n' roll, whenever the stillness of an early morning is broken by the ringing of a telephone, it's usually bad news. This particular call came at 6:30 A.M., on October 26, 1991, from Cameron Sears, the Grateful Dead's manager. There had been a tragic fire in Oakland about two weeks earlier, and the night before I got the call, Bill Graham had gone to the Concord Pavilion to work on a benefit concert for the victims of the Oakland fire. A freak storm hit the Bay Area that night, and unfortunately Bill decided to fly home to Marin County anyway. He and two of his assistants, Steve Kahn and Melissa Gold, were killed when their helicopter went down in the storm.

"Can you do me a favor?" Cameron asked.

"Sure."

"Call Jerry . . . before he hears about this on the news."

I called Jerry around 7:30, and he suspected right away that something was wrong. After all, we never talked on the phone at that hour.

I'm sorry," I said. "There's been a terrible accident." I swallowed hard. "Bill's dead."

There was a long pause.

"Bill who?"

"Bill Graham."

Another pause, this one even longer. And then, finally, he sighed. "Oh, no . . ."

I loved Bill; losing him was like losing a brother, or maybe even a father. But Jerry took it even harder. He changed after Bill died. He became darker, quieter, almost as if a piece of him had been cut away. Bill was the guy we all looked up to, the only semiauthority figure we respected and loved. There was nobody else quite like him, and there never would be again. I think Jerry knew that, and it saddened him immensely.

Jerry's heroin habit was no more or less severe than that of most junkies I've known. It ebbed and flowed, depending on his mood and his health, the company he kept, and the quality of his various romantic relationships. His usage may or may not have actually increased in the late eighties and early nineties; but I was more directly affected by it for the simple reason that much of my daily life revolved around Jerry.

It's been said that a rock 'n' roll manager is a doctor, psychiatrist, friend, and motivator—all rolled into one. This was especially true when working with Jerry. As warm-hearted as he was, he could be slippery and difficult and almost childlike in his approach to the business of running a band. In the beginning he was merely disinterested, so complete was his focus on the creative end of things. Later, though, as heroin took its toll, he became sloppy and lethargic. I existed in a perpetual state of anxiety because I was so worried about overworking Jerry or having him drop out completely, which was something he discussed from time to time. I felt pressure from several directions. The guys in the Garcia Band—musicians and crew—often complained that they weren't getting enough work; meanwhile, the guys in the Grateful Dead complained that Jerry was spending too much time with the Garcia Band, which because of its lower profile, they argued, created an atmosphere that made it even easier for Jerry to indulge his addiction. I didn't find that to be true, incidentally, but I was sympathetic to the notion that he had to be coddled from a physical standpoint because he simply wasn't capable of working as hard as he once had.

I tried to keep tabs on his health, especially after the diabetic coma, but he was difficult and sometimes belligerent about that stuff. We all had conversations about health and diet, not only because we wanted to improve our own quality of life, but because we hoped that it might have some influence on Jerry. For a while he went vegetarian, and we all went along with him. Then he gave up and I immediately hit the nearest steak house. When Jerry tried to quit smoking, we all threw out our cigarettes. That lasted about a week.

You have to understand something: Jerry was an extremely intelligent, well-read man. He knew exactly what he was doing to himself. There were some things you could discuss with him, such as health and diet and exercise. He wasn't going to make any major changes, but at least he was willing to listen. But heroin? Forget it. That was impossible. As with most junkies, there was a wall around Jerry when it came to the subject of drug addiction. I tried nudging, manipulating, psychoanalyzing, but I got nowhere, so after a while I just gave up. I'd been around enough junkies to know the futility of intervention. You might as well take your head and slam it in a door repeatedly, because the effect is the same.

I wanted to work with Jerry. I loved him like a big brother and I wanted desperately to keep him alive, but he was so resistant and tricky . . . you could never pin him down. Once in a while you could get him to talk a little bit about his problem, but it went only as far as he wanted it to go. If you pushed it beyond the line he had drawn in the sand, he'd get pissed off, and then he'd turn it around on you somehow. Jerry was smart—he knew how to cut right to the core of your being.

"Well, what about you?" he'd say. "Let's talk about your problems." And then he'd proceed to expose some weakness in your moral fiber. I went through this with him several times, and it always ended with Jerry on the attack and me throwing up my hands in surrender. True, I didn't have a heroin habit, but he knew I liked to smoke a lot of weed and that I'd led a pretty depraved life on the road in the past. He knew

I had a ferocious temper that sometimes got me into trouble. There were always other things you could zero in on, other scabs to pick. So when you approached Jerry on this subject, you did so at your own risk.

We all tried to reason with him, but if one person made a greater effort than most, it was Bob Weir. I can't begin to describe what a wonderful man he is, how much he cares for his friends and family. Bobby opened his life to me, let me live with him, tolerated my inexperience when I first started working with the band. I'm sure there were times when he became exasperated with me—Bobby is, after all, someone who believes in pushing the edge of the artistic envelope—but he never let on, never made me feel bad. He's the kind of guy you can't help but love, and I'm proud to say he remains one of my closest friends. No one tried harder than Bobby did to reach Jerry. He was the cleanest guy in the group, the one who didn't like having the Hells Angels hanging around and who became squeamish at the very mention of heroin. Bobby ached for Jerry—he even wrote songs about their friendship and Jerry's addiction—but ultimately he was as impotent as the rest of us. There is nothing quite as sad and painful as living with a junkie. You watch him die, inch by inch, and there's nothing you can do about it. Trying to *force* someone to quit junk is like trying to drive a car with your hands cuffed: it's an exercise in frustration.

When Jerry reconnected with Deborah Koons in 1993, I was optimistic that his life might take a turn for the better. I thought she was good for him—we all did. Back in the seventies, when they first dated, Jerry and Deborah were the cutest little lovebirds. She came on the road with us from time to time and didn't have much trouble fitting in. She understood the scene and the pressures we all faced—especially Jerry—so it wasn't like she'd be shocked by anything she encountered this time around. Deborah was an adult. She had her own career as a film maker, she had her own money. Most important of all, she seemed to have fallen in love with Jerry all over again, and he seemed to have responded in kind. They were happy, which made everyone else happy.

I wasn't completely shocked when I learned that Deborah and Jerry planned to marry; Jerry could be sentimental and romantic, and he liked having a woman in his life. I was surprised to hear that they intended to have a big wedding. To me, that seemed a bit odd. Jerry was by nature shy and private, and I couldn't imagine him wanting to share such a personal thing with a large audience. Many members of the band and crew had gotten married over the years, but the ceremonies were always small and quiet, witnessed by only a handful of friends and relatives. If anyone seemed least likely to break that pattern, it was Jerry.

So you can imagine my shock when he and Deborah approached me at a show and not only told me of their plans, but also asked me to be the best man. Actually, it was Deborah who extended the invitation, and when I hesitated for a moment (only because I was so surprised), Jerry jumped right in and said, "Come on, man. Would you do it for us? It'll mean a lot to me."

"Sure," I said. "No problem."

As with almost anything involving Jerry's personal life, though, being best man at his wedding was not a simple thing. I accompanied the two of them during a trip to the Tiburon Yacht Club, where we discussed the arrangements for the reception, and then I did what every best man is supposed to do: I organized a night of debauchery for the groom and his friends. Not that I wanted to, you understand. It was, oddly enough, Deborah's idea.

"You're going to throw a bachelor party for him, right?" she had asked me one day.

I didn't even know how to respond. I knew Jerry well enough to know that he would not have wanted a bachelor party. He was the type of guy who wouldn't even go to a *friend's* bachelor party. He was very uncomfortable around strippers and prostitutes or anything related to that type of atmosphere. I presumed that Deborah knew that much about him, too. But apparently not.

"You're kidding, right?" I said. "He'll hate it."

Deborah shook her head, smiled. "No, no, no. Trust me, he'll have a good time."

I shrugged. "Whatever you say."

Deborah was blinded by her desire to have a traditional wedding, which I guess included a traditional send-off for the groom. So I talked to Jerry about it, told him Deborah was pressuring me to plan a bachelor party, and asked him how he felt.

"If you want this," I said, "I'll make it happen. But be honest with me."

Jerry kind of half-smiled and drove his hands deep into his pockets like a schoolboy. "I don't know. I guess it's all right."

That was as close to a confirmation as I was likely to get, so, knowing full well that it was sure to be a disaster, I put together a bachelor party at our new studio in Novato, where we'd recently moved after so many years on Front Street. A former Coca-Cola bottling plant, the place was still in the midst of a transformation, so we had plenty of room. There were offices in the front, a parking lot out back, and thousands of square feet of warehouse space just waiting for the newest electronic equipment. All of the guys from the crew came, as well as a few guys from the band. And, of course I hired a stripper to pop out of a cake. The party started promptly at 8 P.M., and by ten we were all pretty loaded. But there was no sign of Jerry. Eleven o'clock came and went. Still no Jerry. Midnight . . . 1 A.M.

The party ended without Jerry making an appearance. The stripper did her thing, we all raised our glasses and offered a toast to Jerry, in absentia, and then we went home. No one was terribly disappointed or surprised. The next day, when I saw Jerry, I didn't really give him a hard time. I just told him he had missed a good party. Clearly embarrassed, he just mumbled something under his breath. I still don't know exactly what happened, whether Deborah changed her mind and decided it wasn't such a great idea for Jerry to have a bachelor party after all, or whether he simply didn't want to come. Like so many things involving Jerry in those later years, it was all rather strange and mysterious.

The same could be said of his wedding to Deborah in February of 1994. I was waiting at the church when Jerry was delivered by his personal limo driver, Leon Day. I could tell by the look on Leon's face that something was wrong, and Jerry's behavior quickly confirmed my suspicions. Dressed in sweatpants and a T-shirt, and not looking at all like a man who was supposed to be getting married in two hours, he was as angry as I'd ever seen him. He slammed the door shut and began ranting about being late. I tried to calm him down as I led him to the sacristy, but Jerry was apoplectic. He kept screaming, cursing, kicking doors, which I thought was rather strange considering this was his wedding day. I'd heard of wedding-day jitters but this was ridiculous.

A short time later Leon returned with Jerry's clothes. I handed them to him, but he was so nervous and upset that he was shaking.

"I can't do it," he said, trying to pull on his shirt.

My heart skipped a beat. I was afraid something like this might happen.

"You mean you can't get married?"

Jerry shook. "No . . . I can't get dressed."

I breathed a sigh of relief. "Ohhhhhh."

So I literally had to dress him. Just as the bride was being helped into her gown somewhere, the groom was getting an assist from the best man. As I straightened his tie, I could see the sweat beading up on Jerry's brow. He was clearly suffering from a massive case of stage fright.

"Do me a favor, man," he said.

"Anything."

"Light up a joint."

I looked around the sacristy. "Oh, Jerry, I don't know, man. I feel kind of funny about that in here."

He just stared at me, kind of pathetically, and pretty soon I caved. I took out my rolling papers, some weed, lit it up, and the two of us sat there at the edge of the church, on Jerry Garcia's wedding day, and proceeded to smoke a joint.

Chapter 29

Ironically, Jerry died at a time when he seemed most committed to changing his life. We were on tour with the Grateful Dead—our last tour, as it turned out—in the summer of 1995, and Jerry was talking a lot about getting off the merry-go-round once and for all.

"I can't do it anymore," he'd say. "I have to make some changes."

He told me he was tired: tired of feeling sick all the time, of being a slave to his own addictions, of trying to hide the problem from Deborah; tired of never having enough energy to play the music he loved so much. Jerry was having real physical problems by this time: circulatory problems, blockage in his arteries, adult-onset diabetes. But perhaps the thing that bothered him the most was a dexterity problem caused by a weakness in his left shoulder that affected his ability to play the guitar.

The symptoms had arisen shortly after Jerry and Deborah returned from a diving excursion to the Caribbean. Jerry had always dived in Hawaii before; this was his first trip to the Caribbean, and it was Deborah's idea. Jerry loved Hawaii and had lots of vivid and pleasant memories from his time there, but I understood Deborah's desire to create a different atmosphere, one that was unique to her relationship with Jerry. They were, after all, husband and wife. Jerry had told me the trip was wonderful, that the diving had been good and that he and Deborah had a terrific time. But on the night of our first show after he returned, at the Warfield Theater, it was clear that something was bothering him. He was pacing around nervously, rubbing his hands together, making tight, little fists, as if he wanted to hit something or someone.

"You okay, Jerry?" I asked him.

He shook his head. "Do me a favor—get my axe."

So I retrieved his guitar and he proceeded to pick at it a little. Then, after maybe a minute or so, he just stopped and stared off into space.

"What's wrong?" I said. I'd never seen Jerry act like this before.

He flexed his fingers again, over and over. "I'm not sure. There's something wrong with my hand. I can barely feel it."

He went on to explain that he thought perhaps he'd gotten bit by something when he was in the Caribbean—an unfortunate occurrence that is surprisingly common among divers—and that the toxin had somehow resulted in a partial paralysis of his hand. I'd heard of this sort of thing happening, but it seemed unlikely. Jerry had been back home for several days and the problem had presented itself only that afternoon. More to the point, Jerry could not recall having been bitten, and there was no evidence of a bite. It seemed he was grasping at straws. We stood backstage for a while as Jerry stretched and massaged his hand. He kept picking up the guitar and playing, and each time he quit after only a few seconds. Finally he just dropped the guitar and walked away, and we were forced to cancel the show.

This was new territory for all of us, especially Jerry. Through all the years of partying and drug abuse he'd never experienced a physical problem that prevented him from doing what he loved most: playing the guitar. Sure, there had been postponements and missed flights and delayed recording sessions, all related to his heroin use, but never anything that quite so profoundly and directly affected him. I'm sure Jerry had always taken it for granted that he'd play the guitar until the day he died. In a perfect world, he'd pass away while writing a new song. But now he was very much alive and unable to do that which made him happiest; unable to do the only thing that really mattered to him. And why? Because his hand didn't work. It wasn't supposed to happen this way. When you're a heroin addict, you sort of live with the possibility that your kidneys or liver will give out, or that you'll pop an aneurism and die in your sleep. You know, somewhere deep inside, that you're a heart attack waiting to happen. But to not be able to play the guitar? That was more than Jerry could take.

We never did find out exactly what caused the problem. I was concerned that the numbness in his hand was related to a circulatory problem and warranted immediate medical attention. Jerry disagreed. He disliked doctors, largely because any medical consultation would inevitably lead to a discussion of his drug use. Eventually, the pain mysteriously went away. Although he was enormously relieved to be able to play again, Jerry was unquestionably spooked by the whole episode. As was I. Stuff like this had never happened before, and I was really starting to realize that Jerry had done some serious physical damage to himself over the years, and that he was beginning to pay the price. Years of abuse had led to consequences that I didn't normally associate with heroin use. Maybe it was because I was so close to him, or because I didn't want to acknowledge the truth—sometimes you can't see the forest for the trees. I knew he was deteriorating, but I'd never anticipated a scenario in which Jerry wouldn't be able to play.

His mood was increasingly dark on that tour, too. He seemed to have lost his sense of humor, and he became prone to making strange and cryptic comments, like, "Why has God forsaken us?" Once, while setting up for a show, I started bitching about something. I don't even remember what it was, but I'm sure it was small and petty and not worth the energy. Jerry heard me whining and walked over. With a frown on his face he thumped me in the chest and said, "You don't have anything to complain about, man. I wish I had your body."

I realized then that Jerry was fully aware of his declining physical state, and that he wanted to lean on me for help, but I didn't know how to give it to him. And his problems weren't merely physical or emotional. Financially, too, Jerry was a wreck, the drugs having produced an ulcer in his bank account. Heroin and morphine had become huge expenses in his life, and I think he knew that he was on the verge of losing everything.

It's been said that an addict has to hit bottom before he can begin climbing back up. I'm not sure if Jerry had reached that point or not, but I think he could see it coming fast. He was scared—scared of being alone, scared of dying, scared of losing everything he held dear. So he did something about it. I should add, however, that it wasn't entirely Jerry's idea. Once Deborah knew that he was using again, she insisted he enter a treatment program. She deserves credit for that. She was a strong woman and there was no way she was going to tolerate Jerry's drug abuse. She wasn't about to sit back and let him die. In the end, though, it was Jerry's decision to make. No treatment would work if he embraced it reluctantly.

The Betty Ford Clinic was actually Deborah's suggestion, largely because of its reputation for working with celebrities. I wasn't sure it was the right place for Jerry, because even after visiting the clinic and discussing its program, he seemed highly apprehensive. Nevertheless, he wanted to go through with it, so everyone in the band backed him up completely. We encouraged him, told him how much we loved him, and how we wanted him to get better. To be perfectly honest, after so many years of watching Jerry skulk around and indulge his heroin habit, it seemed like a small miracle that he truly wanted to do something about it. Something real, something difficult. We played our last concert at Soldier's Field in Chicago, in front of 70,000 screaming fans—not one of whom realized the historical significance of the show—and as I watched Jerry on stage, struggling to perform, but still loving every minute of it, I could only hope that I was witnessing some sort of a beginning, rather than an end.

A week later, the three of us—me, Deborah, and Jerry—we flew down to the Betty Ford Clinic on a private Lear jet. Jerry said he needed my strength and support. We talked on the flight down about starting over, about making a new life. As always, he tried to be cheerful. He tried to be brave. But I could see in his eyes just how scared he really was.

The program was supposed to last twenty-eight days. The first two weeks Jerry would do on his own; the final two weeks, which focused on intensive "family counseling," would involve daily participation from Deborah and me. Deborah represented Jerry's personal family; I represented his Grateful Dead family. I was packing my bags on the morning I was scheduled to join him when I received a call from Deborah.

"Jerry has changed his mind," she said. "He wants to come home."

I wasn't really surprised. The physical withdrawal Jerry had endured rather bravely; it was the rest of the program—the counseling and the talking and the baring of the soul—that he couldn't stomach. The Eisenhower Hospital is attached to the Ford Clinic, and I had hoped that maybe Jerry would receive the medical treatment he so desperately needed while he was down there, and in that way he would have been forced to stay for a while, really get himself back in shape. But he didn't get any medical help at all, so once he flushed his system, got clean, and was back in the dormitory . . . for a guy with his intellect and creativity and intelligence, I guess the rest of it was just too hard to take. And though he never said so, I'm sure Jerry was appalled by the idea of family counseling. To sit in a room, hour after hour, exposing his demons to those he loved most . . . well, I can't think of anything he would have found more painful.

Deborah and I went to the clinic that afternoon. She hadn't completely made up her mind about whether to support Jerry's desire to leave. She wanted to see him and talk to him. Ultimately, of course, it was his decision to make and there was no way to keep him there, but Deborah wielded considerable influence over Jerry; he wanted her consent and approval. So we flew down and Jerry showed us all around the place. He introduced us to his roommate, a drummer, who smiled and nodded conspiratorially as we shook hands.

"Oh, yeah . . . Steve. I've heard all about you," he said.

"I'll bet you have."

Jerry appeared frail and weak, but he was nonetheless animated. He seemed to be in a good mood, probably because his system had been purged of drugs. But I also think he was pouring every ounce of strength into putting on a good show—he wanted us to believe that he was ready to leave, that there was nothing more to be gained by staying there, except, oddly enough, a more robust sex life than he'd enjoyed in many years. Indeed, that seemed to be the most notable fringe benefit of rehab.

"Steve, this place is wild," he said when Deborah left us alone for a few minutes.

"What do you mean?"

"Everybody in here, as soon as they get off drugs, they get bored stiff. So they go up on the roof to smoke cigarettes and hang out . . ." He paused, looked around to see if anyone was listening, and then giggled. "Then they pair off, man. It's unbelievable."

I have no idea whether Jerry was a participant or a spectator, or whether he simply thought that I, as an old sex freak, would enjoy a titillating story. And it doesn't really matter. The point is, he saw no more value in the program, and he wanted out. I wasn't there to judge him, and I could tell by the way he talked that his mind was clear and that he was resolute, so I didn't try to talk him into staying, even though I realized it was probably a mistake for him to leave before completing the program. Deborah acquiesced, as well, and so we packed up his gear and boarded a plane for San Francisco. On the way home Jerry talked a lot about the next phase of his life, and how he would try to remain clean and sober and healthy. He looked so white and tender and helpless to me, like a child who just wants to be held and protected.

"You can't just be running around loose out here," I told him. "You need help. You need support."

He didn't dispute that, so we talked about other programs that were available closer to San Francisco, both inpatient and outpatient, and he agreed to embark on a new program as soon as he got home.

A few days later, on August 8, Jerry and I had our final meeting at the studio. He was enthusiastic about charting a new course for himself and the band, but his appearance betrayed him. He was clearly still sick. And he knew it. He made a lot of phone calls in those last few days, probably in an attempt to reach out to people for help. Deborah loved Jerry, but she wasn't about to support his self-destructive behavior. Right down to the final day, she was still trying to get him help, to convince him that he hadn't kicked his habit. I'm not sure what happened in those last few hours—my best guess is that Jerry went out and used heroin again shortly after we said goodbye at the studio, and that the relapse so discouraged him that he admitted defeat. Later that night he checked into Serenity Knolls, a drug rehabilitation facility in Forest Knolls, California, although I didn't know it at the time.

Early the next morning, on August 9, my phone started ringing. The first call came from Billy Crowe. He'd heard on the radio that Jerry Garcia had been found dead at Serenity Knolls, not far from where Billy lived, and he wanted to know if it was true.

"I don't know," I said, which was the truth. Although it seemed plausible enough, I couldn't believe that Jerry was gone. One day earlier we'd been together, talking about the future, about a better life. How could this have happened? The answer, of course, was that it was bound to happen. Jerry had been rolling the dice with his health for many years, and the gambling had finally caught up with him.

Later that morning I went up to Serenity Knolls with Deborah and Cameron Sears to retrieve Jerry's belongings. We talked with the owner of the center for a while. He was a cordial, soft-spoken man who offered his condolences and tried to provide a window into Jerry's final hours. He took us to Jerry's room, a spartan place, where, according to the owner, Jerry had sat down with another patient, a kid who talked with him for several hours about music and guitars and writing. Apparently, on the final night of his life, Jerry had the privilege of being a teacher, of passing on at least a kernel of his genius. Even as I cried, I couldn't help but smile at the owner's story, for I knew Jerry would have liked that image—the image of a teacher and a student, the sharing of knowledge.

Who knows exactly what happened during the night? At some point Jerry stopped breathing. He had a history of sleep apnea, and perhaps that, combined with his circulatory problems and diabetes, led his heart to give out. All we know for sure is that when they found him in the morning, he was dead. The coroner determined the cause of death to be cardiac arrest.

The funeral was held two days later, on August 11, at St. Stephen's Episcopal Church in Belvedere, Marin County, and was presided over by the Rev. Matthew Fox, the same man who had married Deborah and Jerry just eighteen months earlier. It was a strange and unforgettable day, at once beautiful and bitter. On one level it was a spectacular sendoff for the man we all loved, a way to deal with our grief by declaring our everlasting friendship and commitment. But there was, beneath the surface, a good deal of ugliness, stemming primarily from the detritus of Jerry's messy personal life. I helped Deborah as much as possible with the funeral arrangements and anything else she needed. One of the first things we had to do was assemble the list of guests for the funeral. Deborah decided right away that the best way to handle Jerry's farewell was to have a rather small, private affair at St. Stephen's for roughly 250 of his closest friends, family members and business associates. Fans would be able to say goodbye at another ceremony in San Francisco a couple days later.

But I knew there were going to be problems, mainly because there were some glaring omissions on the guest list, most notably Mountain Girl, who was understandably hurt and angry. Mountain Girl begged me to intervene on her behalf, so I did what I thought was the honorable thing: I arranged for her to slip into the church before the start of the ceremony, so that she could say goodbye to Jerry, the man she once called her husband. It seemed to me the only sensible and human and decent thing to do—but when I saw Mountain Girl by the casket, taking pictures, I quickly ushered her out of the church.

The ceremony itself was far more uplifting and cathartic, although not without its macabre elements: the press was barred, and yet Deborah brought in a film crew to record the entire event for . . . well, for posterity, I guess. Deborah was a film maker, and this was an important historical event. I didn't really have a problem with her decision—the funerals of many famous artists and politicians and leaders had been documented on film—and yet it was somewhat distracting to see the video cameras. I don't know whatever became of the tape. It's never been shown, to my knowledge.

Jerry lay in full view at the front of the sanctuary, dressed appropriately in matching black sweatpants and T-shirt; at the head and foot of the casket were flowers arranged in the shape of the Dead's trademark lightning bolts. As Jerry's friend and confidante, it fell on me to speak at the funeral, and though it was one of the hardest things I've ever done, I'm grateful to have had the opportunity. I prepared no notes, only thought about a few things I wanted to say, so that I would speak directly from the gut. Reverend Fox handed me a passage from the Bible that Jerry had once mentioned, in which Jesus is told by his disciples, "You didn't choose us—we chose you," and that seemed to give me a good place to start. I talked about what it was like to work for him and with him, and how much he cared about the working man, and how well he treated working people wherever he went. I talked about how it was an honor to be part of all that, to have him as a friend and a mentor. It wasn't a terribly long speech—I didn't want to eulogize him, really. I just wanted to say thanks and goodbye, and I wanted to make it clear that even though we were saddened terribly by his departure, it was important that the rest of us keep going, that we carry on in his absence. Jerry would have wanted it that way.

Other people jumped up around the church after that and delivered impromptu eulogies: Bob Weir, Ken Kesey, Jerry's daughter, Annabelle, and many others. One of the last people to speak was Jerry's friend and lyricist, Robert Hunter, who read the following poem:

> *Jerry, my friend,*
> *you've done it again,*
> *even in your silence*
> *the familiar pressure*
> *comes to bear, demanding*
> *I pull words from the air*
> *with only this morning*
> *and part of the afternoon*
> *to compose an ode worthy*
> *of one so particular*
> *about every turn of phrase,*
> *demanding it hit home*
> *in a thousand ways*
> *before making it his own,*
> *and this I can't do alone.*
> *Now that the singer is gone,*
> *where shall I go for the song?*
>
> *Without your melody and taste*
> *to lend an attitude of grace*
> *a lyric is an orphan thing,*

a hive with neither honey's taste
nor power to truly sting.

What choice have I but to dare and
call your muse who thought to rest
out of the thin blue air
that out of the field of shared time,
a line or two might chance to shine—

As ever when we called,
in hope if not in words,
the muse descends.

How should she desert us now?
Scars of battle on her brow,
bedraggled feathers on her wings,
and yet she sings, she sings!

May she bear thee to thy rest,
the ancient bower of flowers
beyond the solitude of days,
the tyranny of hours—
the wreath of shining laurel lie
upon your shaggy head
bestowing power to play the lyre
to legions of the dead

If some part of that music
is heard in deepest dream,
or on some breeze of Summer
a snatch of golden theme,
we'll know you live inside us
with love that never parts

our good old Jack O'Diamonds
become the King of Hearts.

I feel your silent laughter
at sentiments so bold
that dare to step across the line
to tell what must be told,
so I'll just say I love you,
which I never said before
and let it go at that old friend
the rest you may ignore.

After the ceremony Jerry's body was taken to a crematory. There was no great debate about that decision. Jerry and I had talked many times during our travels about graveyards and the colossal waste of space they represented. Neither one of us wanted to be buried. Cremation, we agreed, was a far more practical and tidy solution.

"Dump my ashes in the bay," Jerry had said many times, "and I'll be happy."

That stuck with me over the years, so when Deborah and I talked after Jerry's death, we agreed to honor his wishes. In addition to being a "waste of space," a traditional grave site for Jerry Garcia would have turned into something spectacularly grotesque, a shrine to which Grateful Dead fans throughout the world would pilgrimage—like a Graceland by the Bay. The very thought of it made me shudder. Jerry would have shuddered, too.

Again, since I was Jerry's closest friend, it was my responsibility to escort his body to the crematory. Understandably, Deborah didn't want to take that final, gruesome part of the journey, and I really didn't want to go alone, so I asked Ramrod and Kid to accompany me. They were my closest friends on the crew, the guys who had been with me the longest, and it seemed somehow right that we say goodbye to

Jerry together. I needed their strength, their help, and they were kind enough to oblige.

We followed the hearse in our van, just the three of us, and once inside the crematory things happened pretty quickly. We stood with Jerry in front of a giant oven, the flames illuminating the room as we said our final farewell. We talked to him for a few moments, and then, instinctively, I reached down and brushed some dandruff off his shirt. It was something I'd done countless times over the years, a gesture Jerry typically acknowledged with a smile and a nod. Now he lay motionless, his face blank and gray. I took one last look at him, saw the guitar pick that I'd placed in his shirt pocket at the funeral—just in case he needed it on the other side—and then turned and walked out of the room.

A couple hours later they gave me Jerry's ashes in a small, sealed box. Deborah had signed the body over to me, so legally I was now responsible for Jerry's remains. I took the ashes home and put them in a closet in my garage while waiting for some word from Deborah and the guys in the band on how we would handle their dispersal. Bob Weir came up with the idea that some of the ashes should go to India, to be sprinkled into the Ganges River. I had trouble getting my mind around that concept; it just didn't seem like something Jerry would have wanted. But I knew Bobby's heart was in the right place. I knew what the Ganges River symbolized, that it was the place where Gandhi's ashes had been spread. I believed in my heart that all waters of the Earth were one—that Jerry was a great soul, and that he should go where all great souls go. And yet, it wasn't what Jerry had requested.

"Dump my ashes in the Bay . . ."

So when Bob asked me to go with him to India, I declined. Instead, I brought the ashes over to Deborah's house, opened the box, and took out a few scoops. On April 4, 1996—Buddha's birthday (and the day he supposedly achieved Nirvana and thus escaped the endless cycle of reincarnation)—Deborah and Bobby sprinkled the ashes into the Ganges River, approximately 150 miles north of New Delhi. "May you have peace," Bobby said by way of farewell, "and travel to the stars."

Their journey was a nice idea; unfortunately, it created some familial friction. You see, Jerry's daughters hadn't been informed of the trip, and naturally they weren't happy to read about it in the newspapers. To be honest, I felt bad about it. I thought they should have been told and been given an opportunity to make the trip with Deborah and Bobby.

The discord only heightened later, when, on April 15, another ceremony was held in San Francisco Bay. A hideous scene occurred at the dock, just as we were about to board a sailboat and head out onto the water to scatter the remaining ashes. Mountain Girl, of course, wasn't invited, but she showed up anyway. The moment she saw Mountain Girl, Deborah started screaming at me.

"Steve, get her out of here! She is not welcome!"

It was a horrible moment, one that couldn't have been less reflective of the spirit of Jerry Garcia, a gentle, peaceful man who hated confrontation in all forms. Personally, it tore me apart to see them like this, fighting at a memorial service for the man they had both loved. I found myself wishing that Deborah would just let it go. They could have simply stayed on opposite sides of the boat. Hell, they could have gone out in separate boats. But that's not the way it turned out.

Mountain Girl was turned away and left teary-eyed on the dock. Some other people were so appalled and embarrassed by the fighting that they jumped off the boat and skipped the ceremony. It was a shame. Even as we got out into the bay and everyone took turns tossing handfuls of Jerry's ashes into the water, there was no sense of closure, no sense of peace . . . no sense of joy. As the last of the ashes swirled down beneath the surface in the shadow of the Golden Gate Bridge, I couldn't help but wonder whether Jerry was watching. I wondered what he would think.

Epilogue

The unraveling of the Grateful Dead occurred not overnight, but over the course of weeks, months, even years. We hadn't been a band in the traditional sense of the word for some time. There hadn't been a studio album, after all, in the six years prior to Jerry's death, and even touring had become problematic and unwieldy, given Jerry's health and the other band members' involvement in their various side projects. Nevertheless, the Grateful Dead, as a corporate entity, continued to thrive. Revenue came from live performances and album sales as well as from the sale of ancillary products, such as T-shirts, sporting goods, and toys, distributed by the increasingly active marketing arm of the company, Grateful Dead Merchandising.

As Dennis McNally, the band's publicist, said at a press conference the day after Jerry died, "We weren't really in the music business anymore. We were in the Grateful Dead business."

That's a little harsh, I think. Jerry, Bobby, Mickey, Billy, Phil—all of us, really—we loved making music and playing music. To suggest that it became nothing more than a mercenary enterprise is to demean the integrity of everyone involved in the band. That said, I can't deny that the Grateful Dead had become quite a successful business enterprise, one that supported more than thirty full-time employees, and allowed people like me and Ramrod and Kid to lead comfortable, interesting, fulfilling lives. Jerry's death left us all in limbo. We had no idea what would happen to the band, to the company . . . to the music.

The answers came slowly and were sometimes presented in ugly, public fashion. There was tension between band members, tension between the band and management, tension between members of Jerry's family. I had this crazy notion in my head that we could hold it all together, that we could find a new guitar player and carry on in Jerry's memory. He would have wanted that, I thought. We had everything we needed: stages of iron, trucks of steel, people of strength and talent. What we didn't have was Jerry. I'd thought of us as a giant, powerful machine, one that could withstand almost anything, when in fact we'd been more like a delicate crystal. One chip and we shattered.

As it became apparent that the guys in the band weren't interested in continuing without Jerry, the corporate side of the Grateful Dead began to shrink. Most of the crew and office staff were laid off. Ramrod and I hung on. We worked in the studio and helped out wherever we were needed. Deborah Koons helped me replace my Garcia Band salary by letting me work for her company (she asked for my assistance in sorting out Jerry's estate, and also let me produce an album called *How Sweet It Is*, culled from the vault of the Jerry Garcia Band).

Deborah was executor of Jerry's will and the beneficiary of the majority of his estate. But there were several lawsuits that arose in the wake of Jerry's death, the most contentious of which involved Deborah and Mountain Girl. Apparently, Jerry had made some sort of tenuous agreement with Mountain Girl that he would support her financially for twenty years following their separation. Deborah, however, questioned the legality of the agreement and took Mountain Girl to court in an effort to stop the payments. I wanted no part of this dispute, and I told Deborah as much. I begged her in person to leave me out of it, but she felt it was her duty to right this perceived wrong.

My testimony was important, of course, because I'd had many conversations with Jerry about his personal life. I'd spent countless hours with Jerry and Mountain Girl, and with Jerry and Deborah. I guess they figured I was as qualified as anyone to comment on the nature of these relationships. The thought of it, though, made my stomach turn. I'd always been reluctant to talk with the press about Jerry. I'd never cooperated with any book projects about the Grateful Dead. As far as I was concerned, these were all private matters, and they should have been handled quietly, discreetly, and with at least a modicum of dignity. But I was alone in that sentiment. I received a subpoena from Deborah's lawyers and was compelled to testify under duress on national television (the trial was carried on Court TV).

The irony is that my testimony, which I gave only reluctantly, and which Deborah had demanded, turned out not to be what Deborah wanted or expected. And so she broke off contact with me.

I guess we really were like a family, inasmuch as we lived together, loved each other, supported each other, and occasionally fought like crazy. As with any family, there were unresolved personal issues within the Grateful Dead, wounds that had been left to fester, and that now needed time to heal. Jerry had been the nucleus of our group, and his departure sent us all spinning off in different directions. There were so many bad management decisions, lawsuits, petty, stupid arguments, that for a while it seemed we might never recapture the spirit of the Grateful Dead.

I wasn't immune to any of this, by the way. For a while I worked with Phil Lesh's band, helping him with his equipment. He backed me up in every way possible. Phil got sick in 1997 and eventually needed a liver transplant. He made a miraculous recovery, went back on the road in '98, and then started another band, Phil Lesh and Friends. When that band went out on tour, Phil asked me and Ramrod to go with them, and we agreed. I'd forgotten what it was like to be on the road, to deal with the stress of traveling and setting up a stage and all the other craziness. I realized that I had some demons of my own, things I had ignored over the years. I didn't party the way I used to or try to kill myself with drugs. But I discovered that my temper, which had gotten me into trouble on occasion in the past, was worse than ever. I just wasn't ready to be back out on the road, but rather than admit my mistake, I provoked arguments with nearly everyone, including Phil. In the middle of the tour Ramrod and I left. This wasn't at all like us, and it left a hole in our relationship with Phil. And I'm sorry that I let it happen.

Thankfully, everything is cool now between me and Phil—I love him like a brother, and I'd do anything for him. In fact, most of the anger within the Grateful Dead family has withered or subsided. Each of the band members has his own project and is making music with a vitality and joy I've not seen in many years. Phil Lesh and Friends released a new CD in the spring of 2002, as did Billy Kreutzmann's band, the TriChromes; I helped Billy put that band together.

I guess you could say life is pretty good. I know I'm fortunate to be alive, to have a beautiful and loving wife, two healthy children, and work that I enjoy. Although many of my old friends are gone (and others are suffering from a variety of illnesses), I'm not alone. Not even close.

In August of 2002 the surviving members of the Grateful Dead performed together on one stage for the first time since Jerry Garcia passed away. I was with them for weeks beforehand, as they rehearsed in the studio, all of us together again, working hard, playing the songs Jerry had written. And I was with them in Alpine Valley, Wisconsin, when they took the stage in front of more than 80,000 fans, a roiling, tie-dyed ocean of Deadheads. They used the name The Other Ones, out of respect for Jerry, but there was no mistaking what this was: a Grateful

Dead reunion, with Jerry's spirit looming large over the whole affair.

Perhaps it was the first of many such concerts; perhaps not. So successful and enjoyable—so free of selfishness and anxiety—was this event that a minitour was quickly scheduled for the fall. What happens after that remains to be seen. I don't think any of us wants to step into a time capsule, to try to recapture an era that has long since faded away. We had our own little Camelot for a while, and while we wasted some of our good fortune and perhaps did not use our resources as well as we might have, there is no point beating ourselves up over the past. When I look back now, I don't see Jerry as some tragic figure in history or anything like that. I did for a while, I guess, and maybe that's part of the grieving process. But now I see the fullness of it all, the richness and the beauty of our friendship, and the joy that we found in our work. I remember the great American writer and mythologist Joseph Campbell, who was a close friend of Mickey Hart, standing by the side of the stage during a Grateful Dead concert, smiling and patting me on the back, telling me how lucky I was.

"This is modern mythology," he shouted over the band. "And you guys are the heroes of this new culture, this new world."

Well, the culture isn't new anymore and the world has changed, but I can't shake the feeling that he was right, that we were part of something special. For a while we were giants, striding together across a vast canvas. Like all great artists the Grateful Dead made mistakes. We did silly, foolish things. But we did a lot of good things, too. And we left our mark. How many people get to say that?

Ramrod once told me something, back in the carefree days when we all rode motorcycles, when we were young and invincible and the world was our stage.

"If you ever think you're not going fast," Ramrod cautioned, "just look down at the ground for a minute." I did that occasionally, and when I'd see the asphalt unwinding beneath me, shedding its skin in great gray ribbons . . . when I'd feel the wind beating against my face and hear the apocalyptic roar of my bike, I'd understand exactly what he meant.